LEGENDARY LOCALS

OF

WASHINGTON

NORTH CAROLINA

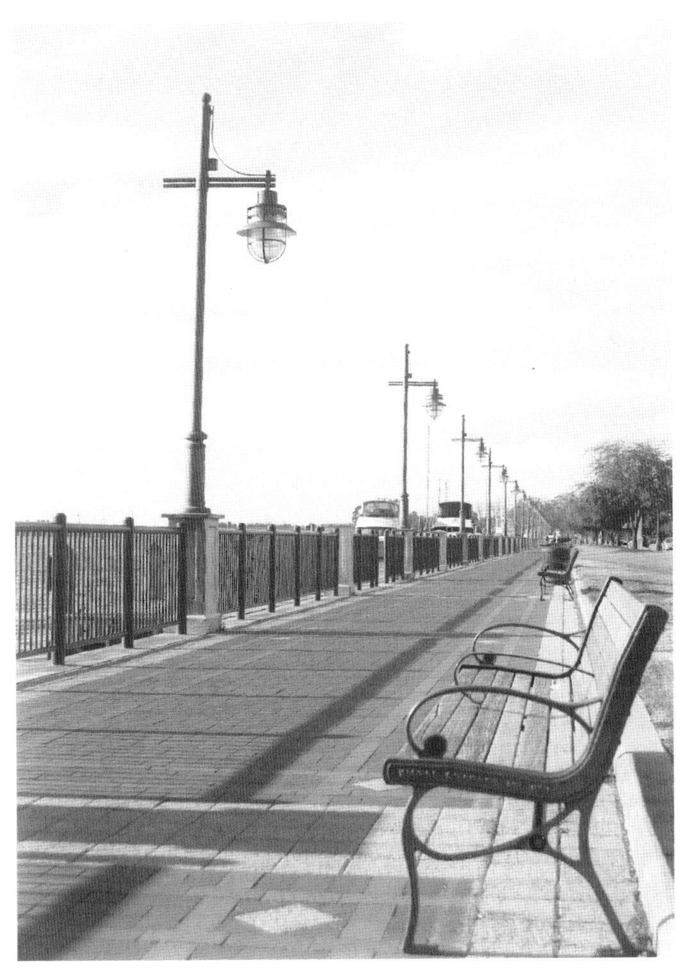

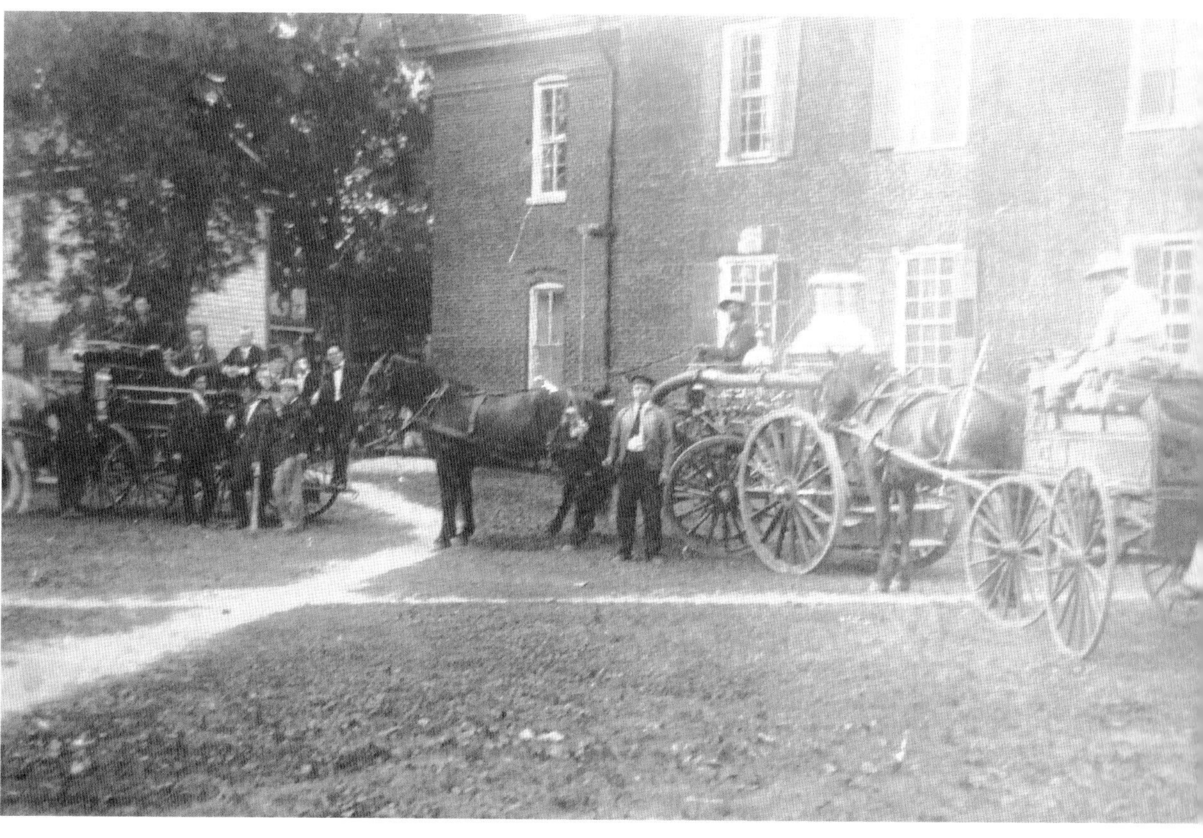

Washington Fire Department
The Washington volunteer firefighters line up their horse-drawn fire trucks. The wagon shown in the center of this photograph is currently on display at Station No. 1 of the Washington Fire Department at the corner of Fifth and Market Streets. (Courtesy of the Washington Fire Department.)

Page 1: Washington Waterfront
Under the guiding eyes of several former mayors, the Washington waterfront has evolved from a center of shipping to more of a leisure area for residents. Boat docks, swings, and gazebos now stand where wharfs and mills once dominated the waterfront. While large sailing ships do not appear in Washington anymore, there are plenty of smaller commercial and personal boats always visible from the shore. (Author's collection.)

LEGENDARY LOCALS

OF

WASHINGTON

NORTH CAROLINA

SUZANNE STOTESBURY

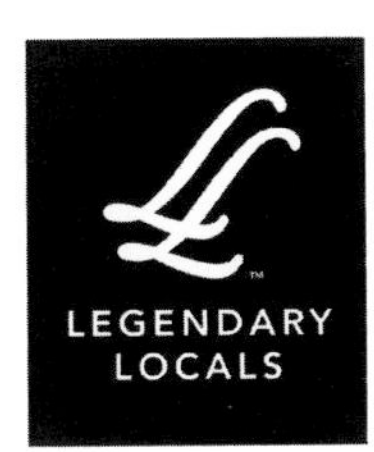

ISBN 978-1-4671-0238-4

Legendary Locals is an imprint of Arcadia Publishing
Charleston, South Carolina

Printed in the United States of America

Library of Congress Control Number: 2015952787

For all general information, please contact Arcadia Publishing:
Telephone 843-853-2070
Fax 843-853-0044
E-mail sales@arcadiapublishing.com
For customer service and orders:
Toll-Free 1-888-313-2665

Visit us on the Internet at www.arcadiapublishing.com

Dedication
To the people of Washington, both past and present. These are your stories, and I am honored to share them.

On the Front Cover: Clockwise from top left:
Blount Rumley, local historian (author's collection; see page 31), William Blount, congressman (courtesy of the US Senate; see page 12), Katie Paul, forerunner in nursing education (courtesy of Beaufort County Community College; see page 122), Joan Little, defendant in landmark sexual assault case (Wikimedia Commons; see page 57), Herbert Covington Bonner, a Democratic representative (courtesy of the Washington Fire Department; see page 51), Judy Jennette, former mayor (author's collection; see page 54), Sylvester Dibble, local barber and fire brigade leader (courtesy of the Washington Fire Department; see page 41), Choppy Wagner, former Washington High School football coach (courtesy of Milton Parker; see page 115), Fred Potts, former fire chief (courtesy of the Washington Fire Department; see page 39).

On the Back Cover: From left to right:
Protesters during Joan Little trial (Wikimedia Commons; see page 57), Dan T. Smith, member of the fire department (courtesy of the Washington Fire Department; see page 37).

CONTENTS

ACKNOWLEDGMENTS

I thank each and every person who spent his or her time and effort to assist me in completing this text. Without your help, this book would not be what it is. When I began this project, I did not realize how little I actually knew of the history of Washington. However, there were many people who helped me. The Historic Port of Washington helped give me a start on the project, as did historians Leesa Jones and Blount Rumley. Locals Judy Jennette, Archie Harding, and Betty Bonner Brashaw added many more legendary people to my list. I must also acknowledge the works produced by Washingtonians. From Milton Parker's well-preserved history of Coach "Choppy" Wagner to the guiding hand of Loy and Worthy's *Washington and the Pamlico*, each person and text I encountered opened more doors to the history and the people of Washington. Finally, I want to thank the Brown Library and the Beaufort County Community College Learning Resources Center for access to their archives and knowledge, which greatly contributed to this book.

INTRODUCTION

As an early settlement of the country, Washington's long and diverse history is enthralling to the historians, artists, and scholars who settle here. The people here reflect a proud tradition of growth, industry, and appreciation of the natural beauty and convenience of the waterways. Washington's unique combination of location and resources is what brought the first American settlers to the Forks of the Tar.

Nestled on the north bank of the Pamlico River, the area's proximity to water was particularly appealing to the first explorers in the late 1500s. By the end of the 16th century, small settlements had started to form. At the same time, the town of Bath was growing. The area upriver was quiet but near, which drew in more settlers. The county where Bath and the future town of Washington would be located went by many names until 1712, when it was officially named for Henry Somerset, the second duke of Beaufort. He inherited a portion of the Carolina lands after the death of his stepfather, John Grenville, the first Baron Granville of Potheridge. Neither Somerset nor his brethren ever visited the land named for them in the New World, but Beaufort County continues to honor their name.

From the Lords Proprietors, the land where Washington now stands changed hands several times before landing in Thomas Bonner's possession. It was then passed to his son James Bonner, who established his home in the area of present-day Washington; for a while, the area became known as Pea Town. More people came to reside at James Bonner's plantation, which on maps of the time is listed as Bonner or Forks of the Tar.

Bonner realized that his land had a strategic advantage. The Tar River was slow and had many sandbars, making his land the farthest inland that ships could navigate. He applied for and received permission from the colonial assembly to establish a town in 1771. By 1776, the town had begun to take shape, and Bonner sold off lots of land by lottery. These lot owners were elected as the first town commissioners, which included Joseph Blount of the well-known Blount family. Bonner bestowed the streets and two lots of land (one for public use, the other for a church) to these first town officials.

With around 30 houses, Washington was not very large at the time, but businesses kept growing. Much like Bath, Washington also had its share of privateers. John Gray Blount and Richard Blackledge, prominent town merchants, armed ships that would stalk British vessels on the coast. Many goods were brought into the town through privateering. However, these men's businesses would be the basis for market and industry on the Washington waterfront.

Washington was officially incorporated as a town in 1782. Records show that it was called Washington as early as 1775, making it the first town to be named for the president. More prominent landowners in the area donated their property to the town, and Respass, Van Norden, Gladden, and other streets are named for them. Three years later, as the prosperity of the town grew, the county seat was moved from Bath to Washington.

Large sailing ships brought goods into the wharves of Washington, and smaller flatboats were used to navigate the shallow and twisting waters of the Tar River. In this way, goods from Washington could be delivered as far inland as Tarboro. Congress officially established Washington as a port in 1790.

Washington served as a supply port during the Revolution, the War of 1812, and the Civil War. Many of the area's founding families rose in the ranks of the early armed forces. Many of these early veterans moved into politics, where they helped shape the beginnings of the state and federal governments, for better or worse.

The first great fire of Washington came during the Civil War. Early in the war, Washington fell to federal troops. On April 30, 1864, while under attack by the Confederates, the Union army finally vacated the town, setting it on fire in their escape. Most of the early buildings in town were lost in the great blaze.

The citizens were tenacious, however, and rebuilt. Unfortunately, fire once again destroyed the business district in 1900. A faulty flue was to blame. Many of the historic buildings still standing in town today were built after the second great fire.

Today, Washington's focus remains on its strategic location, both on the river and in history. Washington's citizenry works to preserve both the area's history and its contributions to early America. Several historical tours are conducted around town for visitors highlighting these accomplishments. Most recently, the Washington Waterfront Underground Railroad Museum has been established, highlighting the contributions of Washingtonians to the historic flight of slaves to the North.

It would be impossible to name each and every contributor to this diverse community when so many people work to make it stronger each day. However, this text provides a sampling of some of the known contributors to the philosophy that with a little work and dedication, people can build a town that assists and enhances the talents of its citizenry.

While Washington is not a town of great size, it still draws in the curious and the nostalgic. It is the center for arts in the county, with many venues featuring local artists. The waterfront continues to draw in visitors for water recreation and festivals. The vintage architecture of downtown, the historic houses, and the family-based industries provide a unique cross section of beauty and convenience that make Washington, to locals and new arrivals alike, a unique place to call home.

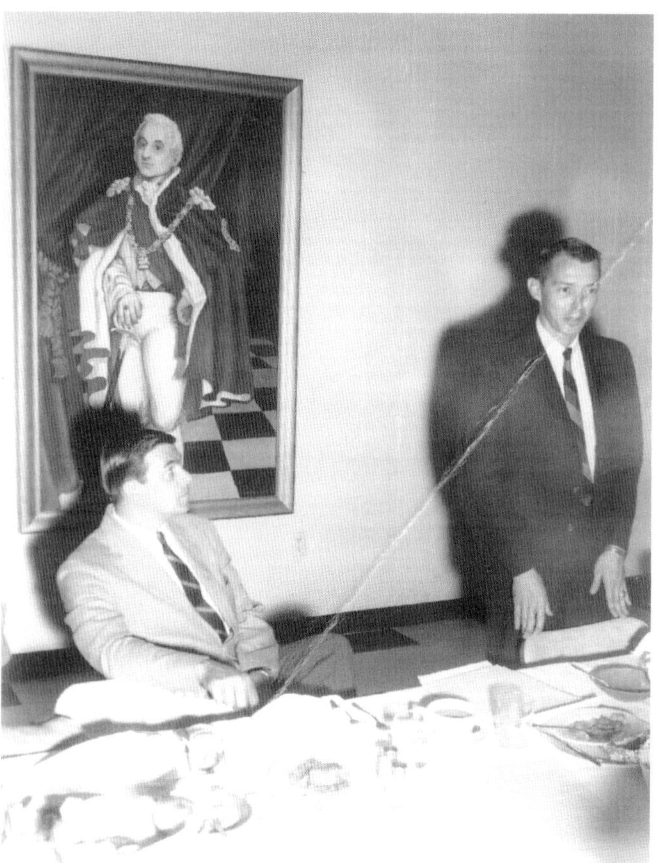

Duke of Beaufort

The county of Beaufort was named for Henry Somerset, third duke of Beaufort. He and his brother Lord Charles Somerset obtained the Albemarle region after the crown bought out most of the Lords Proprietors. Henry, who is pictured in the painting by Whiting Toler seen here, did not visit the land that was later named in his honor. (Courtesy of Whiting Toler.)

CHAPTER ONE

Founding Fathers

The future site of Washington grew into the beginning of a town through the actions of Col. James Bonner. Bonner gave a portion of his landholdings in the area then known as Forks of the Tar for the formation of a town. The name was changed in 1776 to honor Gen. George Washington of the Continental Army. Washington never visited the town, but it does hold the distinction of being the first town named for him.

Over the course of its history, Washington has contributed many great minds to the battlefields and government of North Carolina. The Blount family was especially influential in the area. Jacob Blount helped build commerce at Forks of the Tar, and his son John Gray Blount donated more land to build the town. The Blounts' wealth and political influence reached as wide as their landholdings. It is said that in his youth, John Gray explored the lands of Kentucky with Daniel Boone. Rubbing elbows with the legends of early American history was a part of everyday living for the Blounts, as the family's businesses grew along with their influence. John's sons William Augustus and Thomas Harvey, both veterans of the War of 1812, continued the family's legacy in Washington and across North Carolina and Tennessee. In fact, had William not perished in 1900, it is thought that he would have become governor of Tennessee. The family's contributions to their hometown and several early states were numerous. John's sons Reading and Thomas both served with distinction in the Revolutionary War. Another son, Willie, personally funded three Tennessee regiments during the War of 1812. As a result of their many interests in commerce and politics and close ties to the community, the Blount name and the names of many other prominent early families persist in Washington today.

George Washington

The town of Washington was the first in the country to be named for Gen. George Washington following the Revolutionary War. Incorporated in 1776, the town was named in his honor a full 13 years before Washington was elected the nation's first president. Washington never visited the town, but Col. James Bonner, who donated the original public lands for the town, served under Washington at Valley Forge. (Courtesy of the Library of Congress.)

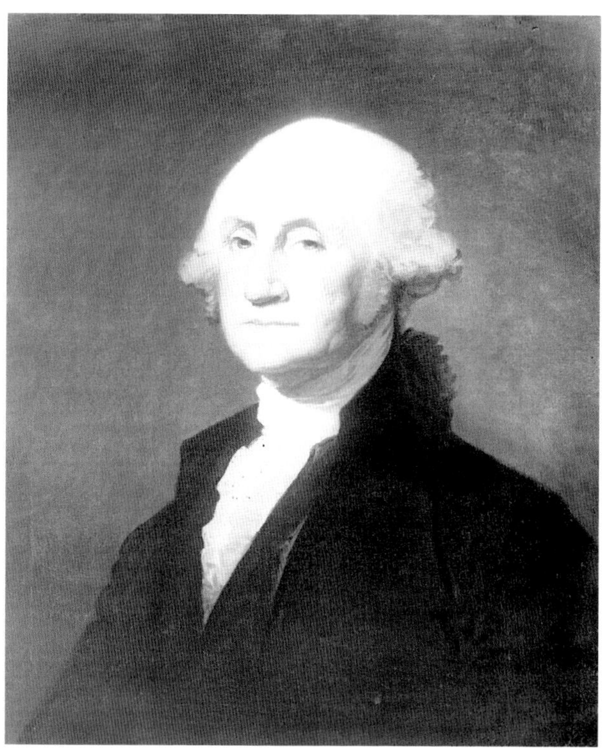

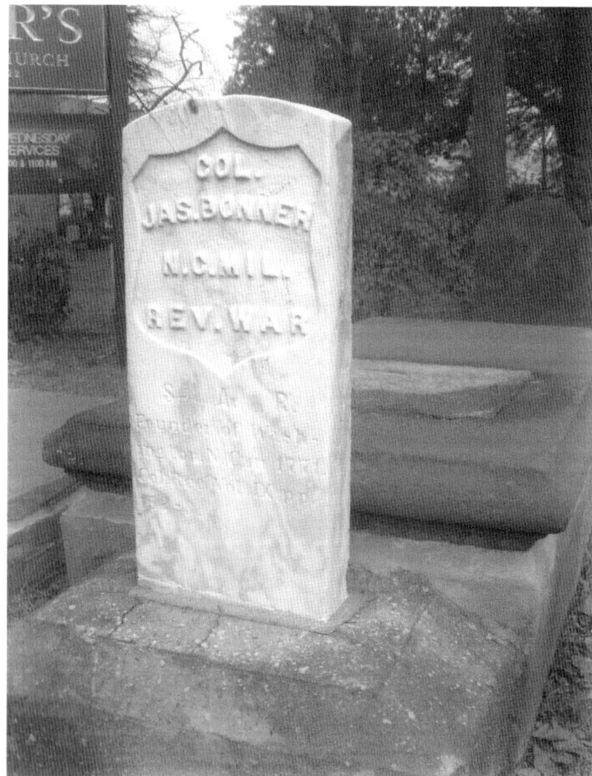

Col. James Bonner

Born in Bath County, North Carolina, in 1719, Colonel Bonner is Washington's founding father. He provided public lands for the town, then known as Forks of the Tar, on his farm in the 1770s. He became a colonel of the Beaufort County Regiment in 1775. His sons James II and John continued to build the town following their father's death in 1782. (Author's collection.)

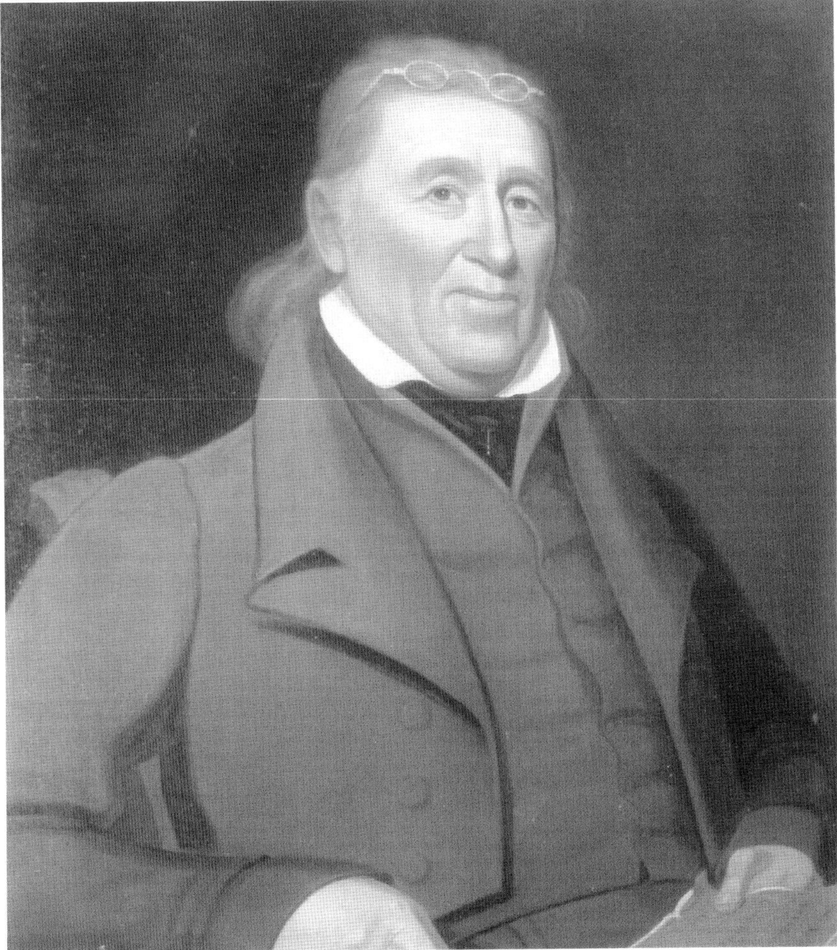

The Blount Family

The Blount family has had a stake in the area since Thomas Blount sailed from England and settled on a plantation near the Pamlico River in the 1660s. His sons rose to great influence. Son Jacob Blount was born in Beaufort County in 1726. An active political figure prior to the Revolutionary War, Jacob later served as an officer under Gov. William Tryon in the Battle of Alamance. He reached the rank of captain during the Revolution and served as paymaster for the North Carolina troops. He served as a state congressman and was a member of the 1776 Halifax Congress.

While his son John Gray Blount (pictured) did not have a proclivity toward politics, it was said that anyone running for public office should seek his support because he was not only well known in early America but his opinion also carried a lot of weight with people from all walks of life. This may be because he was the largest landholder in the United States at the time. His land interests spread from the Atlantic Coast all the way to the Mississippi River.

Born in Bertie County where his mother's family resided, he later moved to his father's land at Forks of the Tar, where he built what might have been the largest mercantile in early America.

He and his brothers diversified the family business, and their empire grew much larger as the brothers acquired wharves, warehouses, riverboats, and seaworthy freight vessels. The Blounts shipped products from their sawmills, gristmills, cotton gins, and other interests, including the slave trade. The Blounts were instrumental in the founding of Washington, and the family held influence in the town, state, and country for years. (Courtesy of the Historic Port of Washington.)

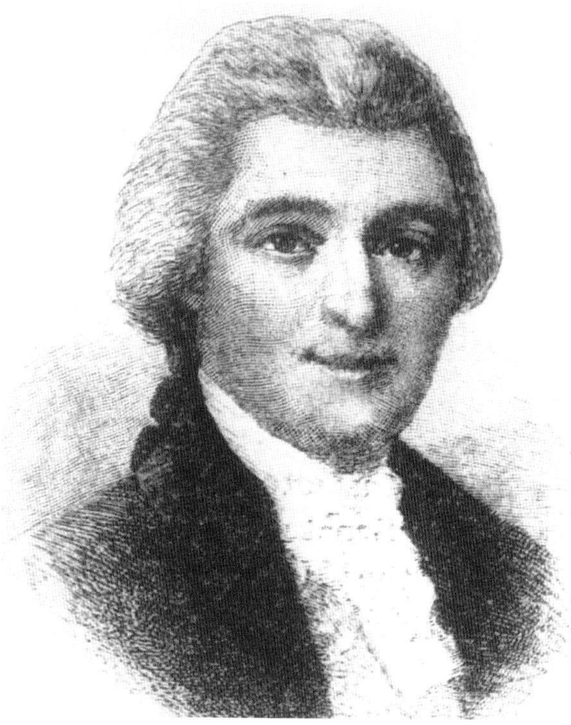

William Blount

William Blount, son of Thomas Blount, represented North Carolina in many political arenas. Following his service as paymaster of the 3rd North Carolina Regiment during the Revolutionary War, he was elected to the North Carolina legislature and served for many years, with the exception of 1782 and 1786, when he served in the Continental Congress. He attended the Constitutional Convention, but it is said he reluctantly signed the Constitution. Blount had hoped to be a US senator, but when that fell through, he moved west to Tennessee, where he owned and controlled millions of acres.

George Washington named Blount governor of the Southwest Territory, western land that had been formally ceded by North Carolina to the federal government. In this position, Blount attempted to protect his citizens from native attacks, but became disgruntled when the new government would not provide assistance. His repeated attempts to obtain assistance made him popular among the people in the West. Because the country was new and regulations were still being developed, Blount rather unorthodoxly managed to obtain statehood for Tennessee by holding a constitutional convention where the state constitution was ratified, effectually bypassing the federal government, which had previously turned down Tennessee's request for statehood. To many citizens, statehood meant the area could manage its own issues more effectively without waiting for the federal government's assistance. However, this meant Blount could not serve as the area's governor. Instead, he became one of the state's first two US senators.

Scandal hit when he was caught trying to manipulate land prices in the West. Like many who looked to the West, he had hoped to add to his fortunes by buying and selling land. However, the market was not as favorable as he would have liked. He cooked up a scheme with local native tribes to assist the British in overtaking New Orleans from Spain. Blount felt if the Brits controlled the city, the value of his land would increase. However, the plan was discovered by Pres. John Adams's administration.

A mere nine years after its creation, Congress impeached Tennessee's first senator. Blount refused to appear before the Senate for his trial, and the charges were later dropped amid uncertainty of jurisdiction. Despite the scandal, he remained popular in his adopted state. He continued to serve in the Tennessee Senate until his death in 1799. (Courtesy of the US Senate.)

CHAPTER TWO

Community Builders

It takes people of many different backgrounds to build a community where it is worth living. This is true in Washington as much as anywhere else. Whether it is building a library or a permanent way of preserving the history and information of the town, these people make a difference in such a way that the generations that follow can enjoy the fruits of their ancestors' labors.

Washington has a long history of libraries being constructed and maintained by local citizens. From Turner's library for African Americans to the town library heavily sponsored by the Brown family, libraries have always found a home in the town.

However, in a town with such a long and diverse history, there is more to preserving history than just providing a space to save documents and stories. Groups of townspeople have worked together to preserve the town's historic buildings that have not already been claimed by fires, weather, or time. From the beginning of the historic district to groups like the Washington Bicentennial Historical Committee and Historic Port of Washington, both natives and new residents find themselves vested in the preservation of the town's history.

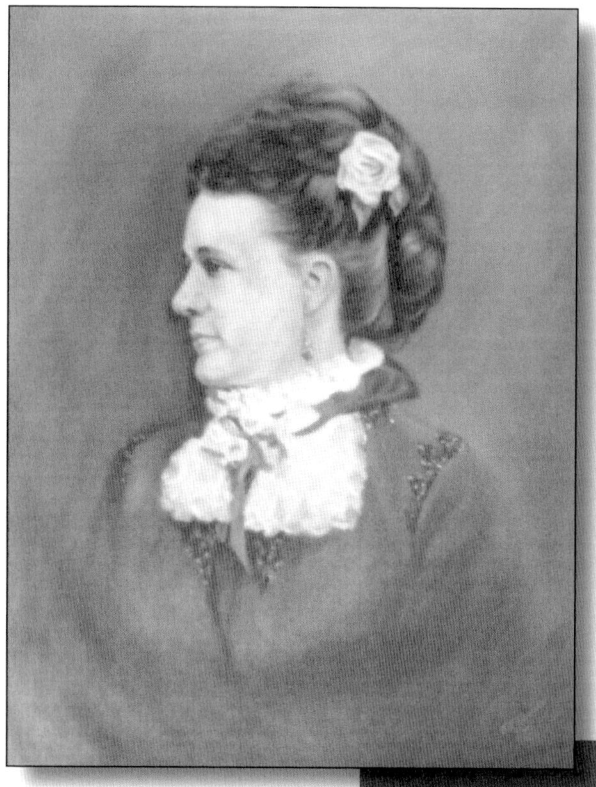

George H. and Laura E. Brown

Laura Ellis Brown was a stylish lady of high standing in Washington. Her husband, George Hubbard Brown, served Beaufort County as a Superior Court judge and presided on the State Supreme Court for 16 years. The Browns were avid readers. They had no children, so they opted to share their wealth by providing their hometown with funding for a new library building. At the time, the facility was dingy, and heating and cooling were not an option. However, the country was suffering shortages in manpower and building material during the Second World War. It was decided that the town would renovate the Browns' home at 122 Van Norden Street (opposite) and use it in the interim to house the library. Finally, the town celebrated the opening of the current George H. and Laura E. Brown Library in 1954. (All, courtesy of the Brown Library.)

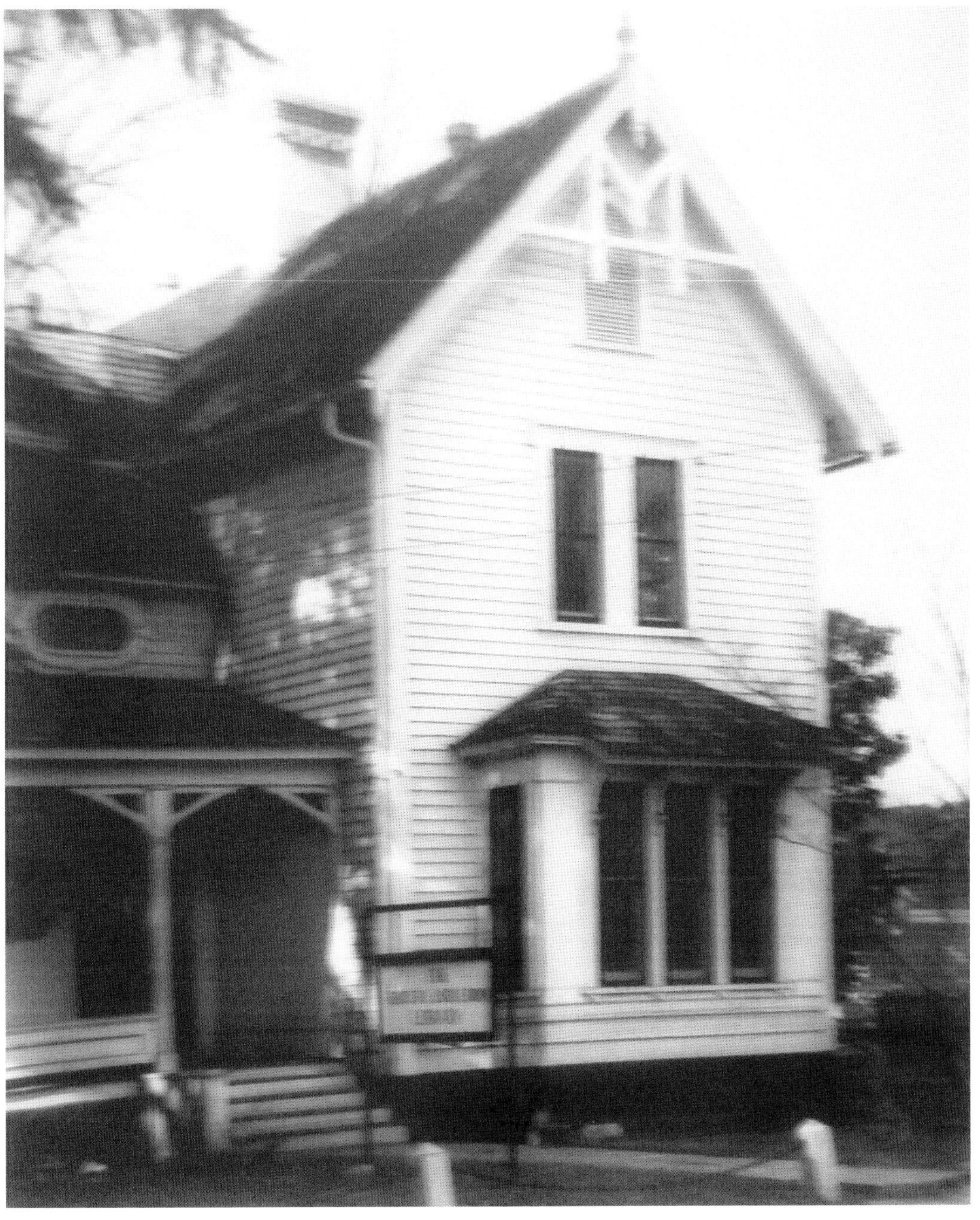

I.B. Turner

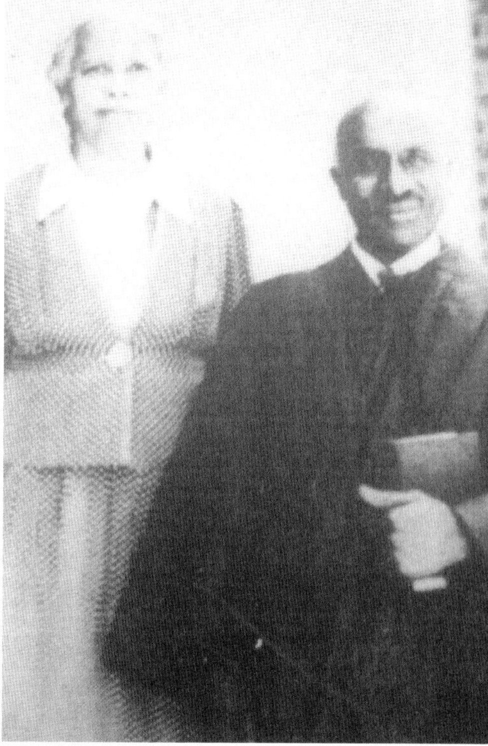

Rev. I.B. Turner was the pastor of the Metropolitan AME Zion Church. A community leader, he noted that there were few cultural manuscripts available for the black population in Washington. As such, he contacted friends in the North, and they sent him some materials. He started a small library in his parish in 1940.

Many local businesses, organizations, and citizens donated to the effort. The Washington Public Library took note of Turner's concern and began soliciting materials that could be shared with the black community. The public library went further and requested funding from the town to aid the black library.

With all this attention, the library quickly outgrew its home at the church. Now named the Public Library for Colored People, it was moved to a building on Gladden Street, and then later moved to even larger facilities on the corner of Ninth and Pierce Streets. High school boys were solicited to do necessary construction for the library, adding bookshelves and other needed architecture. In 1950, the town renamed the library for Turner to honor his dedication and contribution. (Right, courtesy of *Washington Daily News*; below, author's collection.)

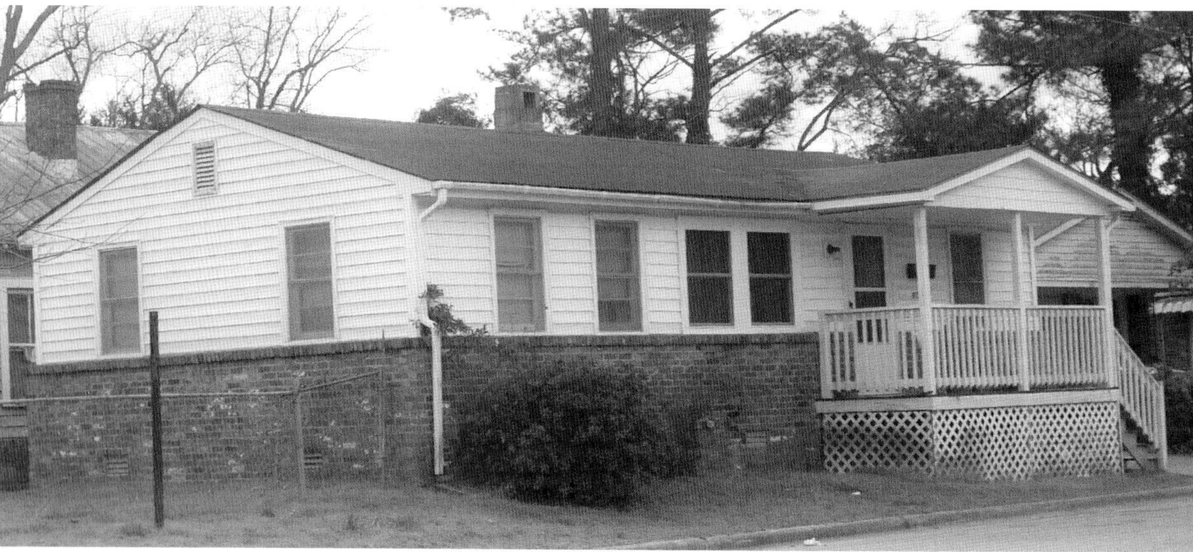

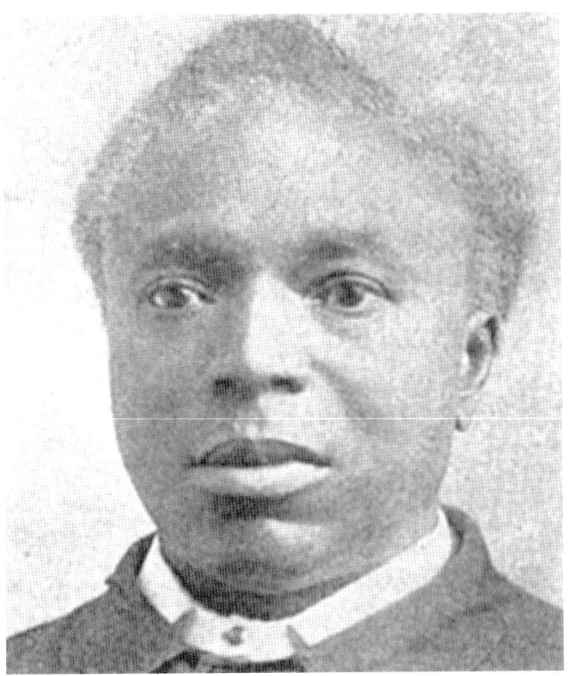

Joseph A. Beebe

Rev. Joseph A. Beebe came to Washington in 1871 by way of Edenton. He quickly became a well-known and respected man in the area. With assistance from both sides of the racial divide, Beebe built the first Methodist church in the state. The first members of the church were former slaves and free blacks. Beebe spent only two years organizing and leading the church as a pastor and elder, but the efforts he made did not go unnoticed. When the original building burned down, it was rebuilt in the 1920s and renamed Beebe Memorial CME Church. The town also later dedicated Beebe Memorial Park to Beebe's memory. (Left, courtesy of Judy Jennette; below, author's collection.)

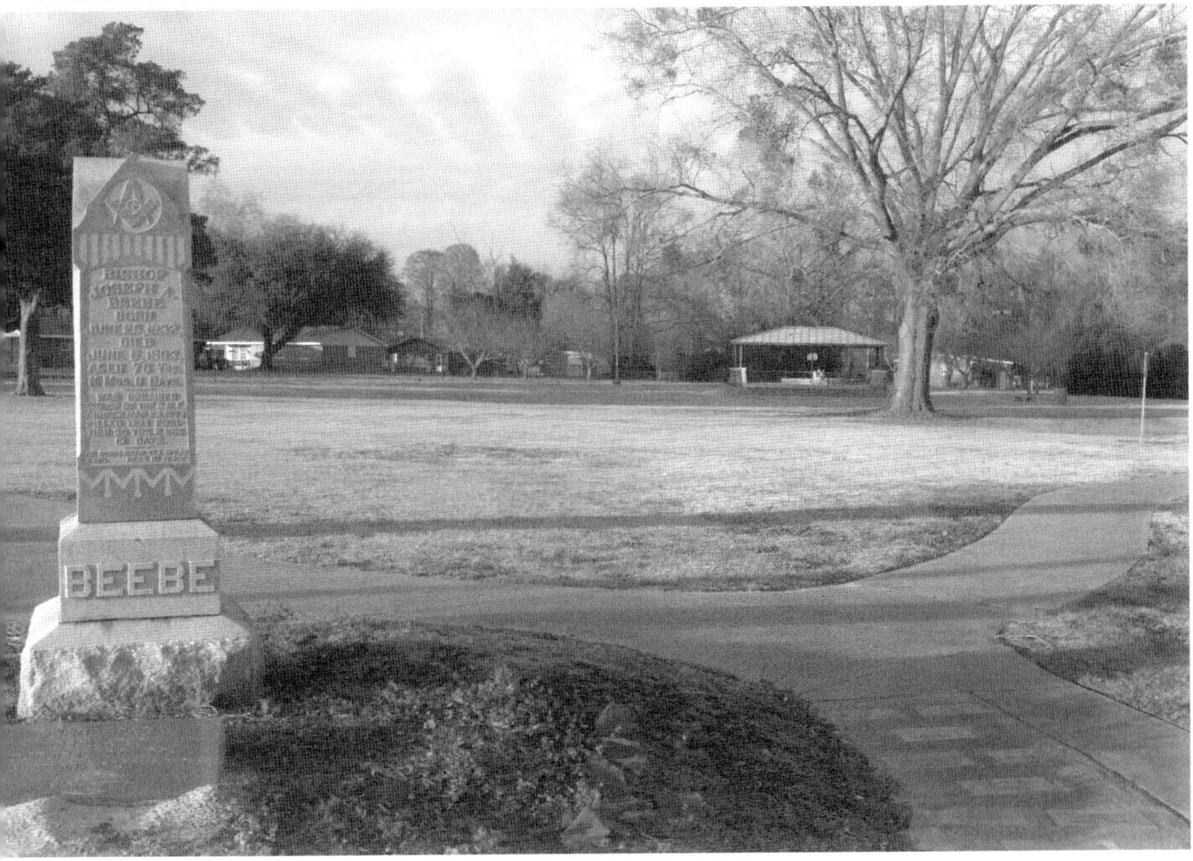

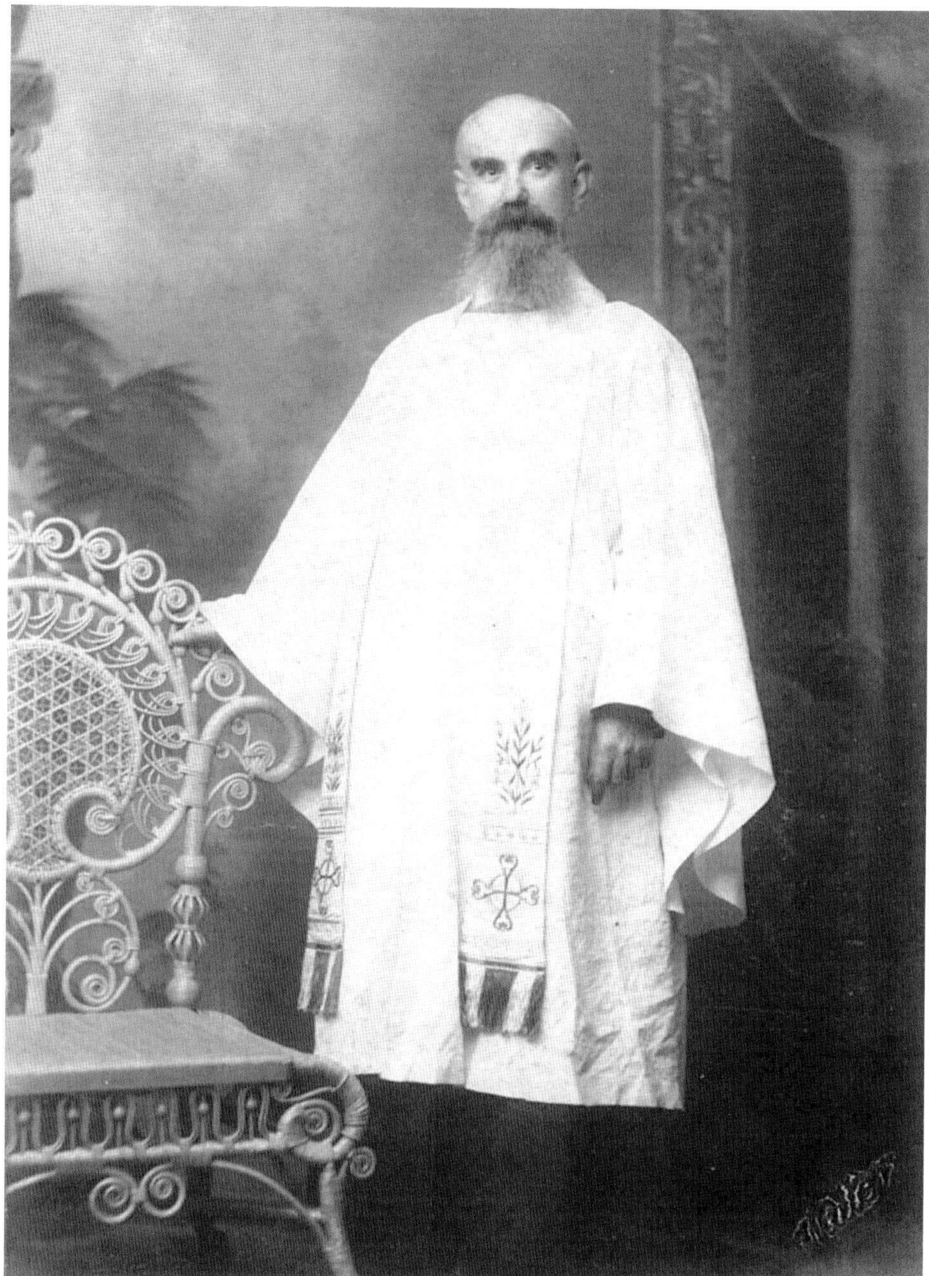

Rev. Nathaniel Harding

Having enlisted in the Confederate army as a teenager, Nathaniel Harding was found in a ditch after being wounded. The Yankee solider who found him later arranged for Harding to attend school in the North, where he decided to go into the ministry. When he returned to Washington, Harding ministered at St. Peter's Episcopal Church for more than 45 years. He believed in education and served as the county school superintendent for 25 years. He traveled all over the county on horseback to work at improving small local schools. He had 11 children, the ninth of whom was Edmund H. Harding, a well-remembered local personality. (Courtesy of Beaufort County Community College.)

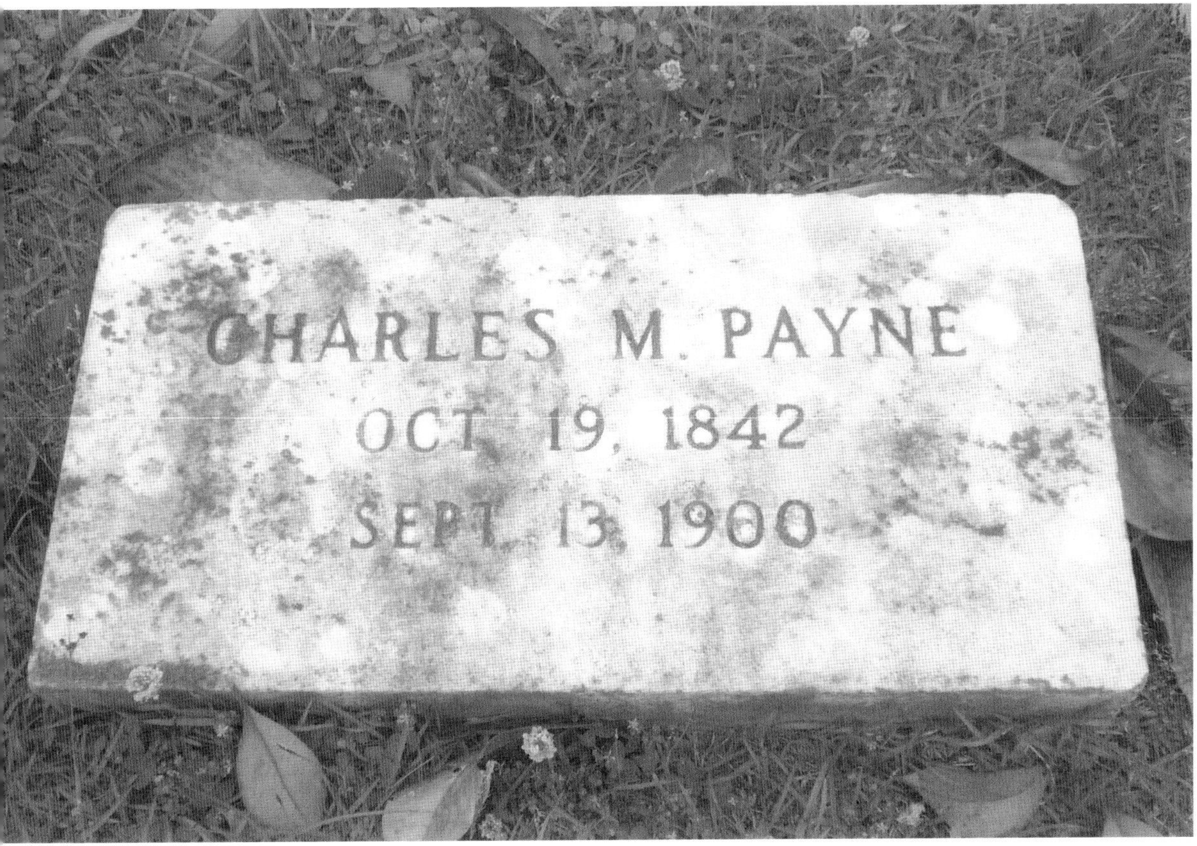

Rev. Dr. Charles Payne

Rev. Dr. Charles Payne was the pastor of the Presbyterian church in the late 1800s. The son of a doctor, he was well educated, ultimately earning a doctorate degree in divinity. He served in several churches across the state before making his way to Washington, where he and Rev. Nathaniel Harding were known and liked by many in the town. The day Payne died, September 13, 1900, was the same day of a great fire in the downtown and waterfront areas that changed the face of the business district. Payne was the father of four children, including Anne Blackwell Payne, who became a poet. (Author's collection.)

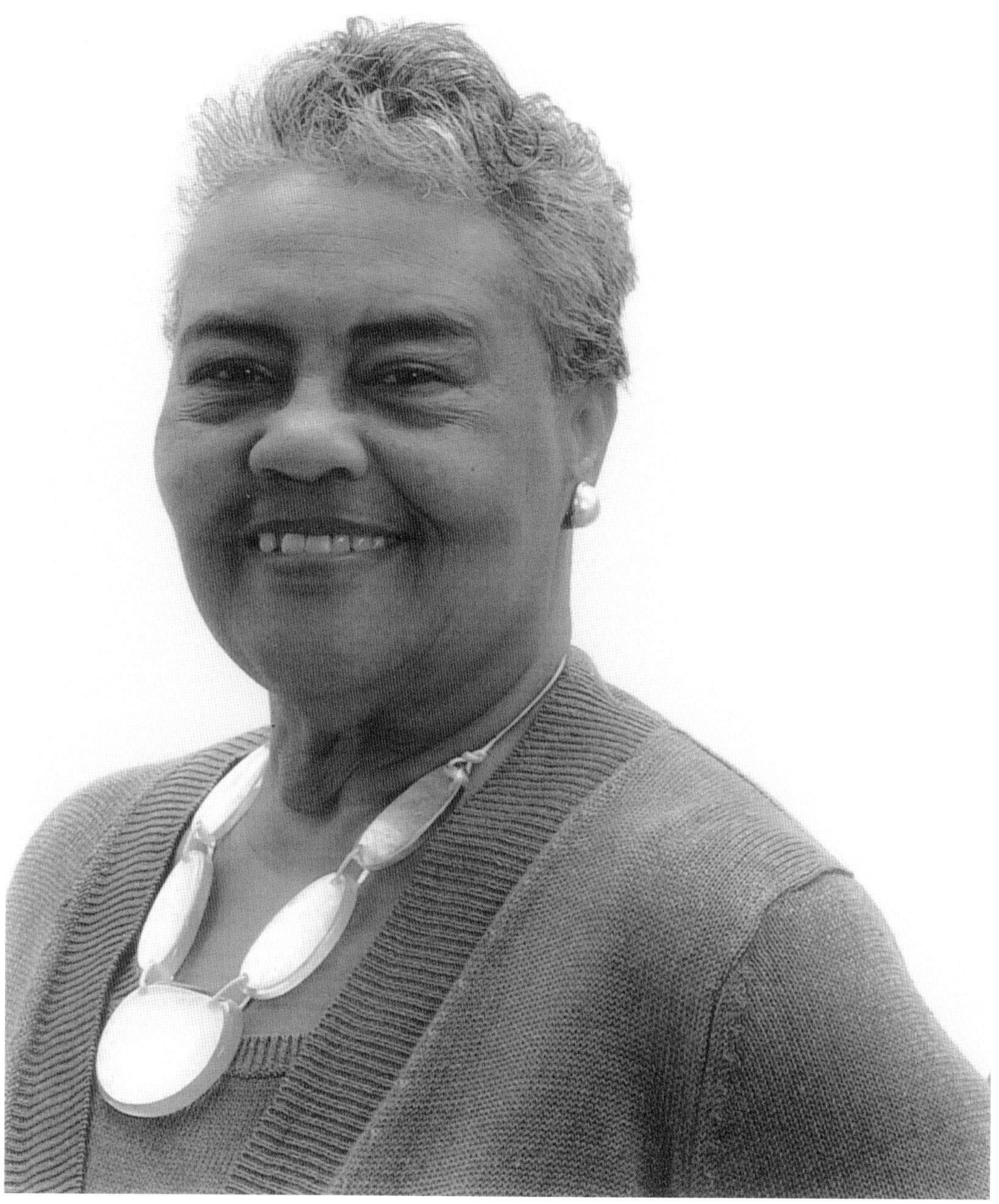

Betty Randolf

In a time when fewer services were offered to the black community, Betty Randolf worked as a home economics teacher for the local extension office. She helped people of color connect with the community development program, 4-H, and other local services. As a teacher and director of Beaufort County Developmental Center, she assisted many in the community. She has served on the local school board and has worked with many local civic groups. Randolf worked with her husband in his family funeral business, and after his death, she began her own business, the New Beginnings Funeral and Cremation Service. She continues to assist with education in the community by serving as a member of the board of trustees for Beaufort County Community College. (Courtesy of Betty Randolf.)

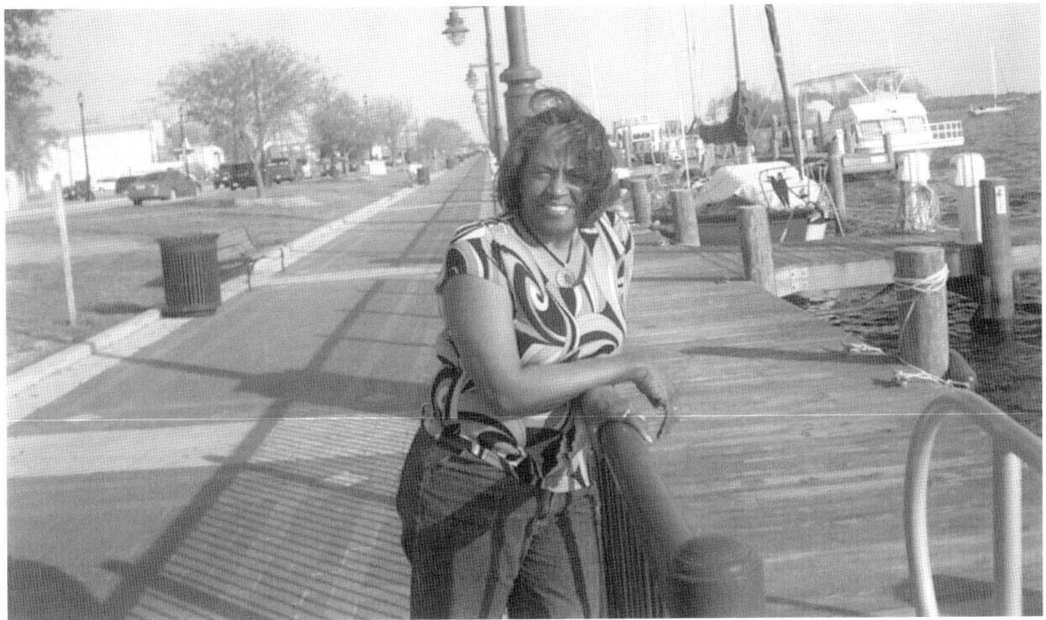

Leesa Jones

A local historian and author, Leesa Jones is a busy woman full of energy. She collects research on the black history and culture of the area and delights in sharing her knowledge. She also leads historical walking tours of downtown Washington. It is not uncommon to find her near the Washington waterfront, where she finds a place of calm and contemplation. Her most recent project is the establishment of the Washington Waterfront Underground Railroad Museum in downtown Washington, commemorating an almost completely unknown history of the area. The museum will be housed in the train caboose in Freedom Park, near the civic center. (Above, courtesy of Leesa Jones; below, author's collection.)

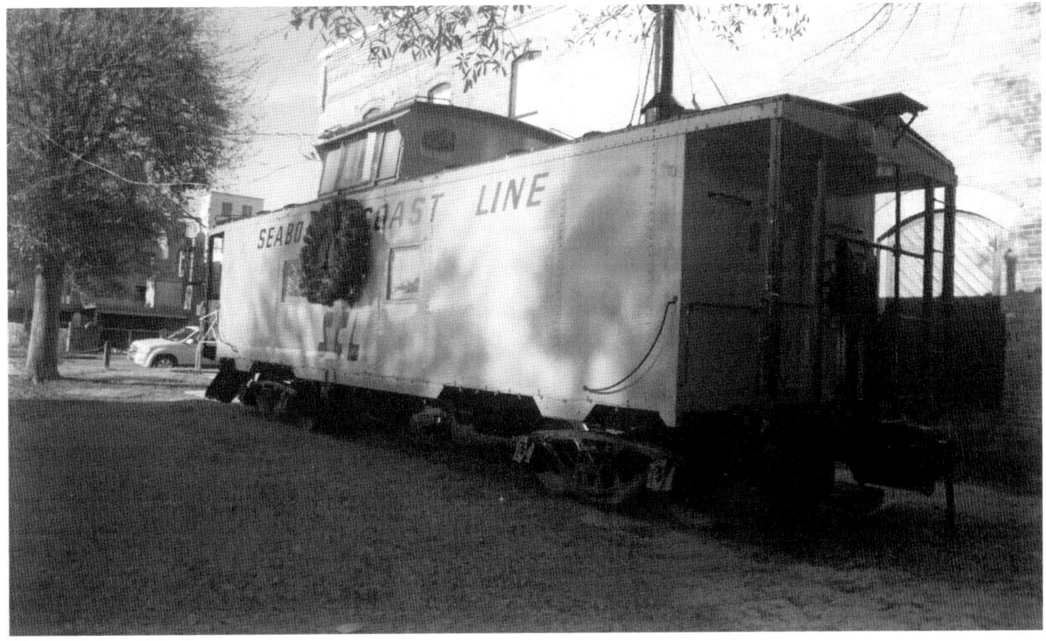

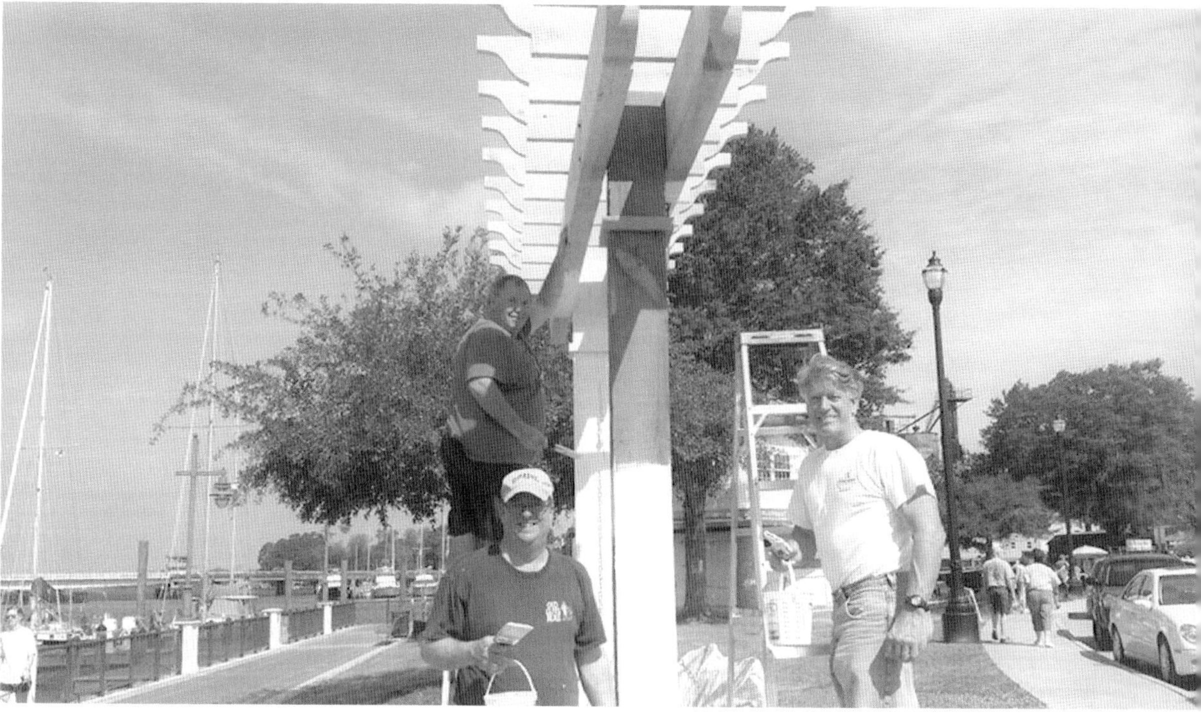

F. Ray Moore Jr.
In addition to years of running his family's oil business, F. Ray Moore Jr. (far right) has always felt a calling to help people. A licensed minister, he is active in his church, where he has organized and led many mission trips abroad. Moore is humble, however, about his contributions to his community despite his many years of service in various organizations. He is particularly fond of the Optimist Club, and has volunteered with it for over 30 years. His efforts helped fund the Susiegray Moore McConnell Sports Complex and the Hildred T. Moore Aquatic Fitness Center. Since his retirement in 2015, Moore has continued to serve his community in various volunteer roles. (Courtesy of F. Ray Moore Jr.)

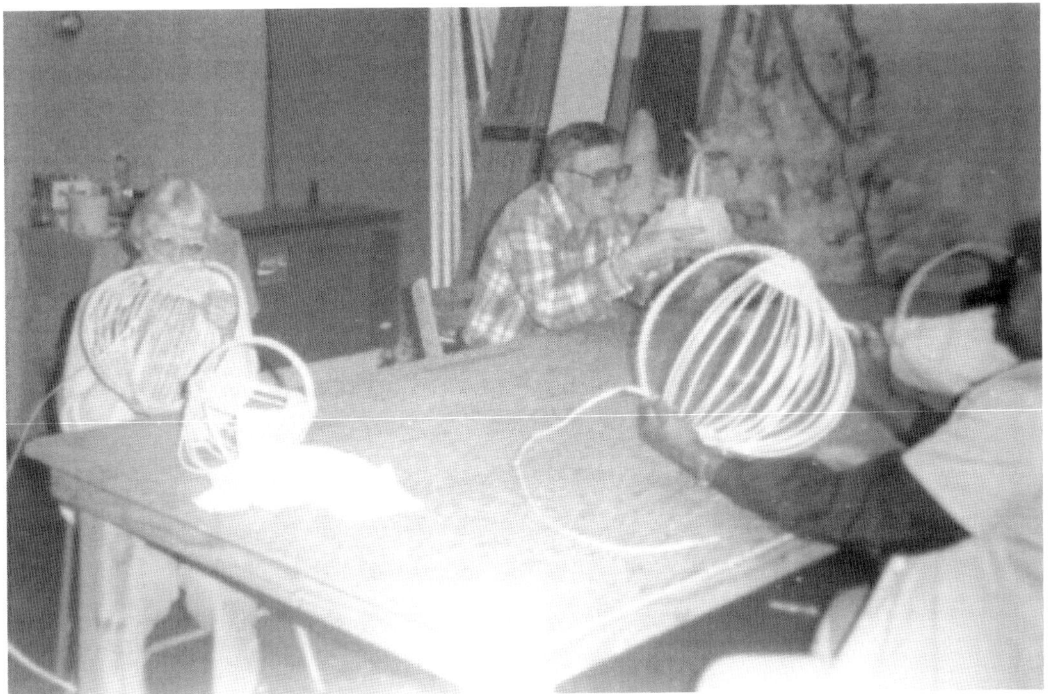

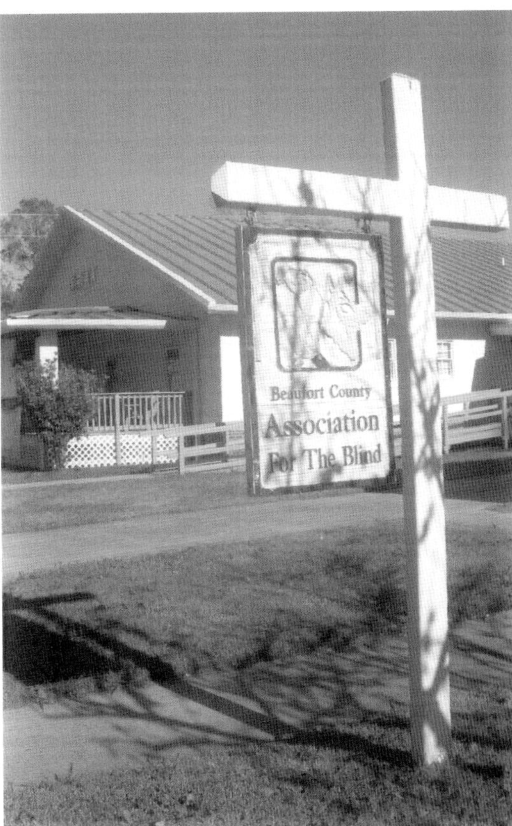

Nancy Boyd

Without Nancy Boyd, the Blind Center would not exist. As a social worker, she often brought the blind into her home to work on social activities. According to Boyd, "My job was to help the blind people become as independent as possible." However, the blind had nowhere to go and nothing to do. No stimulation was available to them, and many often felt useless. So Boyd invited them into her home. In these visits, blind people of all ages learned to become more self-sufficient through tasks such as preparing meals and making crafts. Soon, the blind people were raising money by selling their handiwork. With the assistance of local citizens and civic groups, their efforts allowed for the establishment of the Blind Center of North Carolina. (Above, courtesy of Nancy Boyd; below, author's collection.)

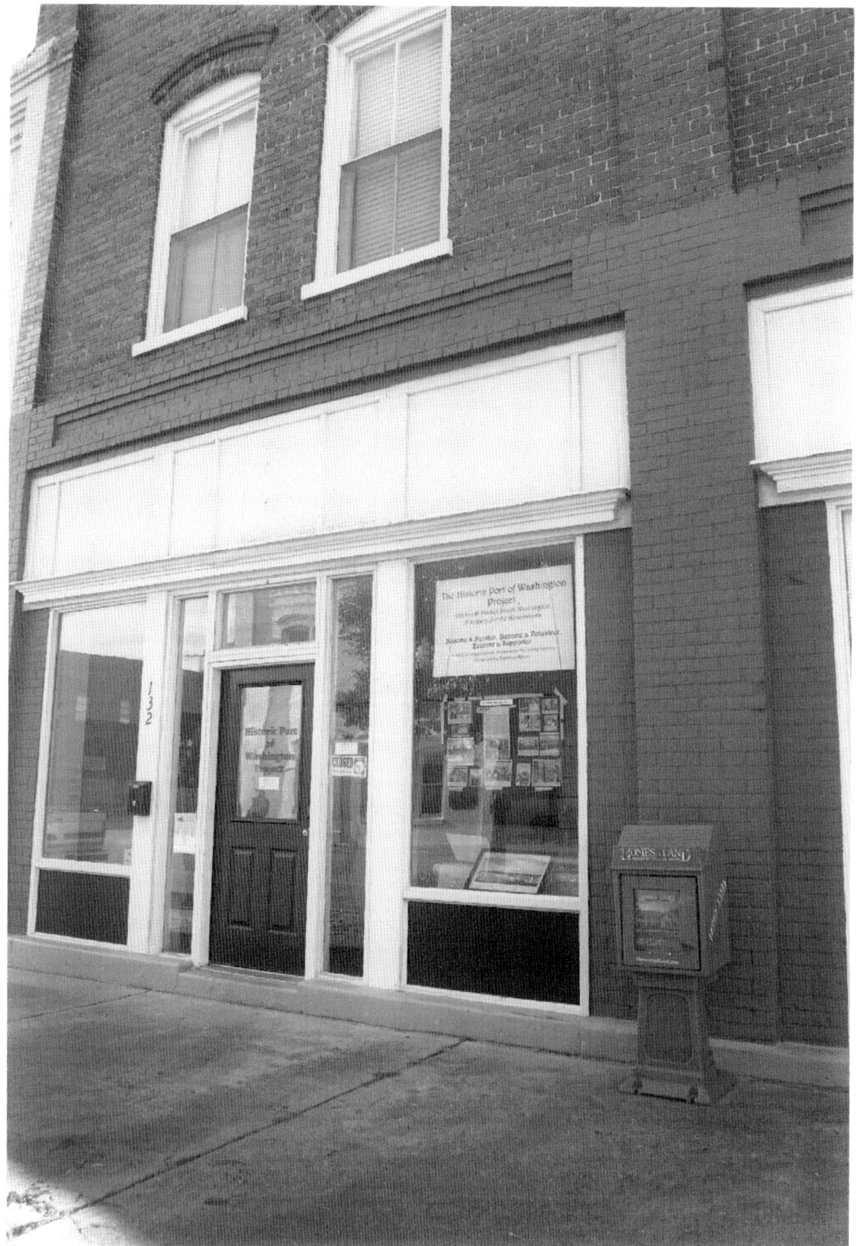

Historic Port of Washington

Under the umbrella of the Arts Council, the Historic Port of Washington project (HPOW) is a loosely associated group of like-minded volunteers who are interested in providing a place to preserve the maritime history of Washington. The group has started collecting as much history about the waterfront and its progression as possible, and as one of its first big projects, the group hosted artist Douglas Alvord, who painted a 10-foot mural illustrating the Washington waterfront as it appeared between 1880 and 1920. The mural, which hangs in the HPOW museum on Market Street, depicts images of Hull Anderson's shipyard and the various mills, wharfs, and businesses that once nestled against the banks of the Pamlico. (Author's collection.)

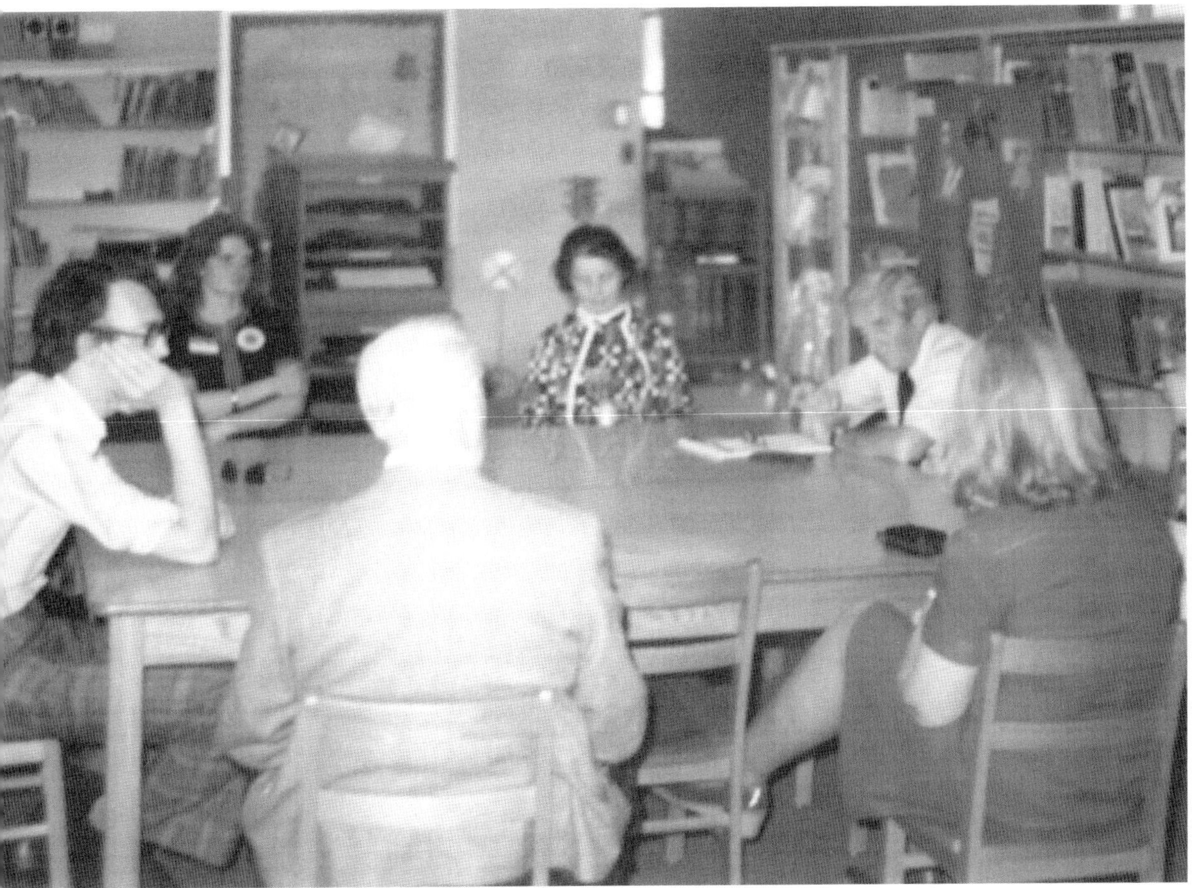

Washington and the Pamlico

The unofficial history of Washington is gathered in the book *Washington and the Pamlico* by Pauline Worthy and Ursula Loy. Any historian would be lost without it because it is one of the most complete historical works about the town and its people. It is the first recommendation that anyone in town makes when someone starts local research. A collection of firsthand accounts of the history of Washington, the text was prepared by the Bicentennial History Committee, which was composed of Pauline Worthy, Ursula Loy, Ysobel Dupree Litchfield, Louis May, Jill High, Daisy B. Parham, Norfleet Daniel Hodges, and John Morgan, chairman. Pictured here is one of the many meetings required to put on the events for the bicentennial celebration. (Courtesy of the Brown Library.)

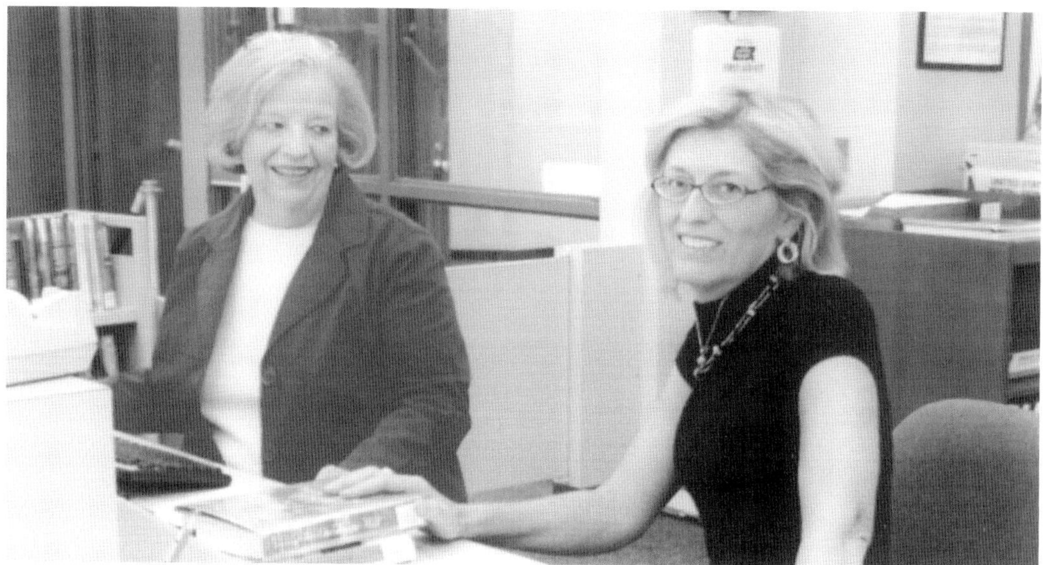

Betty Ferrell

Betty Ferrell (left) is a familiar face in the libraries of Washington. After serving as librarian at Beaufort County Community College for 39 years, she then worked as a part-time librarian at both the Beaufort, Hyde, Martin (BHM) and the Brown Libraries. While Ferrell is not in the library very often anymore, she says she holds fond memories of the many library patrons whom she served in the area. (Courtesy of Beaufort County Community College.)

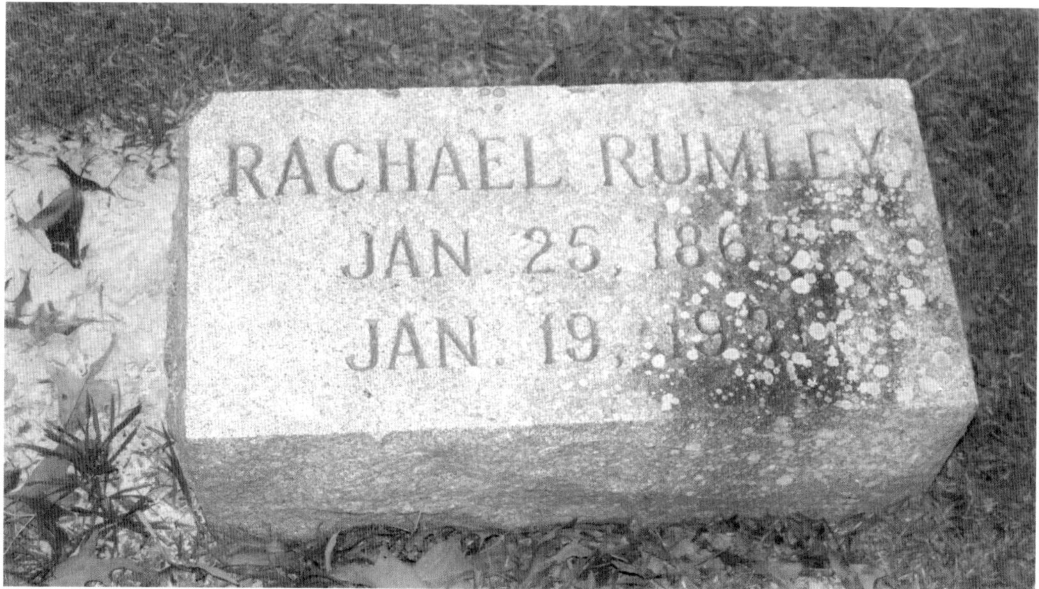

Rachel Rumley

Rachel Rumley is remembered as an attractive woman who worked tirelessly for the unfortunate. She not only fed the hungry, but also actively assisted those in need to find jobs. She partnered with Rev. Henry Searight of the First Presbyterian Church, and along with like-minded citizens, they founded the first local welfare office, which later became the Department of Social Services. (Author's collection.)

Rev. David Moore

Rev. David Moore was the pastor and an elder at Washington AME Zion Church. He was devoted to his community and served it in many volunteer capacities. However, one of his most notable contributions to the community was a lawsuit he brought against the county. At the time, the way the ballot was structured gave unfair advantages to certain candidates during elections for county commissioners. The courts ruled in Moore's favor, so the ballots were restructured and the district lines were redrawn to provide a fair and balanced opportunity for all candidates and voters. (Courtesy of *Washington Daily News*.)

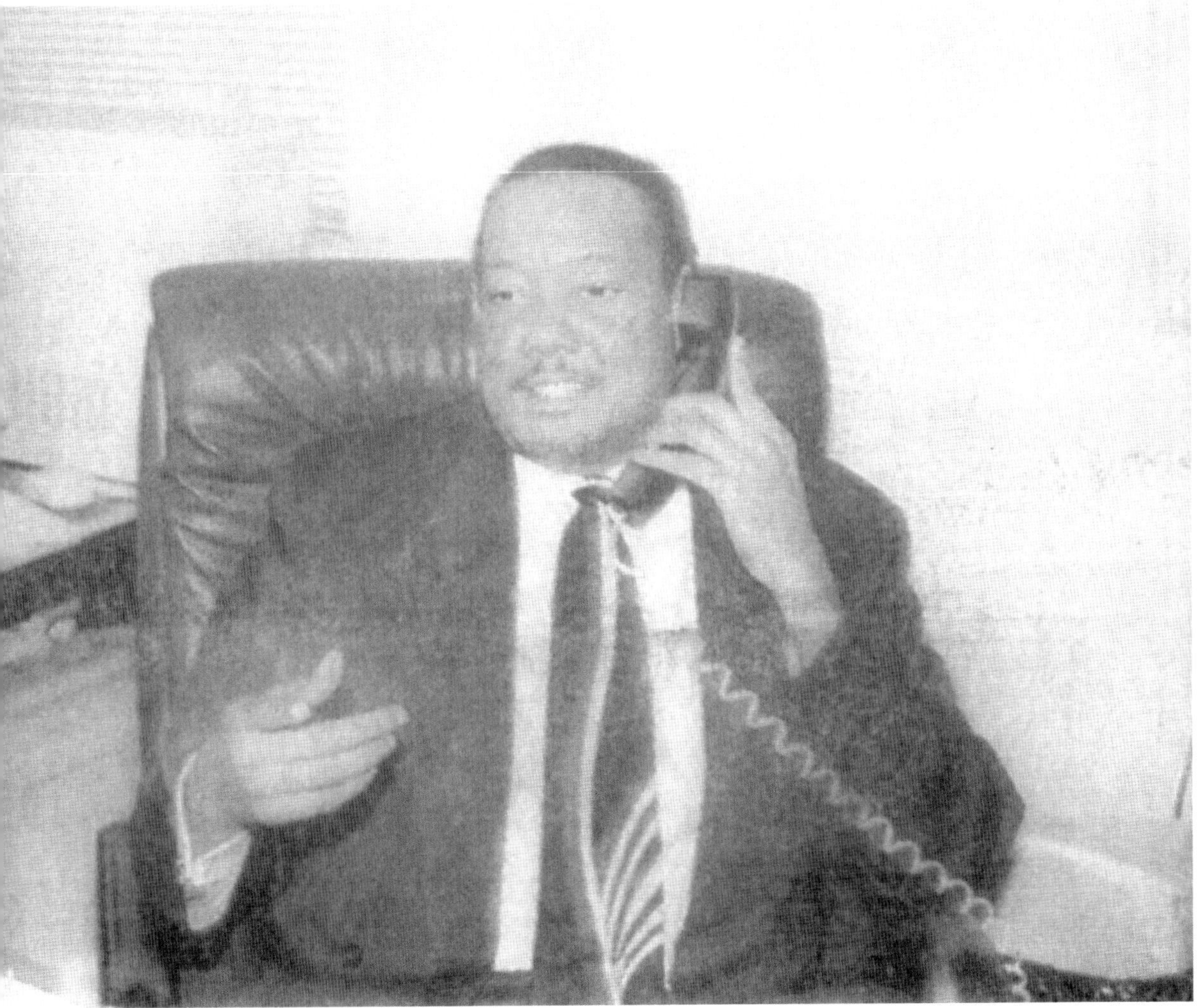

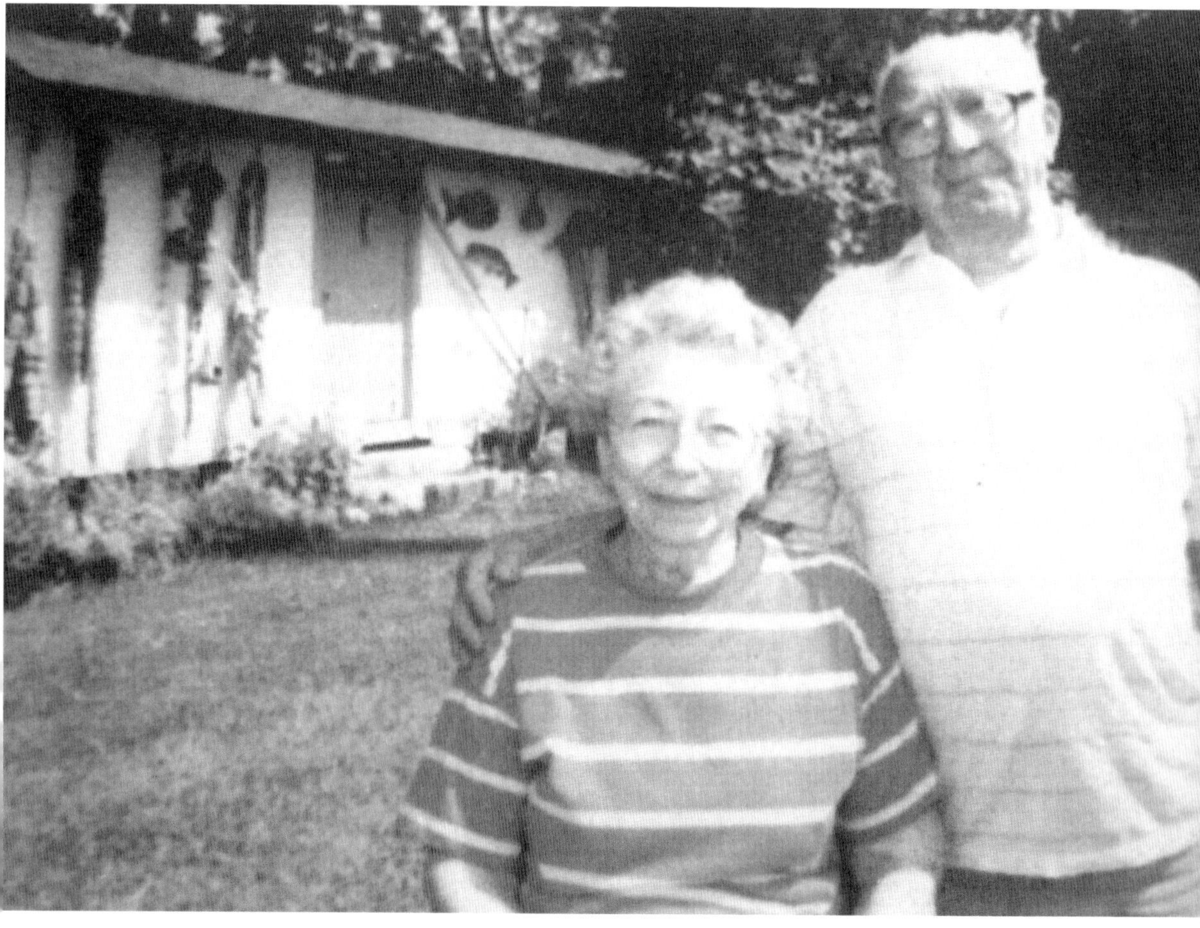

The Bug House

Started by a few local boys, the Bug House was a unique staple in Washington. Later called the Washington Field Museum, it was thought to be the largest amateur museum in the world. Situated near the Washington waterfront where Havens Gardens Park is today, the facility brought ecological education to youth across the county. (Courtesy of *Washington Daily News*.)

Elizabeth and Hugh Sterling

Run by teachers Elizabeth and Hugh Sterling for many years, the Washington Field Museum hosted educational programs for youth and adults for more than 50 years. Unfortunately, with a location so close to the water, the facility often flooded during storms, and finally, it was torn down because of its age. However, a memorial still stands in Havens Gardens to commemorate this place of education and fun in the community. (Courtesy of *Washington Daily News*.)

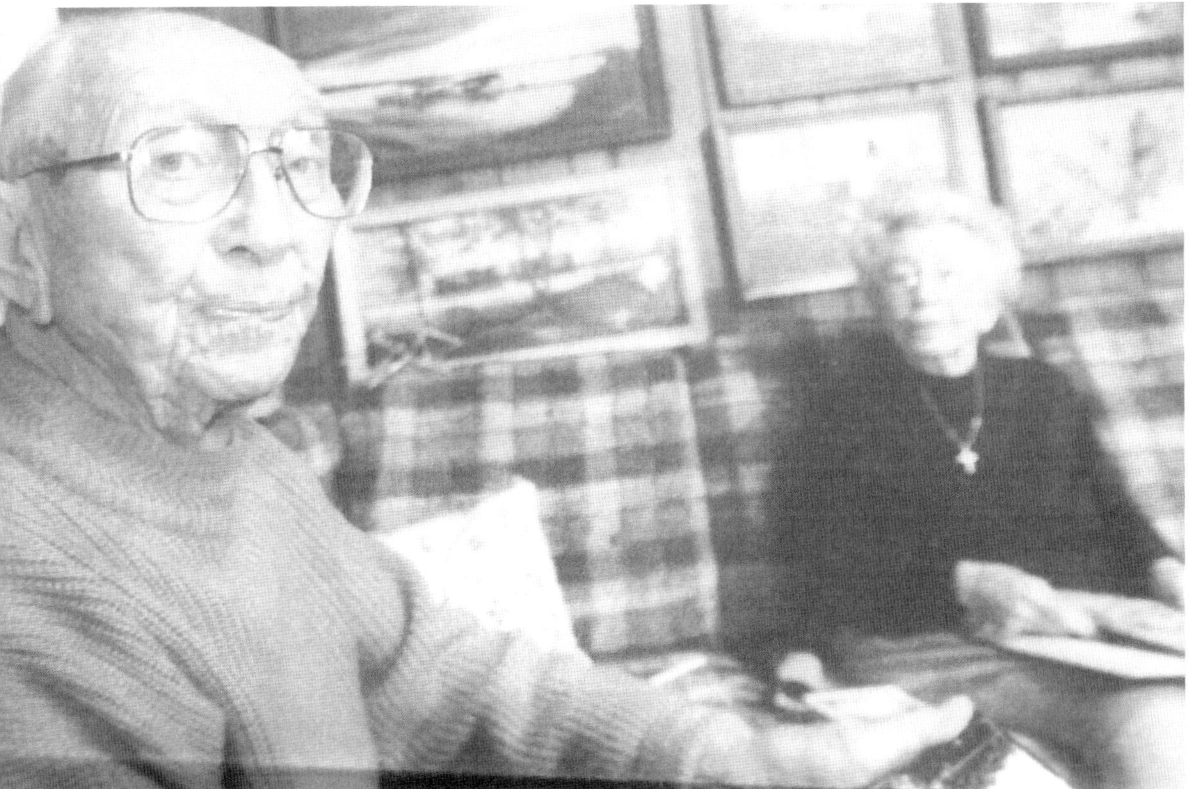

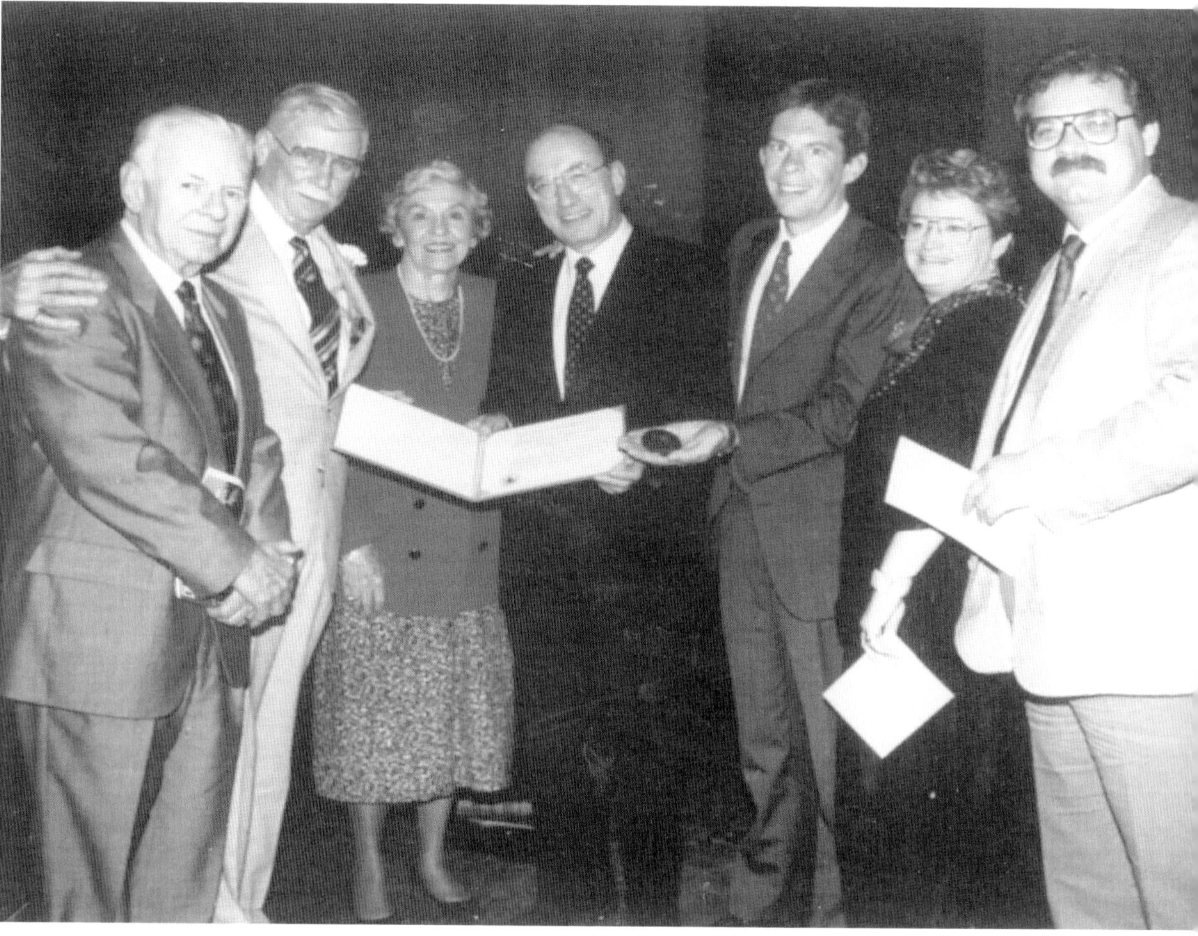

The Washington Daily News Pulitzer Prize–Winning Team

It is not common for small newspapers to gain prestigious awards. However, even in smaller towns, big news stories can fall into a reporter's lap. For Betty Mitchell Gray, the day her editor dropped a water report on her desk changed not only her newspaper's status but also better informed the townspeople of a serious problem with their water. She and Mike Voss researched and wrote about the issue.

Gray and Voss became longtime writers for the publication, but Gray had only been at the newspaper for six months prior to this assignment. Through their extensive research, they found that carcinogenic materials were present in the municipal water and that a lengthy cover-up of that information had ensued. Their series of articles lead to changes in the Environmental Protection Agency's regulatory requirements concerning water in small communities. It also netted the newspaper a Pulitzer for Meritorious Service. The *Washington Daily News* is one of the smallest newspapers to receive a Pulitzer Prize.

This photograph was taken right after the prize was awarded. From left to right are former *Washington Daily News* owner Ashley Futrell, former executive editor William J. Coughlin, Rachel Futrell, Columbia University president Dr. Michael Sovern, former publisher Ashley Brown "Brownie" Futrell Jr., and writers Betty Gray and Mike Voss. (Courtesy of *Washington Daily News*.)

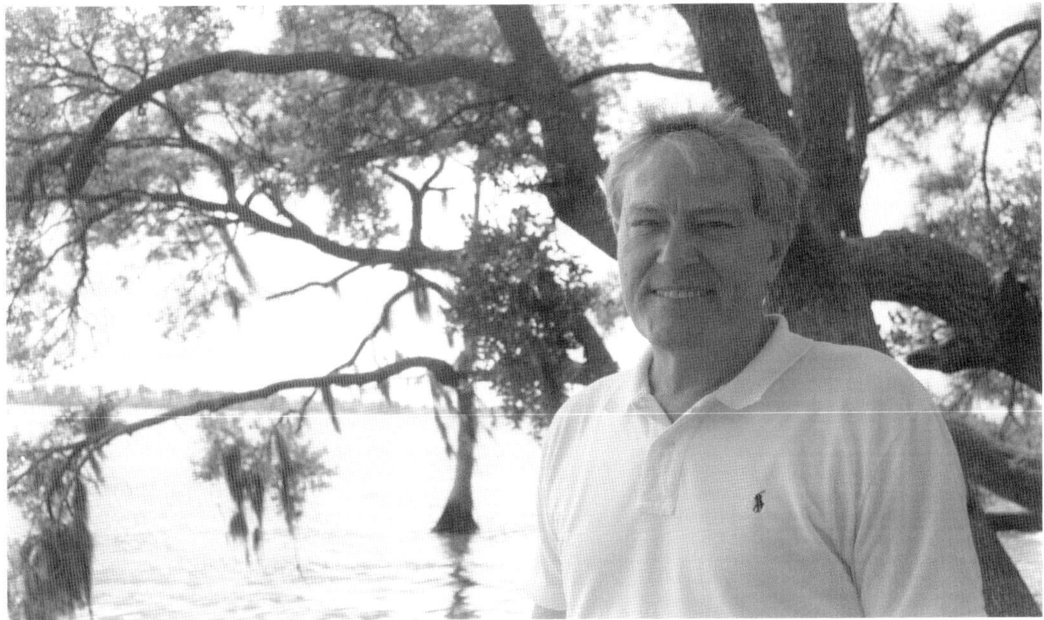

Blount Rumley
After dedicating 27 years to the North Carolina Estuarium, Blount Rumley has retired to his waterfront home in Washington Park, where he spends his time conducting regional and genealogical research. His goal is to compile a written history of the town and its people in a time period that is particularly lacking—from the early 1900s through World War II. In his quest to share the stories of the people in the area, he has collected a unique cache of historical and family research. He is quick to share what he has learned with others; all they have to do is ask, and Rumley will happily talk for hours about the history of his town. (Both, author's collection.)

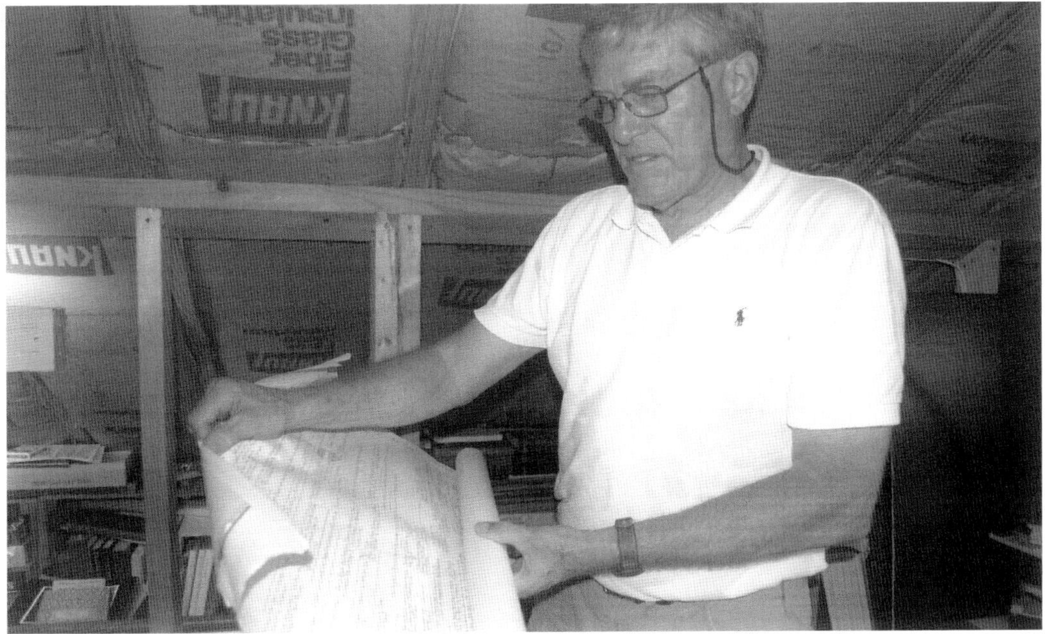

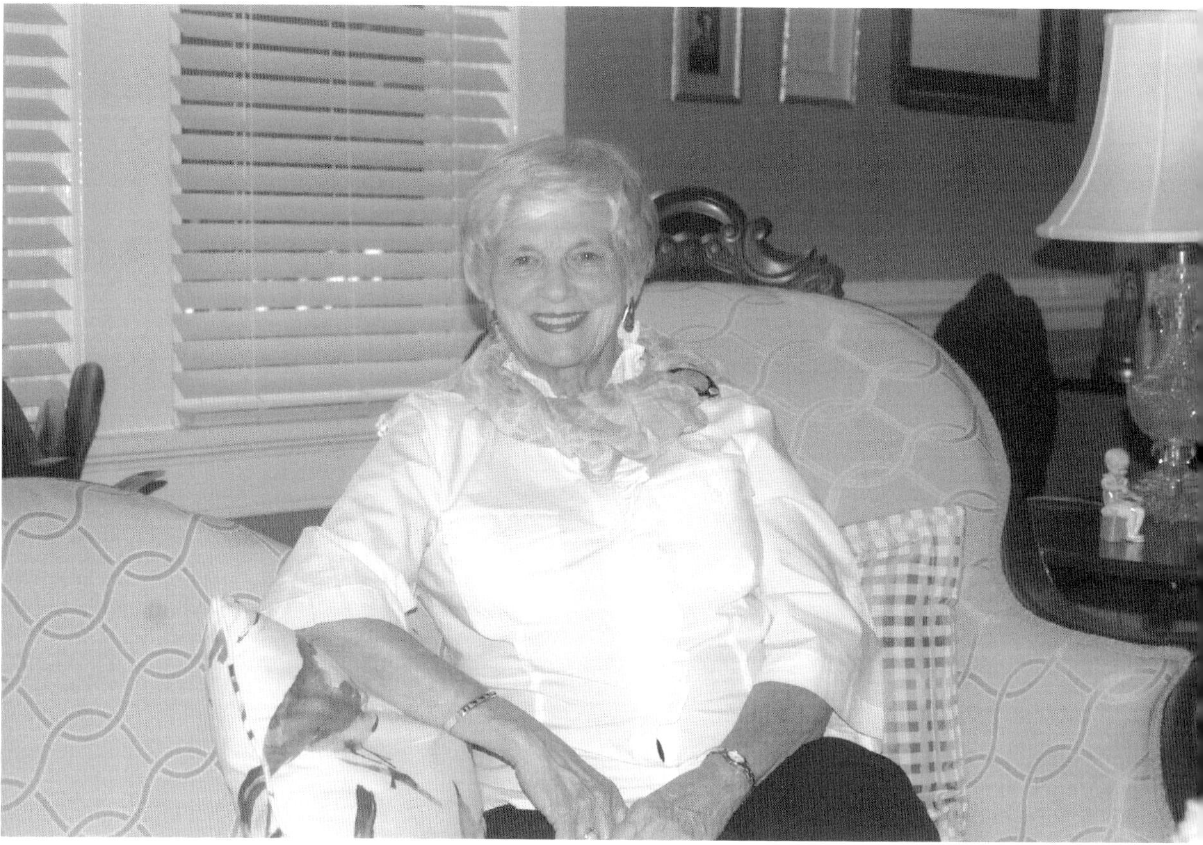

Betty Bonner Bradshaw

As a descendant of some of the first settlers in the area, the Bonners, and other prominent families such as the Havenses, Betty Bonner Bradshaw's connections with Washington run deep. For this reason, she knew the town's past must be preserved when some of its historic homes were being torn down. With the help of other concerned citizens, Bradshaw quickly worked to establish the historic district, which prevented further changes to the area where some of the town's oldest homes stand. Later, she also assisted in the move of the BHM Library into the old county courthouse building as a way of preserving the c. 1786 courthouse, the second oldest of its kind in North Carolina. (Author's collection.)

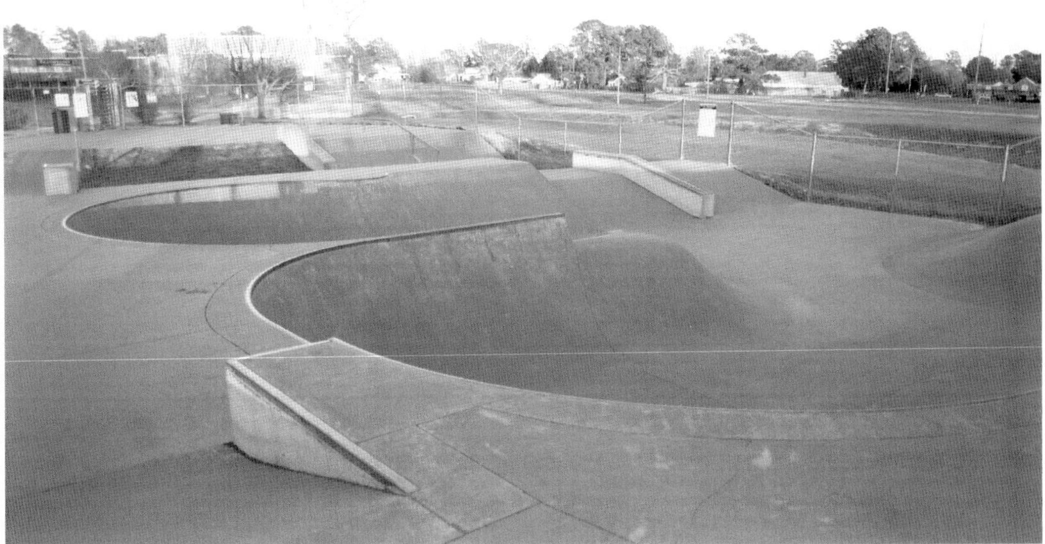

Patrick Harris Cochran

Patrick Harris Cochran was a lively child who enjoyed all types of sports. "Anything with a board on it, he loved it," his father, William, said. He and his twin brother, Kyle, could be found skateboarding, playing soccer, or working with their father. The community mourned when the 13-year-old died in an automobile accident. However, from this tragedy came a positive solution to the local youth's lack of skateboarding facilities. Years of fundraising efforts by the Cochran family and the community raised enough money to assist the town in building a multilevel skate park named in Patrick's honor. His parents and siblings still stop by the park on holidays, as they find it a place where they can feel close to Patrick. (Above, author's collection; below, courtesy of the Cochran family.)

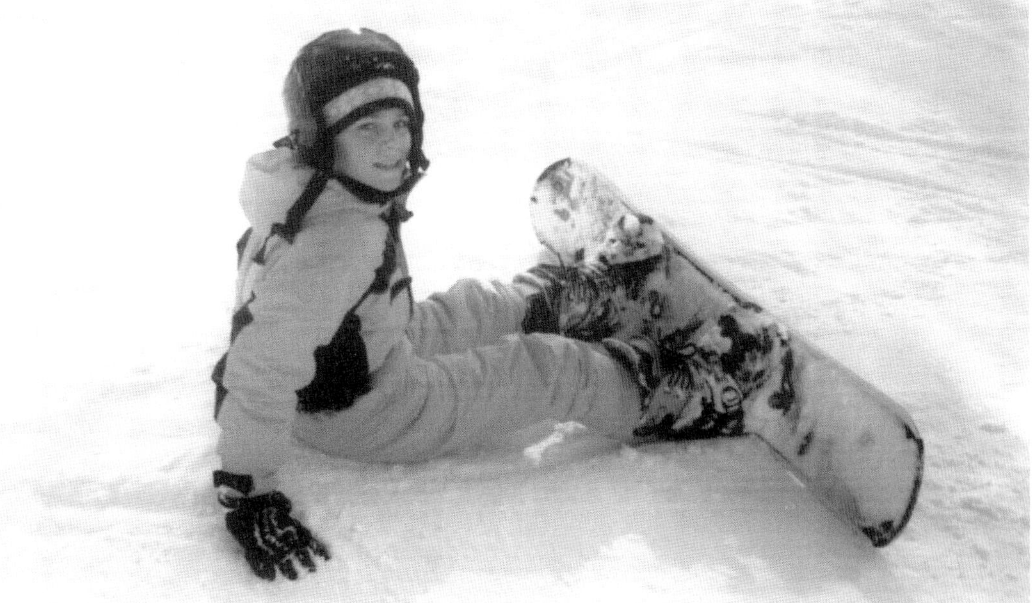

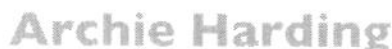

Archie Harding

After retiring from the New York City Department of Corrections, Archie Harding moved back to his hometown of Washington. He had a dream of opening his own business, and ran the Shop'n Bag, a small store on US Highway 264, for nearly 25 years. He often hired students from the community college just a short walk down the street. However, he was not content in just offering commercial services to his community. Harding also wanted to help. He has served on the boards of many organizations in town. A graduate of P.S. Jones Colored High School, he is an integral part of keeping the history of the school alive as a member of the reunion committee. (Courtesy of Archie Harding.)

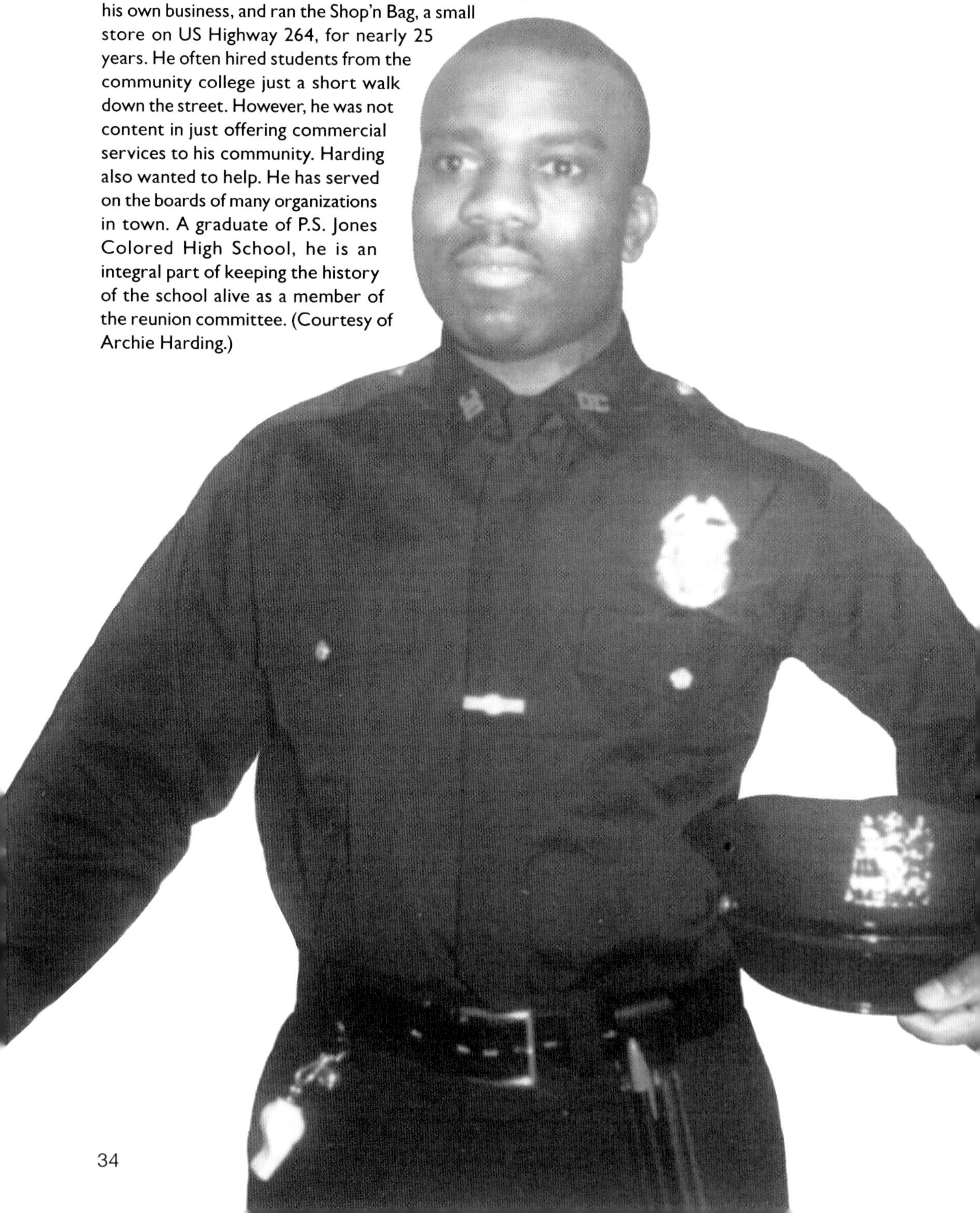

CHAPTER THREE

First Responders

In the years before the Internet and mass media, it was the job of one person in town to warn those nearby when hurricanes and other storms were headed toward the Washington area. With a little effort, they were able to possibly save the lives of their neighbors and friends in the event of severe weather conditions. However, the first responders who are most remembered served as a part of the many fire brigades that operated in town. There were up to 10 fire brigades in Washington during the early years of localized fire services. Several large fires claimed many buildings in the business district over the years, and the wharf saw its share of losses as well.

With the loss of property also comes the inevitable loss of life. Ed Peed of the Salamander Company was the first black man in the state recorded as having died in the line of duty. The town cares so much about its fire personnel that Peed's sacrifice was memorialized. The newer fire department learned of the nearly forgotten Peed, and it now houses the memorial so that it may care for it and preserve the memory of Peed and other firefighters' service to their town.

The history of Washington's fire and emergency services is diverse and long, and many men and women have served decades with the department, while many others have served for numerous years as volunteers, selflessly giving their time to their community. The men and women of today's law enforcement and emergency services continue to show the same dedication to saving lives and property as those who came before them.

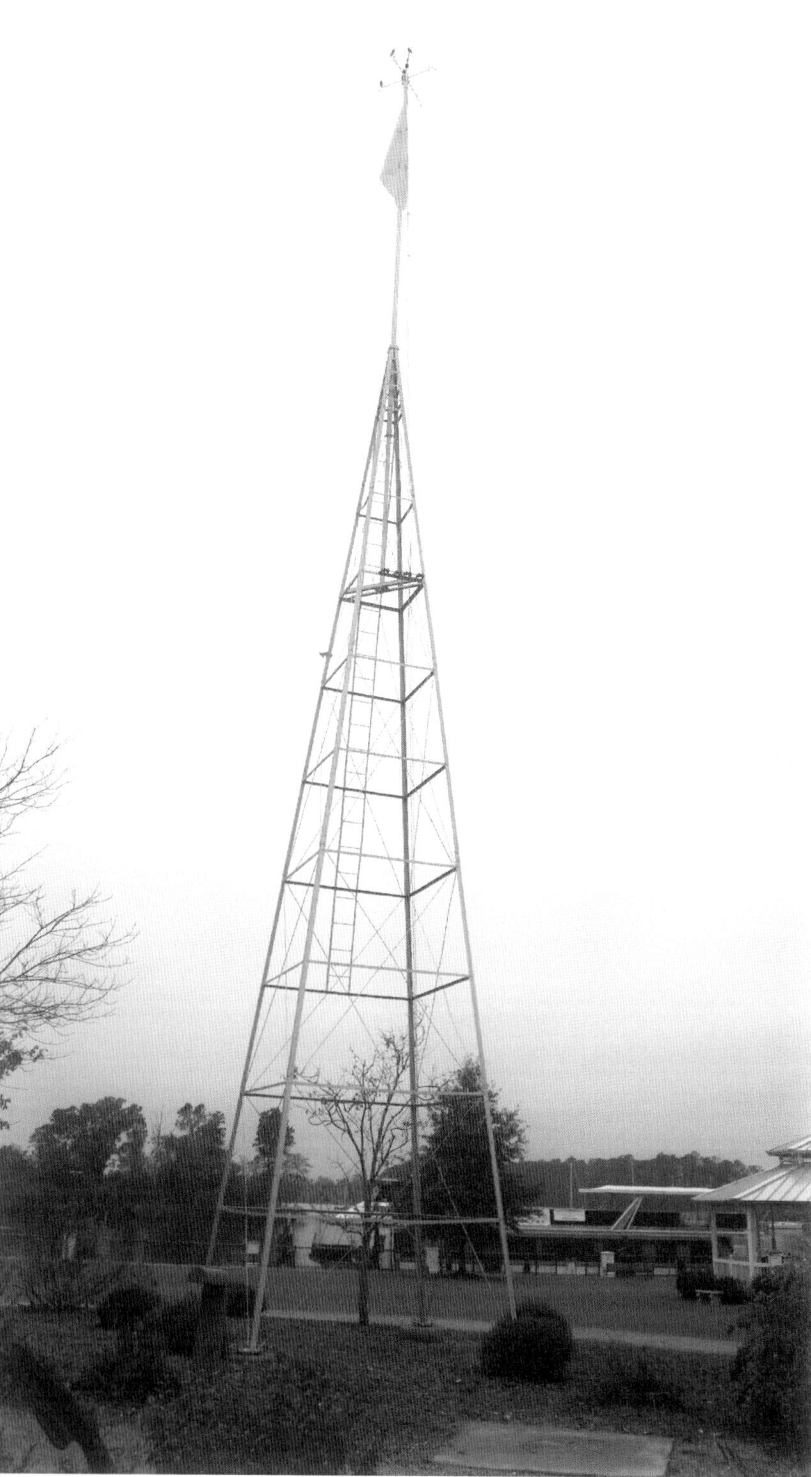

Mary Gallagher and Lossie Waters

Before modern weather radar systems, weather displaymen warned the community of impending storms by erecting combinations of colored flags and pendants. Interestingly, Washington's longtime displaymen were actually women. The first weather warning tower in Washington was erected in 1900 behind the Main Street home of Mary Gallagher, the wife of a local physician. Records from 1906 show that she was paid $12 a month for her service and that she still maintained this post when she was 88 years old. Following her death at age 91, her neighbor Lossie Waters took over the position, and the tower was moved a block down the street to be re-erected in her own yard. Waters was on duty during many memorable storms of the past century, including hurricanes Hazel, Ione, Diane, and Donna. She died in 1983 at the age of 94, just five years before the weather warning towers were discontinued. The monument to the bygone system stood in the yard of 720 Main Street until 2013, when the skeletal structure was donated to the city of Washington. The tower was stored for some time before it was erected at the North Carolina Estuarium by the Washington waterfront, where it continues to stand to this day. (Author's collection.)

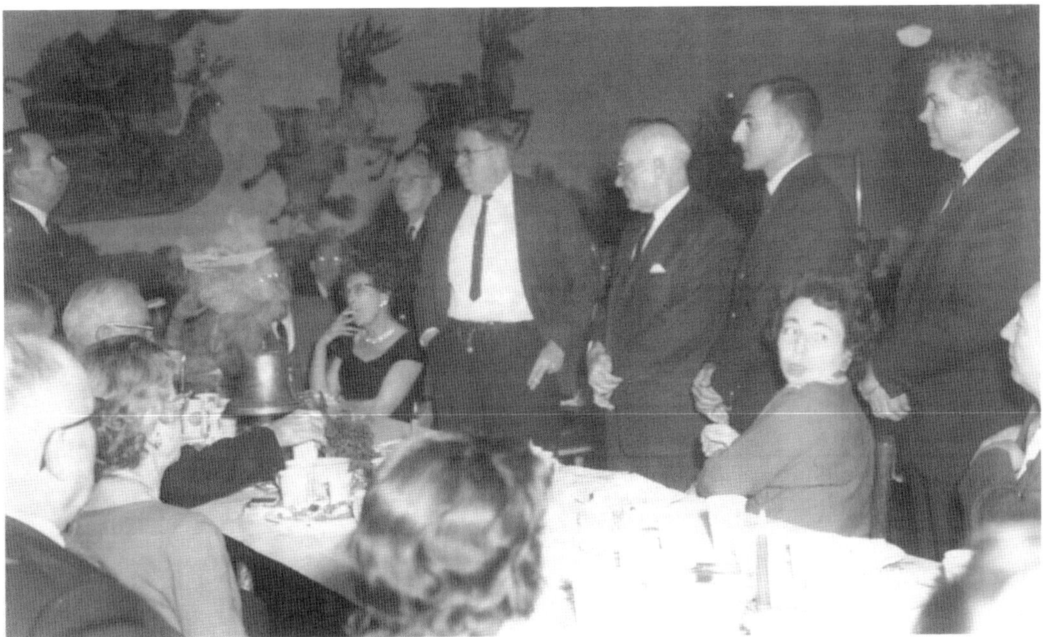

Dan T. Smith

Dan T. Smith was a fixture of the Washington Fire Department for over 34 years. He joined the department in 1924. Known as "Schmidt" around the department, he served the Volunteer Motor Company in many positions, including chief, assistant chief, and captain. He was given honorary status following his retirement due to his many contributions to the development of the fire department. Here, Charlie Yates (far left) presents Christmas checks to the paid firemen. Standing from left to right are Pop Bowen, Jonny Rochelle, Dan Smith, Tony Abeyounis, and Lee Stewart. (Courtesy of the Washington Fire Department.)

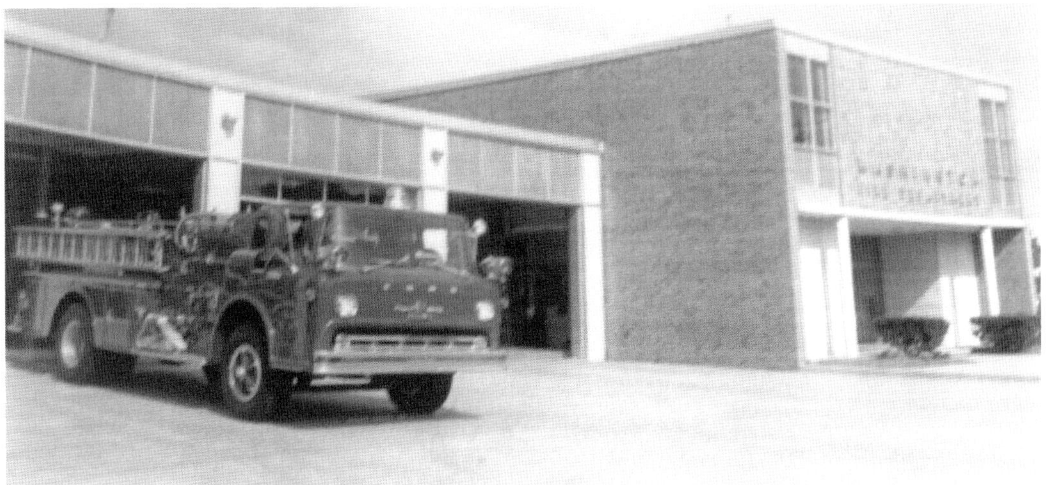

William Finlayson

William Finlayson delivered newspapers and groceries around town on his bicycle. For 54 years, he loaded his bike daily with copies of the *Washington Daily News* and the *News and Observer*. Locals note with amusement that, as a local volunteer firefighter, Finlayson had a fireman's plate on the front of his bike, on which he often arrived to fires. (Author's collection.)

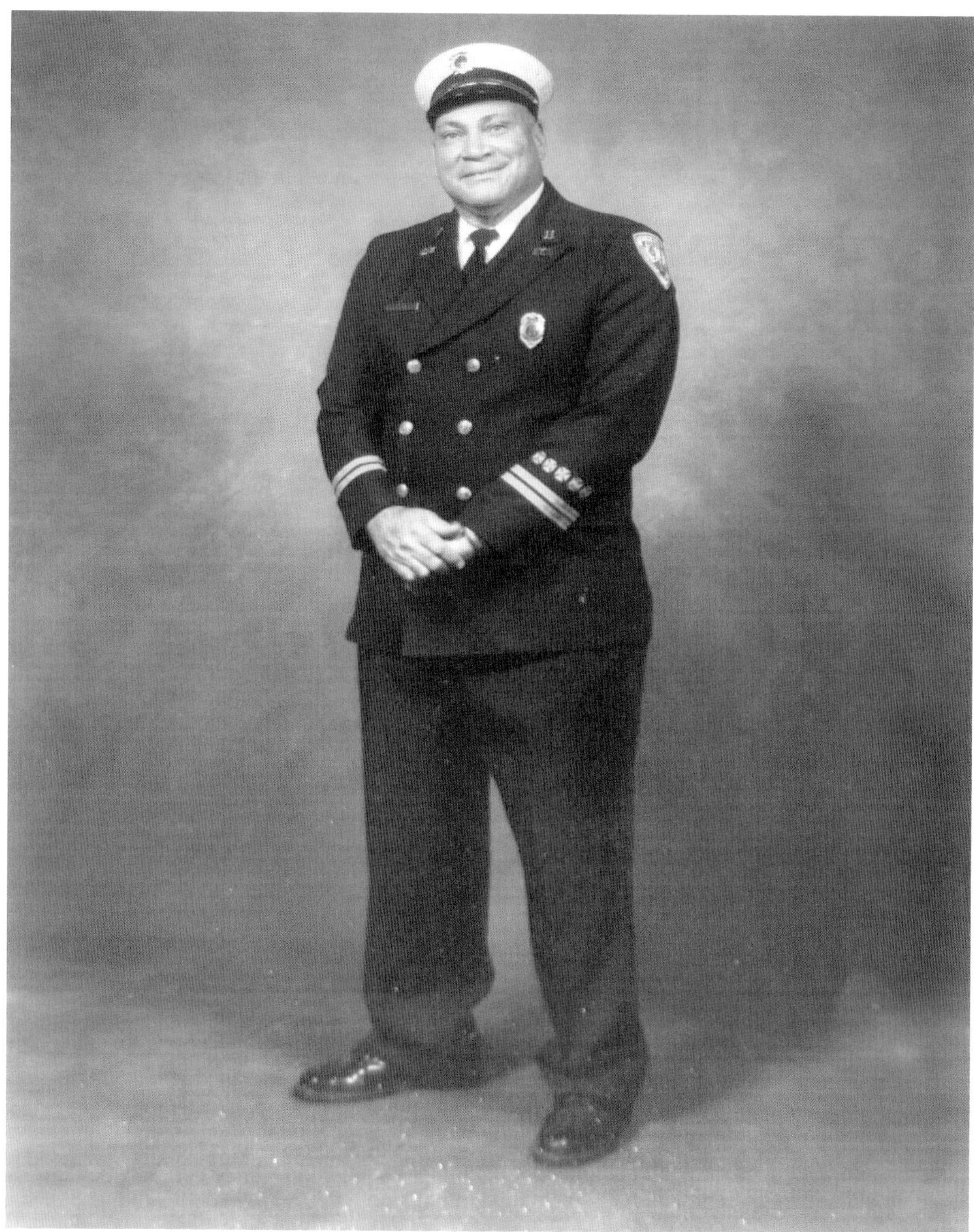

Richard Moore

Richard Moore was young and looking for work when he found employment at the Washington Fire Department in 1974. At the time, he did not know that he would serve the people in his town for 31 years as a firefighter. "It was a job where you can help people in the worst parts in their life," he said. "I enjoyed helping people." Retired as a decorated captain, he now spends his time enjoying his life at his leisure, which includes staying in touch with his two grown sons. (Courtesy of the Washington Fire Department.)

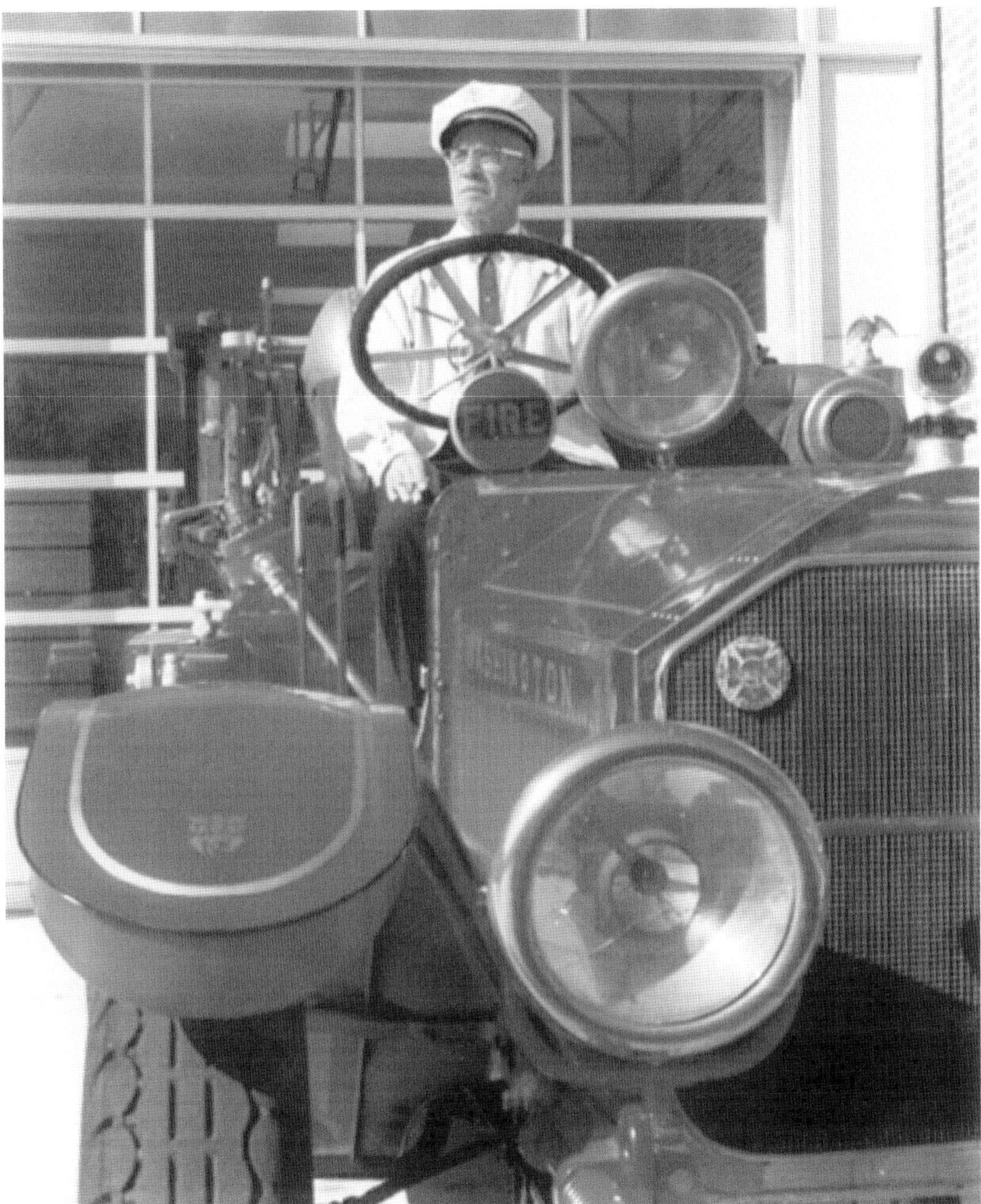

Fred Potts
Fred Potts served as a firefighter for Washington for many years before being appointed as fire chief in 1952, the same year the town's first rescue squad was formed. In 1965, he oversaw the department's move to its current location on the corner of Fifth and Market Streets, an event that brought over 3,000 people to the new fire station. Potts served as chief until 1972. By the time he left the department, it had grown to a staff of 11 paid firefighters and 57 volunteers. Today's generation may be more familiar with his son Zoph Potts, who is a businessman and community leader well known in the town of Washington. (Courtesy of the Washington Fire Department.)

Lonnie Jackson

Lonnie Jackson, one of the first two paid drivers in the fire department, was known to go beyond the call of duty. For many years, he would take out the horse-drawn fire wagon to pick up boys for Sunday school. Jackson was not a member of a church, so each Sunday, the fire wagon was parked outside of a different church. He died from a heart attack in 1930 while standing next to his fire truck. All the fire equipment was brought out to be part of his funeral procession. After his death, the fire whistle sounded each Sunday at 10:45 a.m. in his honor. (Courtesy of the Washington Fire Department.)

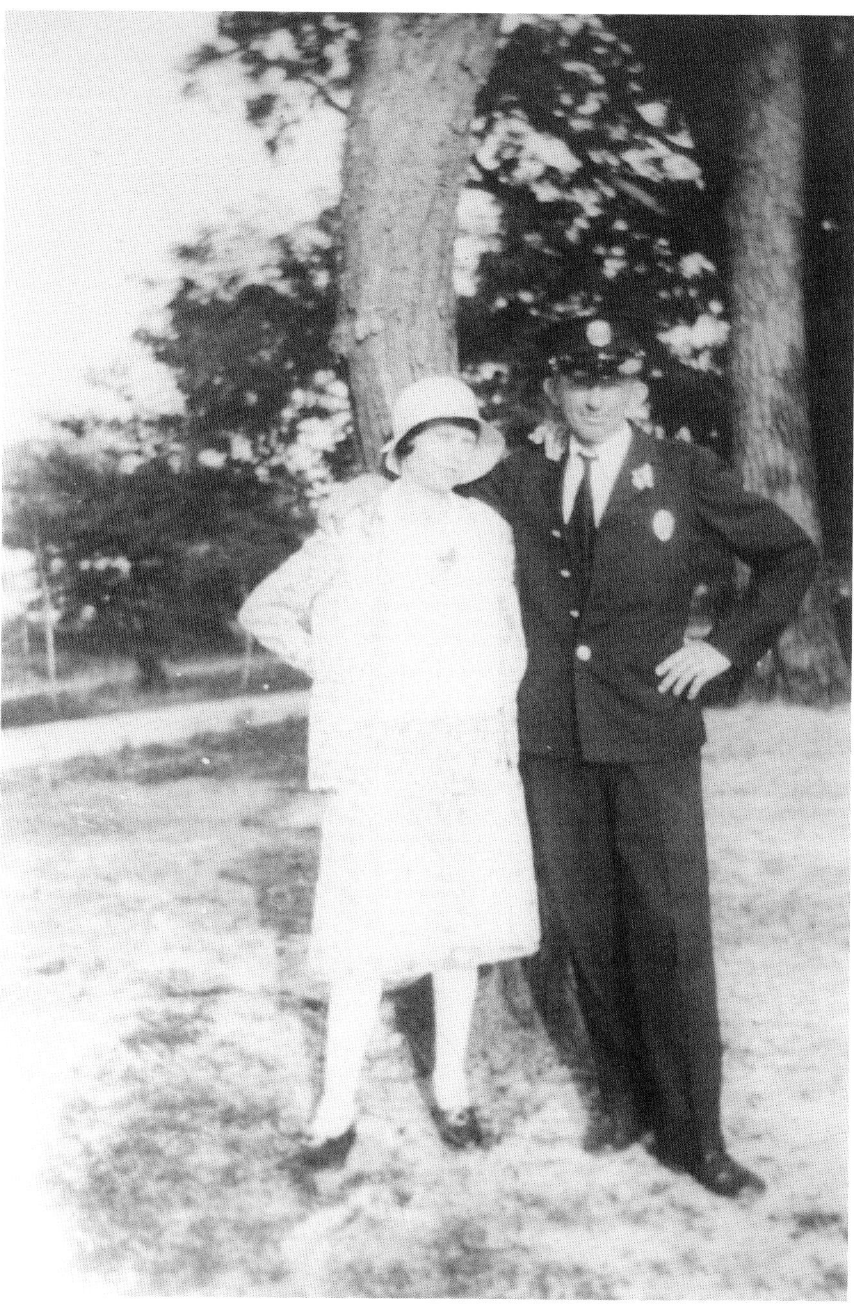

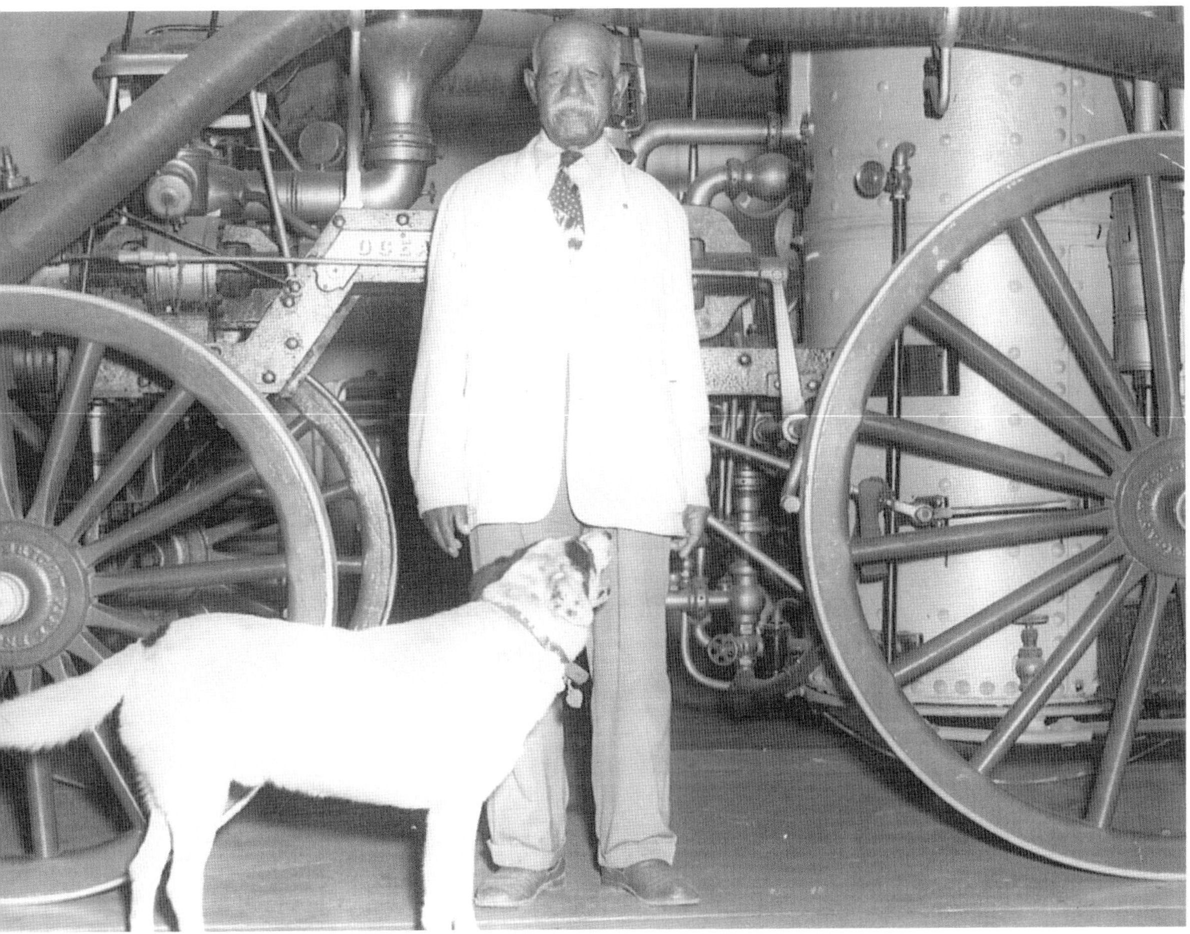

Sylvester Dibble

Founded in 1881, the Salamander Fire Company was the oldest black fire brigade in town. Leading the company was Prof. Sylvester Dibble, a highly respected man. Dibble was a barber by trade, and he and a partner operated Dibble and Brown, the only barbershop in town. His home was at the corner of Pierce and Second Streets. His was the only black family that resided in the main part of town.

Dibble was a commanding force for the Salamanders, who wore red fire helmets and sang hymns as they hand-pumped their cumbersome old fire truck. Black men who wanted to participate as true firefighters coveted a post with the Salamanders. If they were part of another fire brigade in town, these men were usually pumping the fire trucks and rarely participated in the more heroic elements of firefighting. The men on the Salamander brigade had high standards for themselves, as is evident in a contest that was held each year. All the fire brigades (up to 10 at any given time) competed to see who could get their pump trucks to produce a stream of water in the least amount of time. The Salamanders typically won.

Dibble was reelected as captain of the volunteer brigade year after year. His influence with other fire brigades in town only grew; Dibble was even made chief marshal of the firefighters' convention held in Washington in 1905. (Courtesy of the Washington Fire Department.)

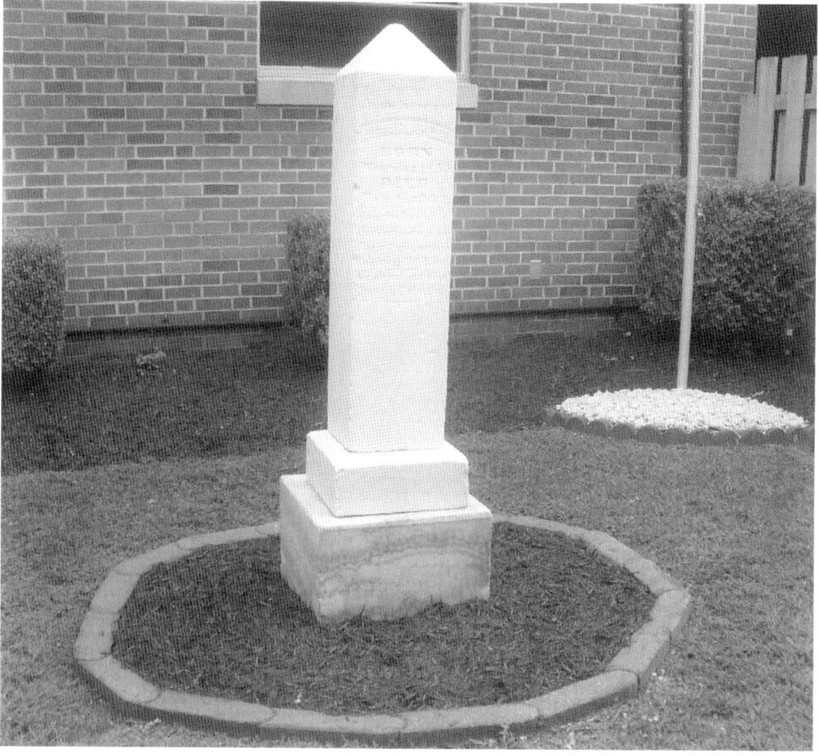

Ed Peed

On the evening of February 8, 1902, a small fire erupted in the Atlantic Coast Line freight warehouse on the Washington waterfront. A small flame from the flue grew in the dry warehouse, and within minutes, flames had engulfed the entire building. Fire crews arrived, but the steam engine failed them. Suddenly, the first responders found themselves at the mercy of a fire they were not sure they could contain.

The fire moved fast, and the old grain elevator building nearby caught fire. It continued to spread to the Hoyt building, then occupied by the E. Peterson Company. Fire crews from all over town came to assist as the fire moved from building to building along the waterfront.

It took three hours to finally contain the blaze. Soon after, Edward Peed, a nozzleman and 20-year veteran of the Salamander Fire Company, was splashing water onto a pile of broken rubbish when the westward wall of the Hoyt building suddenly collapsed, killing him instantly. He was the first firefighter in town to perish while on duty. Peed was mourned by all in the town. The *Washington Progress*, the local newspaper at the time, wrote: "He was a very worthy colored man and all of our citizens regret his misfortune." A group of white citizens pooled resources to purchase and erect a monument "in appreciation of his faithfulness."

Over the years, Peed's story faded from memory. It was resurrected nearly a century later when Charlie Yates, a longtime volunteer fireman, began doing research on the fallen firefighters. He found that the memorial stone had been moved in the 1960s to make way for P.S. Jones School, and in the years since, it and the other headstones in what is now Bebe Park had been neglected.

More research about Peed revealed something the Washington Fire Department did not know: Peed was the first black fire responder in the state of North Carolina to die in the line of duty. Yates and his fellow firefighters knew something had to be done to better preserve Peed's memory.

In 2000, the original monument was moved to Washington Fire Station No. 1 and settled into a small courtyard, where Peed's sacrifice for the town can be appreciated by future generations. Then, 11 years later, the Human Relations Council erected a headstone near his original resting place in Bebe Park. (Author's collection.)

CHAPTER FOUR

Doctors on Call

Washington has been home to many doctors. It is through the efforts of these men and women that advances in medicine and heath care have greatly improved in the area over the centuries. These doctors established hospitals and clinics. Most served the community through civic organizations. While some became businessmen like Dr. Samuel R. Fowle, others like Dr. Charles Payne found different ways to serve their community, such as Payne's most memorable role as a pastor. Still others served in the local government to find another way to help those around them.

While men might dominate history, women in Washington have also made significant contributions. Dr. Susan Dimock, for example, was one of the first female physicians to be formally recognized in the United States. While she did not practice in Washington, she was greatly influenced by the doctors of her hometown. Her primary focus grew into improving the nursing profession, moving nurses from a more passive to active role in heath care. Likewise, that was Katie Paul's goal when she took over the nursing education program at Tayloe Hospital. With the founding and growth of Beaufort Technical College (now Beaufort County Community College), her efforts to establish a professional nursing program in Washington are evident in the popularity of the nursing program at the college today.

Dr. Susan Dimock

Susan Dimock was born to Henry and Mary Dimock in Washington in 1847. Her father owned the Lafayette Hotel and served as editor for the *North Whig State*. As a young girl, Susan found an interest in medicine, and often rode with Dr. S.S. Satchwell, the family's neighbor, on his routes.

After her father died, Susan and her mother moved to Massachusetts. Susan studied at the New England Hospital for Women and Children in Boston, but when she applied for Harvard Medical School, she was denied because she was a woman. That did not deter Susan, who applied abroad and was accepted to the University of Zurich. She received her medical degree in 1871, making her the first female doctor from North Carolina.

Dr. Dimock made many contributions to the medical field. Her specialty was obstetrics and gynecology; however, her lasting contribution was leading improvements in nursing. At the time, nursing was viewed as minimal work based on labor rather than education. Like Florence Nightingale, Dimock thought that nurses could provide more, and under her watch, nurses not only learned as they worked but also attended lectures where they were taught more about human anatomy. Her contributions raised the profession to a respectable level, one that career middle-class women could pursue without appearing unseemly to the rest of society.

Dimock enjoyed her work, but she was still young. She wanted to travel and yearned to visit Europe again. She sailed for England, but she never arrived. Her ship sank after hitting a reef. Susan Dimock was 28 years old when she died. She was buried in Massachusetts.

Today, a small memorial honoring her stands at St. Peter's Episcopal Church in Washington. The Dimock Community Health Center in Massachusetts is also named in her honor. (Right, author's collection; inset, courtesy of Beaufort County Community College.)

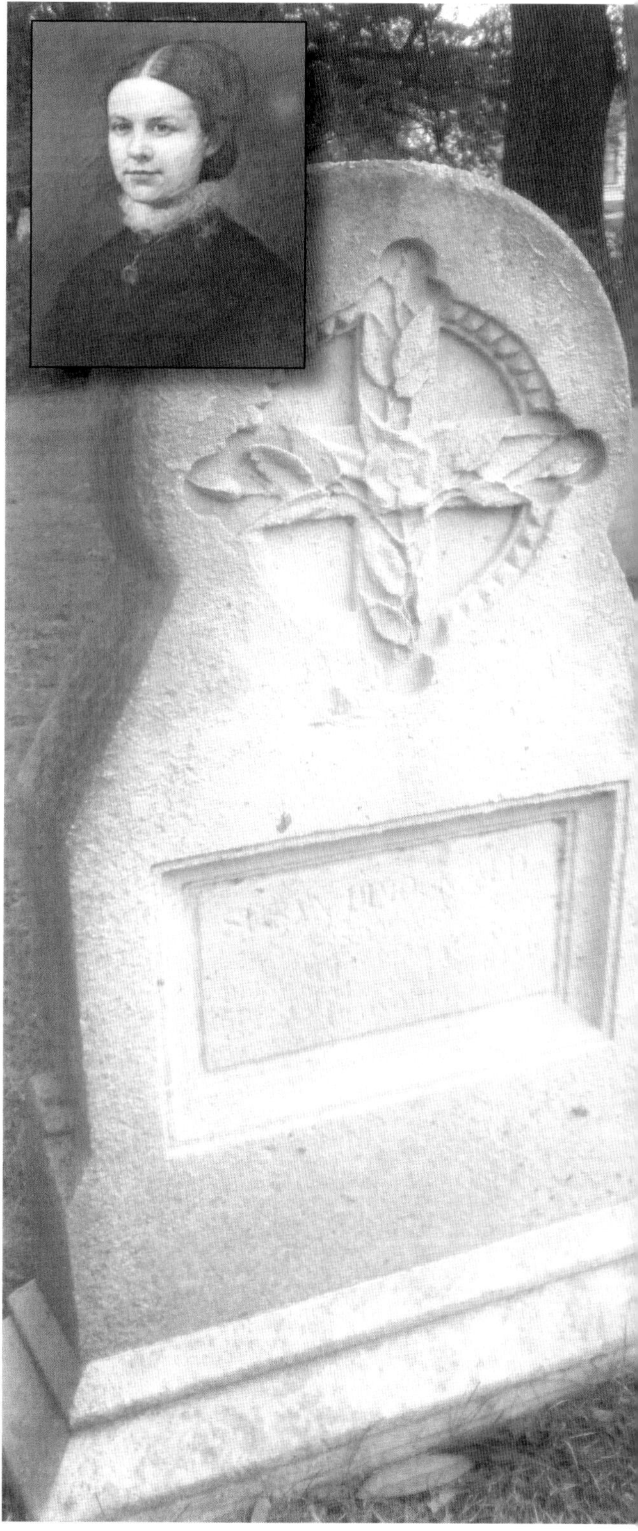

Dr. Patrick Maule

Dr. Patrick Maule practiced medicine in Bath during the early 18th century. He was the first doctor recorded for the Beaufort Prescient, and served the people in the area now known as Washington. He was a successful man, owning a large plantation at Maule's Point (pictured) on the south side of the Pamlico River. He served his community not only as a doctor but also as a statesman and community leader. He served in the General Assembly of North Carolina twice (1733 and 1735), representing the Beaufort precinct. He was also a member of the vestry at St. Thomas Episcopal Church in Bath and a well-known figure in the area.

What really made Dr. Maule a legend, however, was not his skills in state or medical affairs. Instead, many in Washington remember him for how he survived a Tuscaroran raid.

In the 1700s, tensions between the natives and the new settlers were growing. Native peoples were treated poorly, and throughout the summer of 1711, groups met privately to plan an onslaught. The natives gathered at the village of Catechna (now Grifton) to plan their attacks. The raids were set for Saturday, September 22. Just days before the planned attack, surveyor and explorer John Lawson happened upon the village. His was the first of many deaths to come as a result of the natives' scheme. Interestingly, Maule's older brother, William, had once worked with Lawson and later rose to the position of surveyor general.

When the Tuscarorans struck, it was without warning. No one in their path was spared. That morning, Maule was visiting John Porter Jr. in his home at the head of the Chocowinity Bay. Porter's home was one of the first to be hit in the attacks along the Pamlico River. A band of warriors rushed toward the home, scooping up an infant and preparing to smash its head against a tree. Porter's wife, Sarah, ran at the man, snatched the infant away, and darted back to the family home. The men brought out their guns and covered the women and children as they ran for the shore. They were successful in holding off the warriors long enough to get everyone to a boat. They escaped with their lives, but they watched from the boat as the house and all the family's possessions were burned. (Author's collection.)

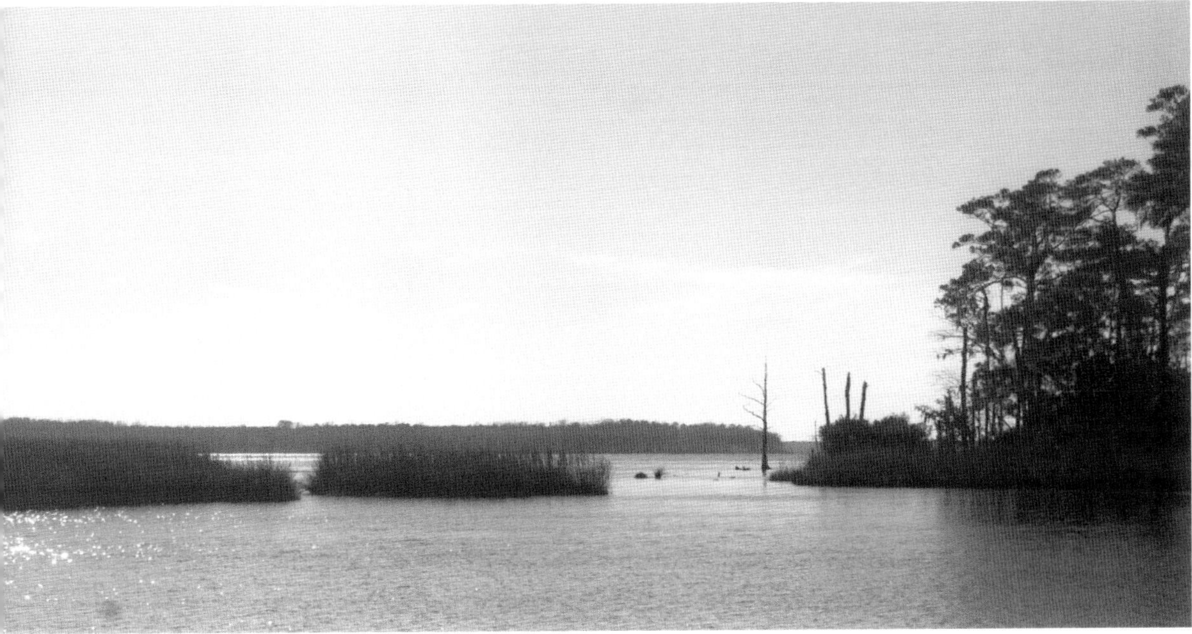

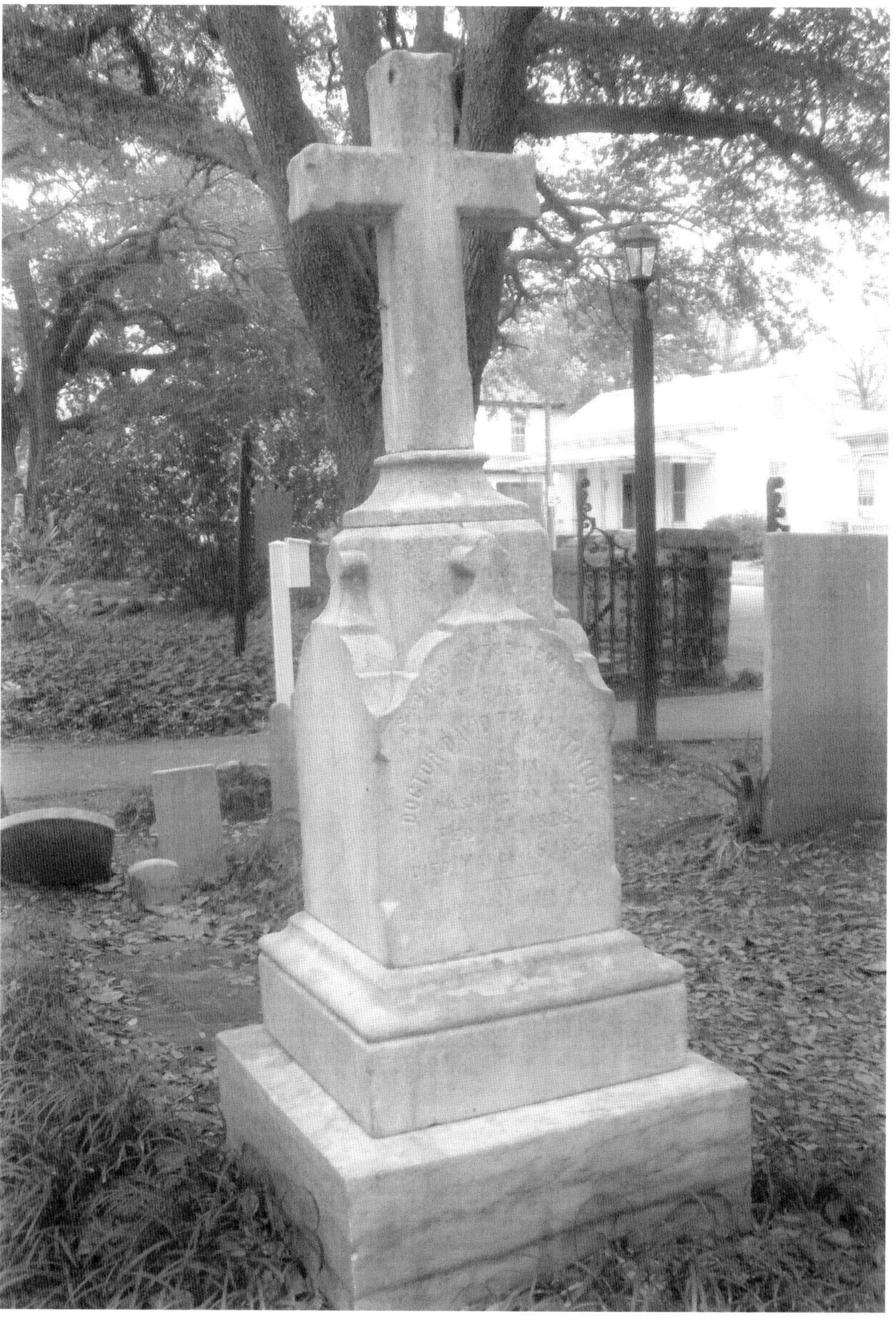

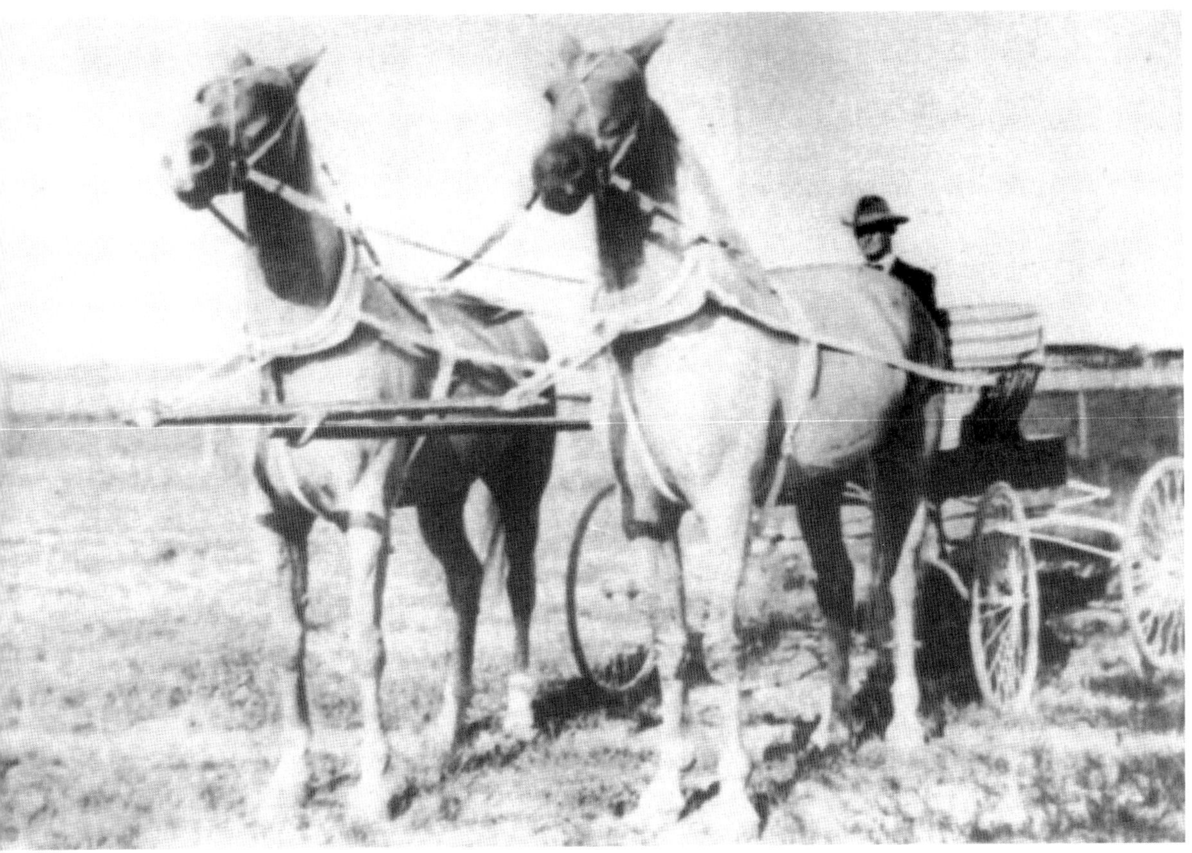

A Family of Doctors

With the town's hospital facilities needing renovation and expansion, Dr. David C. Tayloe acquired a home on Main Street to add to the town's current surgical facilities. Interestingly, there have been five Dr. David Tayloes who have served Washington, but the one many remember most fondly is "Dr. Dave," as he was affectionately known. As a leader in pediatric medicine, he helped improve health care for children across the state. The Tayloe family also had other doctors not named for the family patriarch, including Joshua Tayloe (pictured above). For more than 100 years, the Tayloes have run the town's locally owned pharmacy. (Opposite, author's collection; above, courtesy of the Brown Library.)

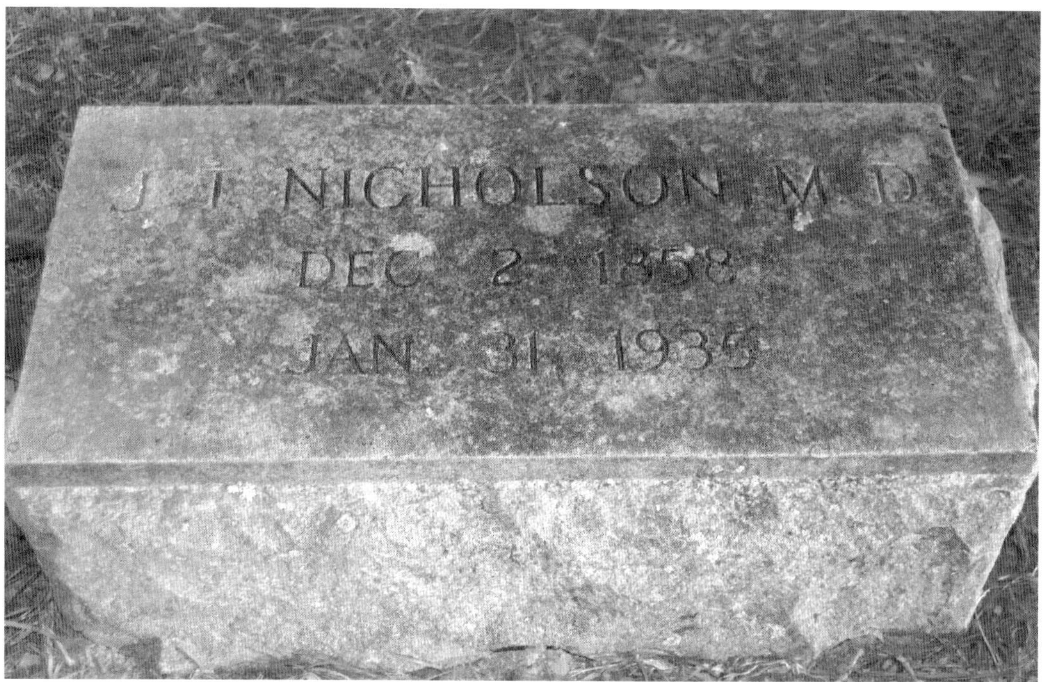

Doctors Nicholson

The spirit of healing also ran through the Nicholson family. Samuel Timothy Plummer and Jack Nicholson were well-liked and respected doctors who served Beaufort County. Jack, who settled in Bath, is remembered as having performed the first caesarian operation in the area. Dr. S.T. Nicholson's son, Dr. Jack Nicholson, became the chief surgeon at Fowle Memorial Hospital before opening his own hospital, Riverview, in the 1920s. (Author's collection.)

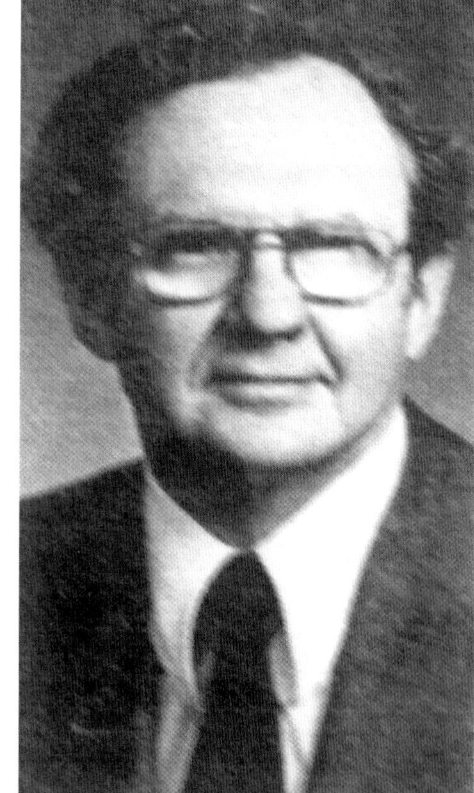

Dr. Lewis Swindell

In 1919, Dr. Lewis Swindell, a native of neighboring Hyde County, came to Washington, where he ran the Riverview Hospital until 1926. He then took over as chief of surgery at Fowle Memorial Hospital until 1958, when Beaufort County Hospital opened. Later, he pursued a career in education, serving as the dean of Atlantic Christian College for 26 years. (Courtesy of *Washington Daily News*.)

CHAPTER FIVE

Political Leaders

Politics are not for everyone. It takes a person with strong will to enter the political arena in order to accomplish what must be done for the people they represent. Washington has had its share of politicians. From those with federal assignments to those who serve as mayor or town commissioner, each finds a way to contribute to their constituents to make their lives better. No matter who they are, their purpose is to make a difference.

Washington's politicians tend to not only work in the area of politics, but they also spend a lot of time helping the community at large. They often are part of civic organizations or are involved in business. Regardless of their background, each contributes to the community in a special way.

However, just as in any other aspect of living in a community, some politicians find themselves embroiled in scandal. These people often leave politics to avoid additional issues from their accusers—although William Blount's escape from US politics into the government of the future state of Tennessee might be an exception. Most are not so lucky. When Robert Tripp Ross's improper connections came to light, he decided to leave government work all together and return to the merchandise business. Luckily, in Washington, it seems more politicians work to bring good than bad to their community, and most scandalous personal agendas are set aside.

In the modern era, politics have become more diverse, including more women and people of color. For example, the town's first black mayor worked diligently to remove the ramshackle buildings, or "blights," as he called them. Through his work with other local leaders, these old buildings were removed, leading the town to receive a prestigious award. Other projects implemented during the reign of the town's first and only female mayor added the well-known North Carolina Estuarium and changed the face of the Washington waterfront. These changes bring more and more visitors to the waterfront and businesses downtown, even today.

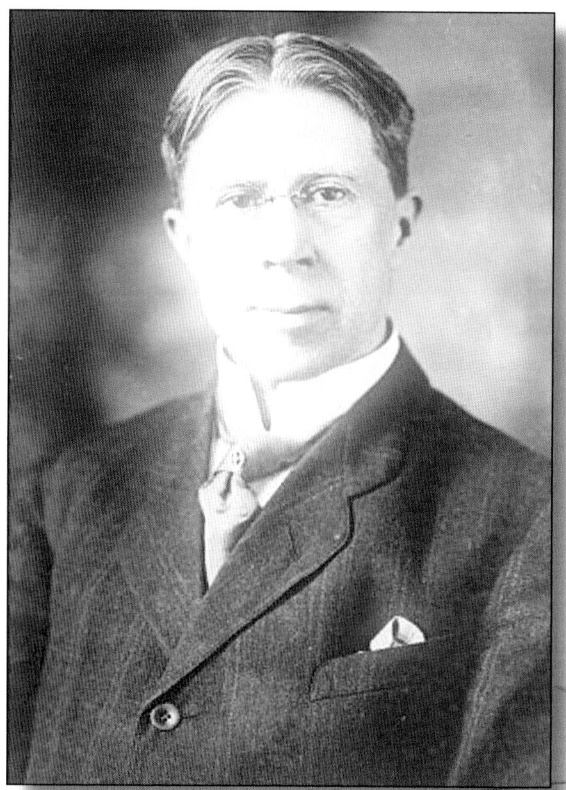

John Humphrey Small

John Humphrey Small was born in Washington. Small was dedicated to the law, but he served Beaufort County and Washington in many positions, including county superintendent of public instruction, town councilman, county attorney, and editor for the *Washington Gazette*. In Congress, he became an outspoken leader for the Democratic Party. He is most remembered for his work in helping to create the Atlantic Intracoastal Waterway, a project that was a hard sell until World War I, when the focus shifted away from commerce to defense. Small diligently served North Carolina's First Congressional District for 11 years and later became a staff member of the Securities and Exchange Commission. Following his retirement, he spent his final years once again living in his hometown. (Left, courtesy of the Library of Congress; below, author's collection.)

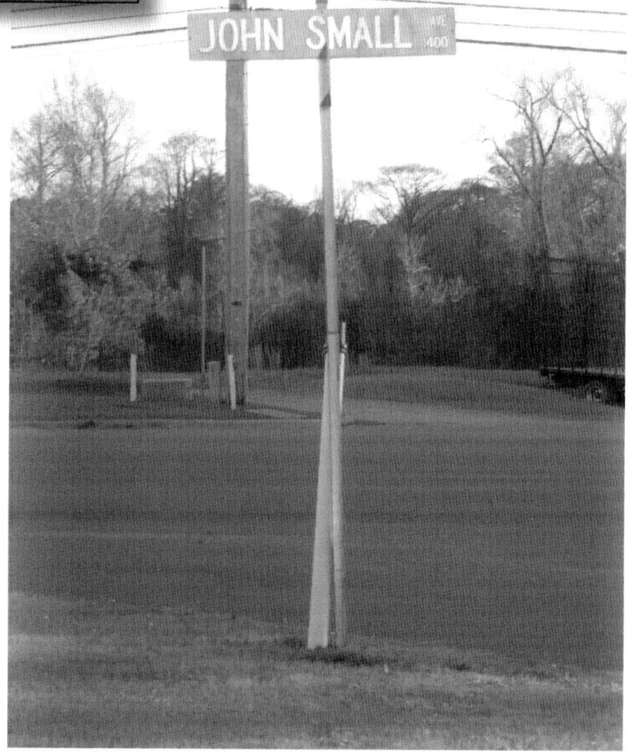

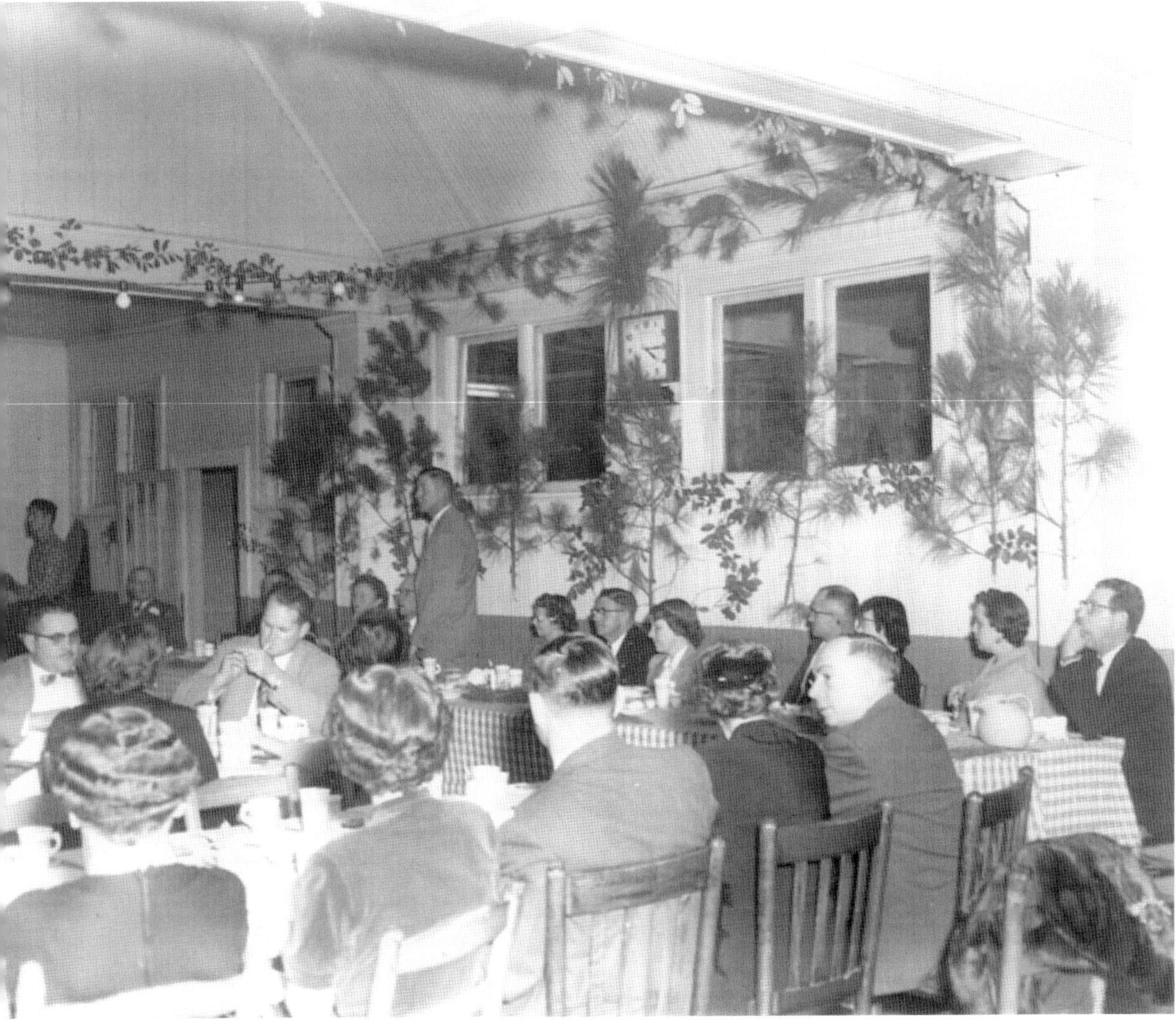

Herbert Covington Bonner

Democratic representative Herbert Covington Bonner (pictured at far right during a Washington firefighters' holiday party) was a native of Washington. In addition to serving many civic organizations, he worked as a salesman, and like many others in the area, he also had a hand in the agriculture business. After serving in World War I, he went to Washington, DC, as an aid for his hometown neighbor Lindsay Warren. His interest in politics grew, and he was elected to Congress, where he served 13 terms. As chairman of the House Marine and Fisheries Committee, he was integral in approving the first nuclear-powered merchant ship and innovations in Coast Guard and water navigation projects. The Bonner Bridge on the Outer Banks is named in his honor. (Courtesy of the Washington Fire Department.)

Robert Tripp Ross

Washington native Robert Tripp Ross served in many posts for the federal government, including two years as a representative for New York. While serving as assistant secretary of defense for legislative and public affairs, Ross's political career was embroiled in scandal in 1957. Wynn Enterprises of Knoxville, Tennessee, owned by Ross's brother-in-law H.D. Wynn, and another company with which the family was affiliated were awarded approximately $5 million in military contracts. Ross had once been an officer for the company, and he was still listed as an officer when he began working for the Defense Department. Wynn claimed this was a mistake. Ross resigned from his post and the Senate's investigation was eventually dropped. He was never charged but moved out of politics, becoming vice president of the Merchandising Apparel Company. (Author's collection.)

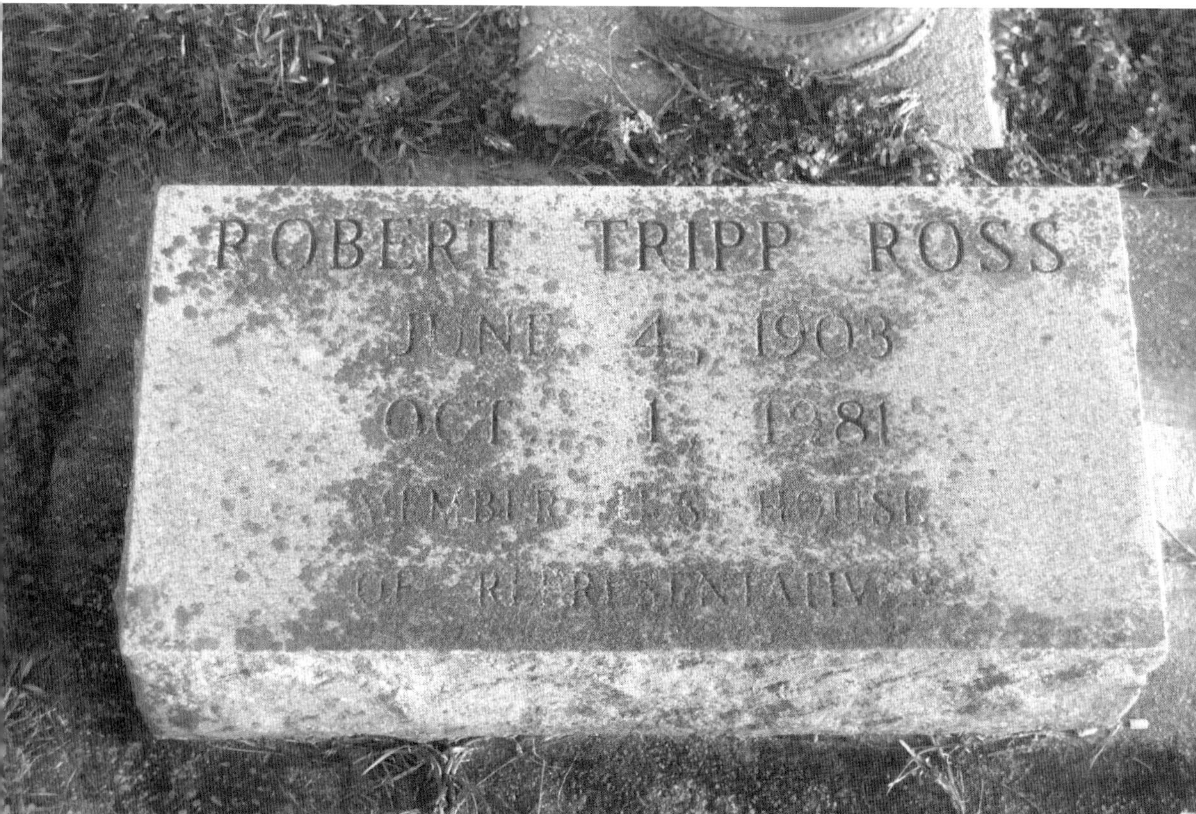

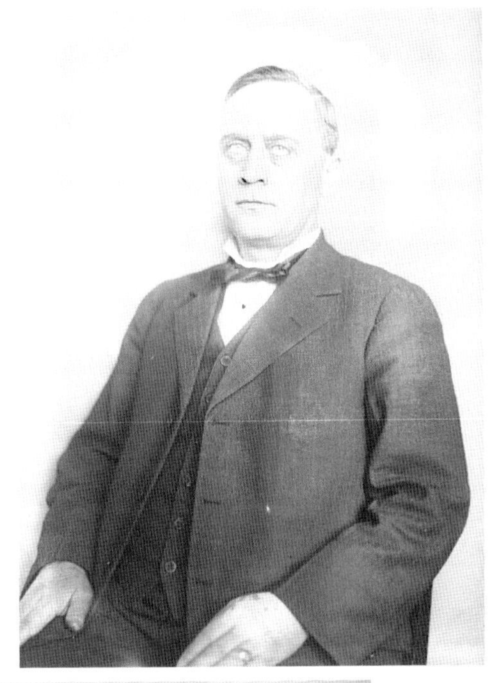

Hallett Sydney Ward

In his years as solicitor of the First Judicial District, Hallett Sydney Ward gained the moniker "Hot Stuff" based on his initials. He was part of many important trials during that period. The Democrat was then elected to Congress. He served two terms in the Senate before moving to Washington to practice law. A devout worshiper, Ward taught the men's Bible classes at St. Peter's Episcopal Church for 34 years. (Courtesy of the Library of Congress.)

Lindsay Carter Warren

A lifelong politician, Warren (left) was named county attorney the same year he entered the bar. He served in both the state and federal governments, where he was a part of many lasting decisions. For example, Warren opposed the ratification of the 19th amendment; however, he was a champion for North Carolina, supporting the creation of the Cape Hatteras National Seashore Act and the Wright Brothers National Memorial. (Courtesy of the Library of Congress.)

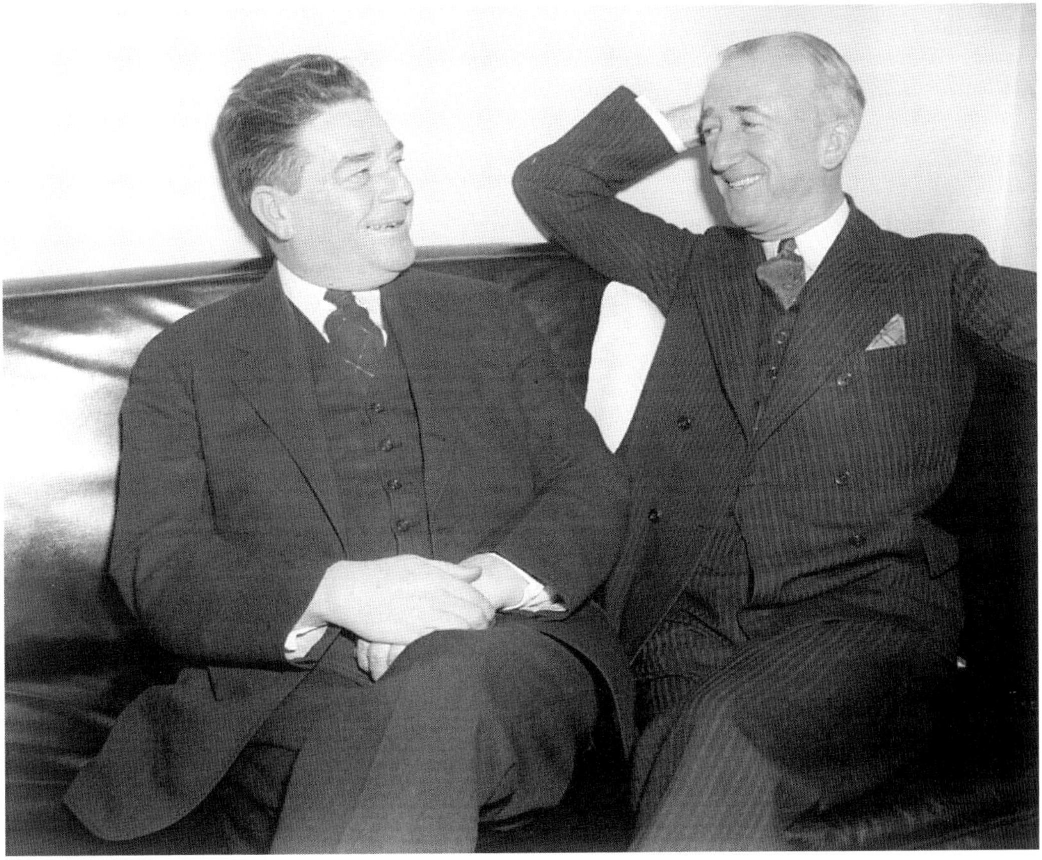

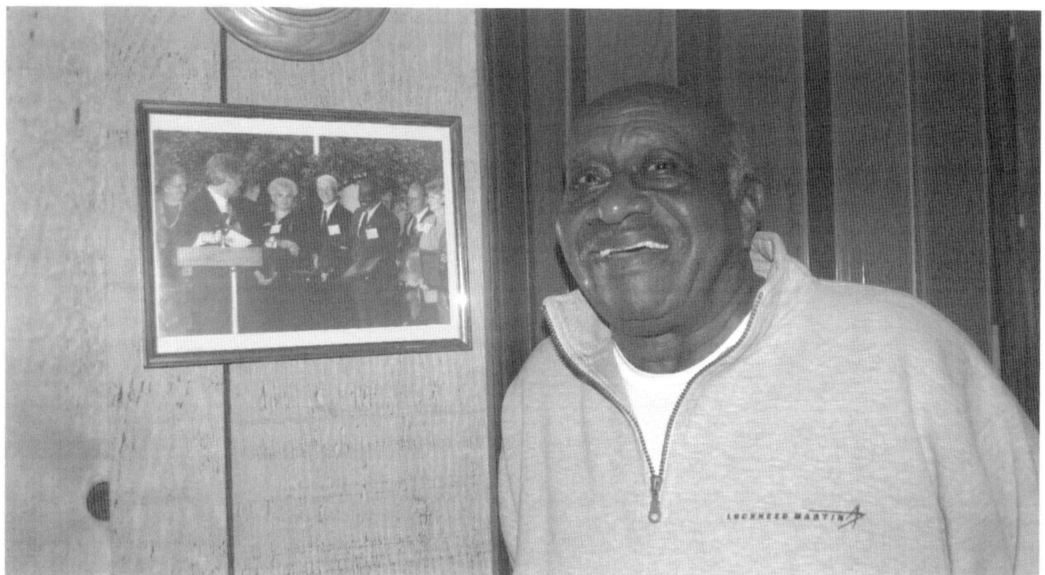

Floyd Brothers

Floyd Brothers took office as the town's first black mayor after the previous mayor had passed away. He was reelected twice, and during his service, Washington was named an All-America City for the many improvements made around town. For this award, Brothers gave a speech at the White House Rose Garden, where he met Pres. Bill Clinton. However, he says his children and grandchildren's successes have brought him the most joy in life. (Author's collection.)

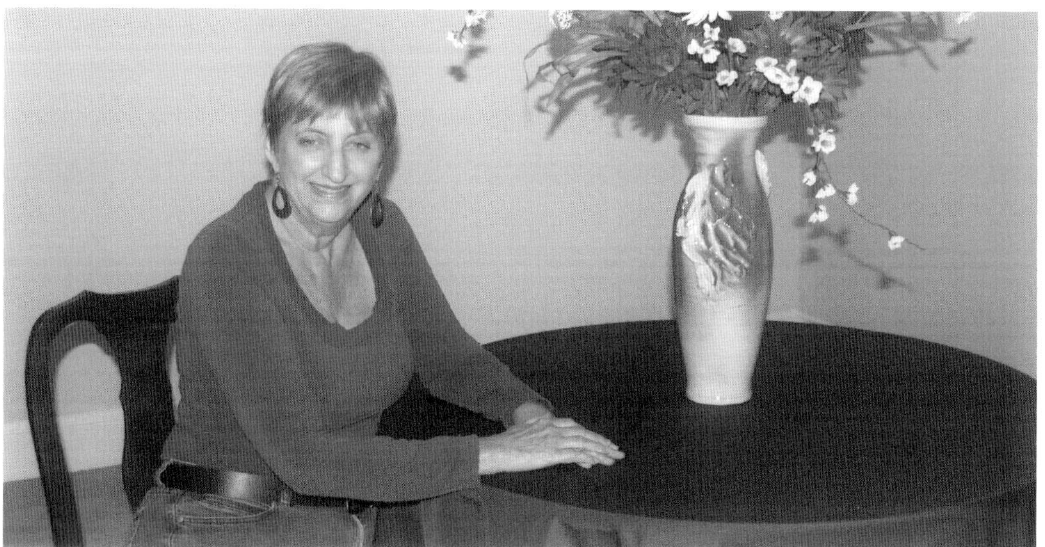

Judy Jennette

Politics is often an old man's game, but Judy Jennette found her leadership role quickly. She led the Beaufort County Arts Council right after college and had become a member of the town's commission by age 29, serving for 16 years. She later served two terms as Washington's only female mayor. As mayor she oversaw many changes, including renovations to the waterfront that have shaped it into what it is today. (Author's collection.)

CHAPTER SIX

Law and Order

Like many small cities, Washington sees its fair share of petty crime, but major crimes often seem like a distant issue only larger cities must endure. However, the quiet serenity of the waterfront town is shattered when a major criminal act occurs. From civil rights to patricide, major crimes do not escape notice. Families and neighbors know the criminals, and they know the victims. Some white-collar crimes, such as those of William Blount, signer of the US Constitution and the first senator ousted from Congress, leave few noticeable victims.

In some cases, like the trial of Joan Little, the outcome sets a precedent still in place today. As both the victim and a criminal, Little's case made people consider possibilities that they might not have before. Likewise, Sarah Keys's arrest for not moving from her place on the bus when asked led to a ruling making segregation illegal on interstate bus routes. The ruling in the case was made just weeks before the issue hit the national stage with the arrest of Rosa Parks. These cases highlight the benefits that can come from fighting for civil rights.

Other crimes, however, have a grislier end. The murders of well-known citizens shake the community in many ways. When certain citizens took revenge on the killer of the toll bridge owner, law enforcement could not find a suspect. But in the case of Lieth Von Stein's murder in 1988, the most famous in recent memory, there was little relief when it was discovered that the person who had planned the murder was Von Stein's own son.

Just as the people who commit crimes are remembered, the town also has many people who specialize in dealing with the law. Judges try cases of people in the community, while lawyers take the time to get to really know their clients so as to clearly and fully represent them in the courtroom. Without these men and women, the system of law and order would not function. In contributing to the system, these professionals make sure that justice is served and those charged are fairly represented to avoid miscarriages of justice.

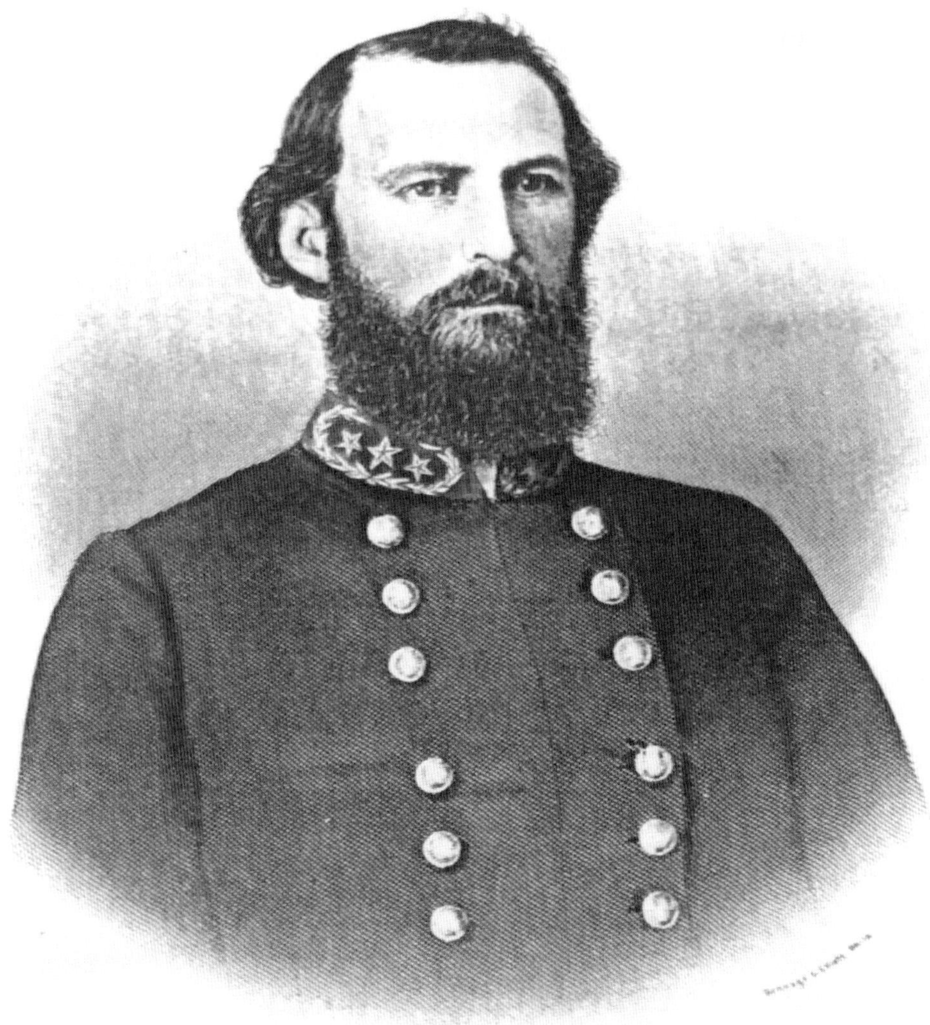

Gen. Bryan Grimes
Heir to the Grimesland plantation, Bryan Grimes was eager to join the political arena during the presidency of Abraham Lincoln. He was said to be a proud member of the state convention that signed the Order of Secession, and he happily gave up his political career for a military one. He was part of many battles during the Civil War, retiring with the rank of general.

Sometime later, he returned to the family plantation just a few miles from Washington to pursue the life of a planter.

However, it was on his way home from a political gathering in Washington that Grimes met an untimely end. Crossing the bridge over Bear Creek, he was shot by an assassin. William Parker, a local man said to be of "bad character," was accused of the crime, but he was later released, stalling the case. It was seven years later when Parker drunkenly confessed to the crime and was brought into police custody. Later that night, unknown citizens took Parker from the jail. The next morning, a local fisherman reported a body hanging from the Grimes family bridge. Parker's death was not investigated seriously, and no one was ever changed for the crime. (Courtesy of the Brown Library.)

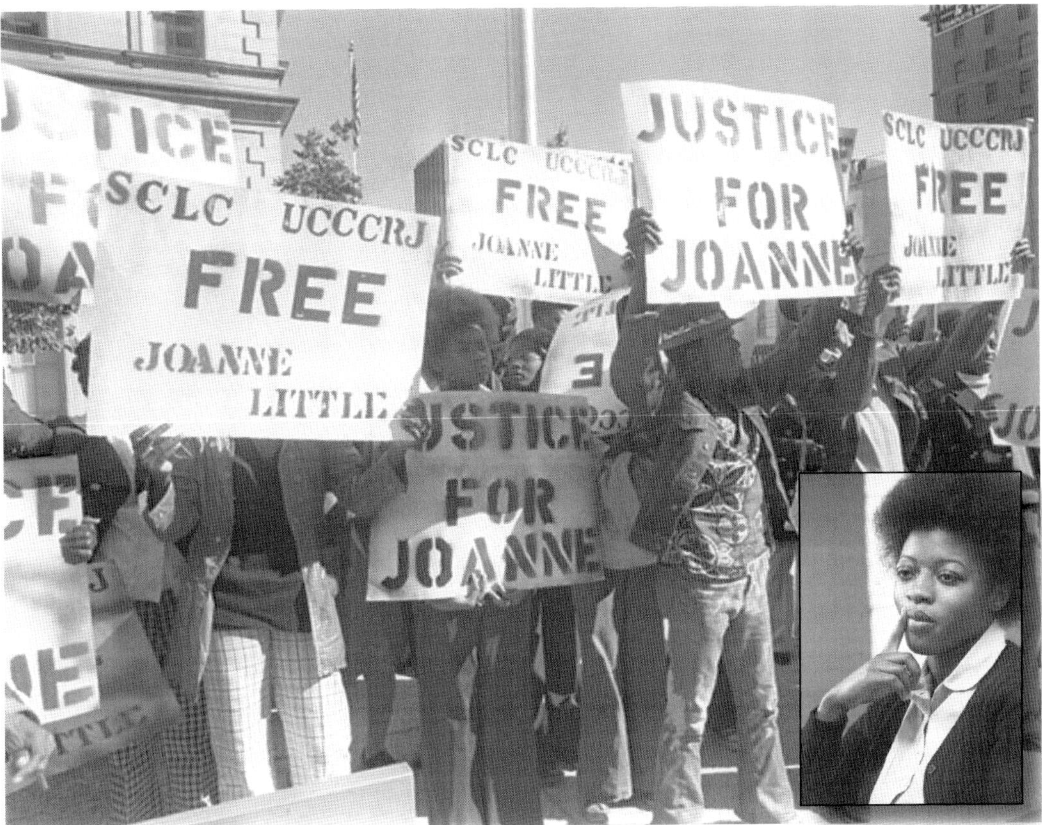

Joan Little

Joan Little was born to a mother who was considered a religious fanatic and an absentee father who lived and worked in New York. In her youth, she took to running away, and over the years, her crimes escalated. She was accused of shoplifting, breaking and entering, and many other small crimes, but many times, she did not receive harsh penalties.

In January 1974, she was caught shoplifting in Washington, but the issue was dismissed. Six days later, however, she was arrested again, this time for felony breaking and entering and larceny. She was convicted and sent to the county jail.

Three months later, a jailer was shocked to see a guard in Little's prison bunk. Guard Clarence Alligood was found partially undressed and had been stabbed many times with an icepick. Little had escaped, but she returned to turn herself in a week later.

In an era when black people were often convicted on little or no evidence, Little was in major trouble. How could she prove that the guard had sexually assaulted her first? She had clearly killed the man, but she had only done so to protect herself. There was no precedent for such a defense, and at the time, a conviction of first-degree murder carried a mandatory death sentence.

The case gained attention for its connection to racial tension, women's rights, and capital punishment. The case leaned on the selection of jurors. A new method of jury selection was used, and it was six white and six black jurors who decided her fate of not guilty. After she had finished serving her previous sentence, Little moved from the Washington area to New York, but her landmark victory continues to assist lawyers defending similar cases of self-defense today. (Both, Wikimedia Commons.)

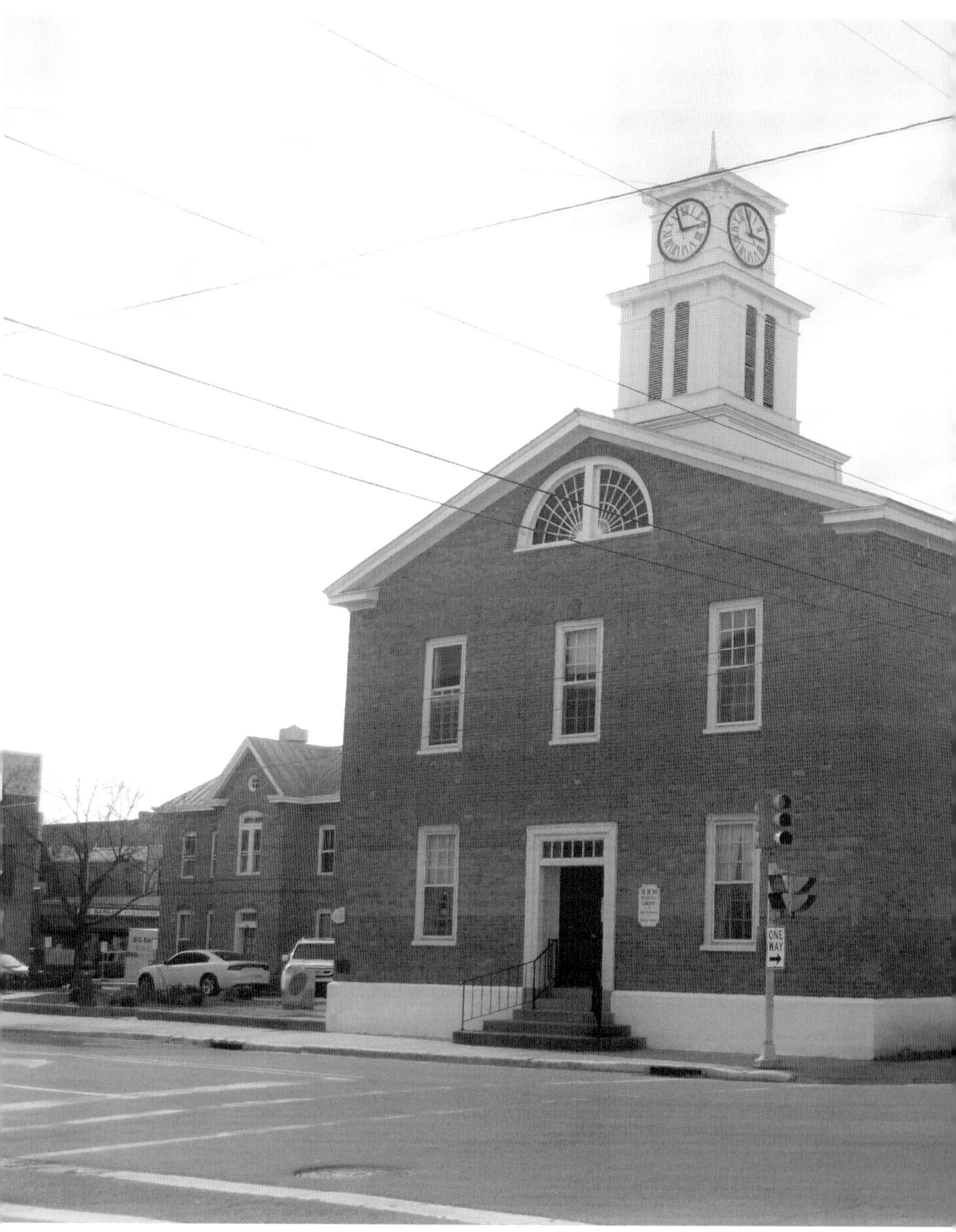
ONE
WAY

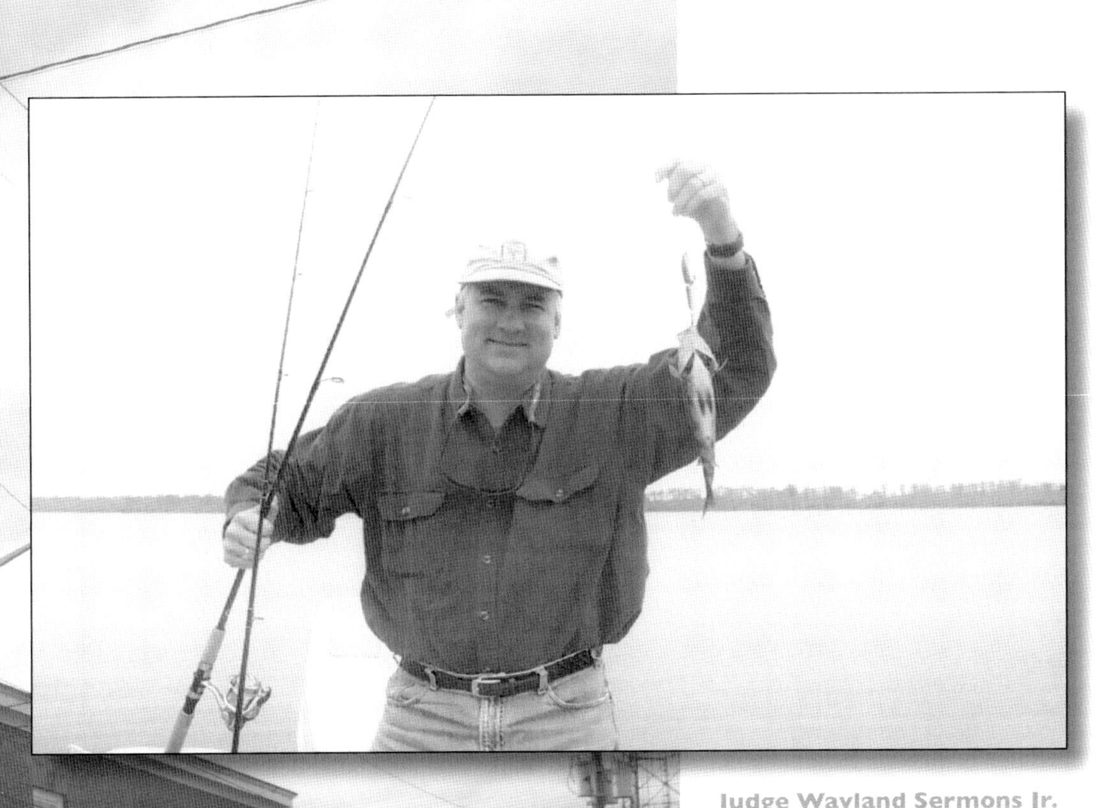

Judge Wayland Sermons Jr.
Washington attorney Wayland Sermons Jr. defended alleged criminals in many cases from 1981 to 2009. Probably his most well-known case was defending James Bartlett Upchurch III in the Von Leith murder trial. He also served his community in the role of town attorney for Chocowinity and Bath. During his time working with Bath, Sermons helped the town as it worked to preserve its historical atmosphere. In 2009, Gov. Beverly Purdue appointed him the senior resident judge for the Second Judicial District after Judge William C. Griffin retired. While his current term ends in 2018, he hopes to continue to serve the local justice system for many years to come. Pictured at left is Old Beaufort County Courthouse. (Author's collection; inset, courtesy of Wayland Sermons Jr.)

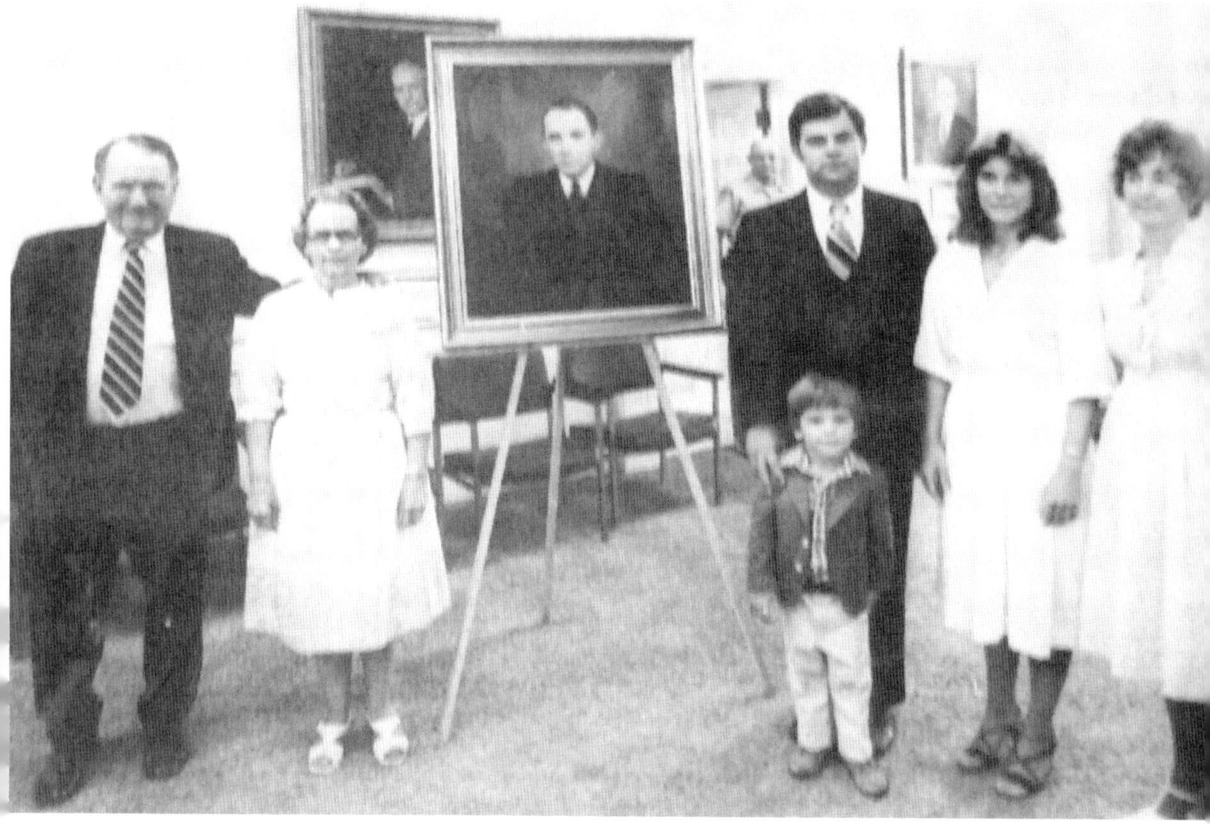

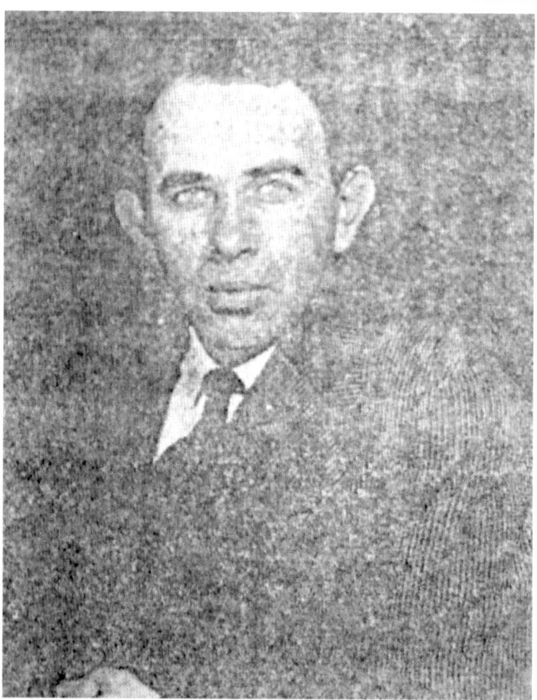

Judge Malcolm Paul

Descended from the Paul family that settled in the area in the 1780s, Judge Malcolm Paul served as a superior court judge in Beaufort County for many years. A native of the Pantego area, he is remembered as a compassionate and considerate man. (Both, courtesy of *Washington Daily News*.)

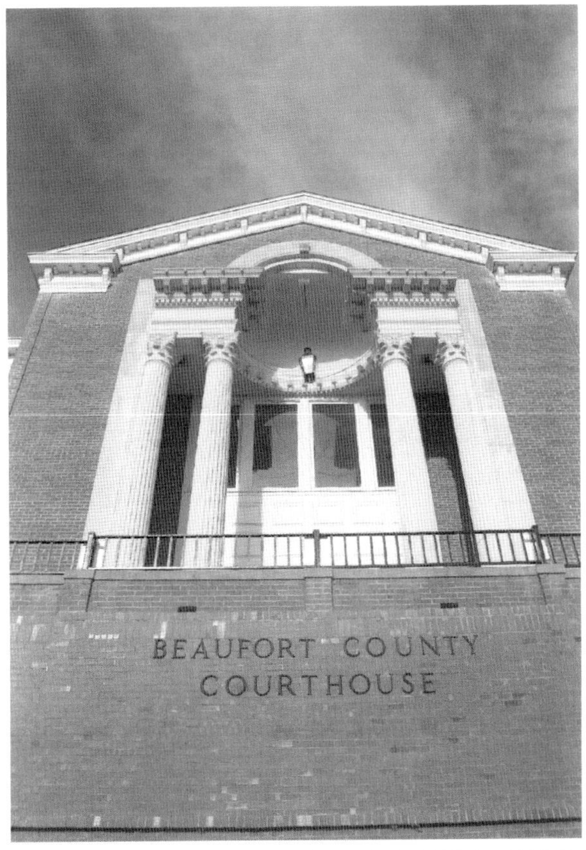

Judge Samuel Grimes

The great-grandson of Gen. Bryan Grimes, Samuel Grimes hails from a line of attorneys and judges serving the Beaufort County and Washington area that stretches over 100 years. He ran a law practice in Washington for a decade before serving on the bench as a district court judge for 26 years. He retired in 2010. Pictured is present-day Beaufort County Courthouse. (Author's collection.)

Seth Edwards

Seth Edwards and his wife, Kimberly, opened Edwards & Edwards, Attorneys at Law, in Washington in 1996. In 2002, Edwards ran for district attorney, and has since served in that position. The law is not his only passion, however. He is a Sunday school teacher at First United Methodist Church and an active volunteer with local youth sports programs. (Courtesy of Seth Edwards.)

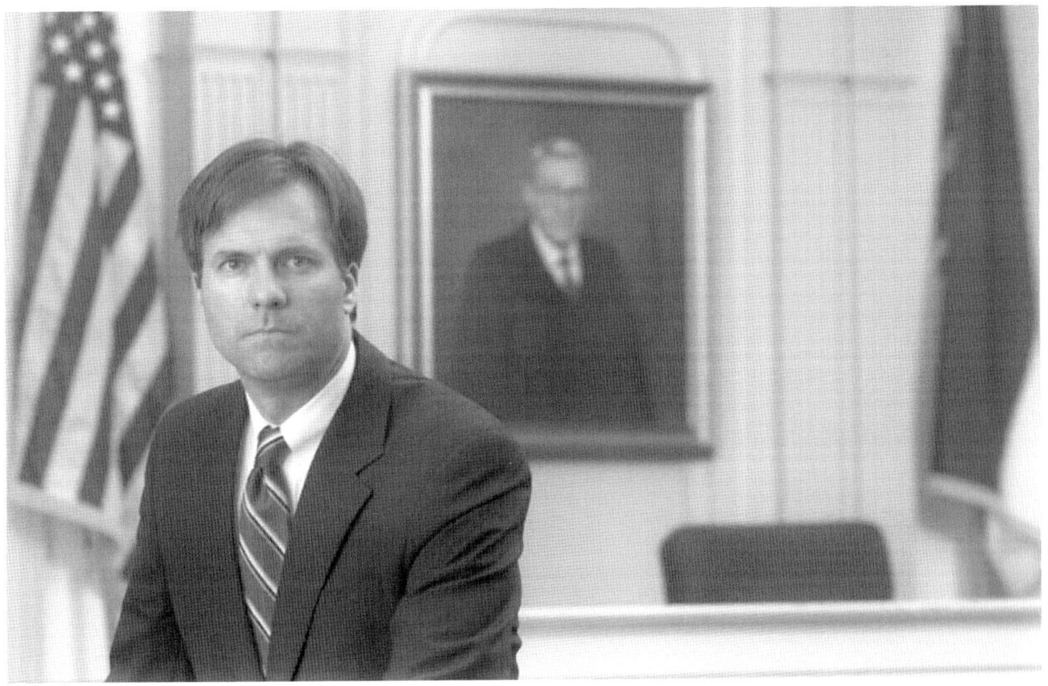

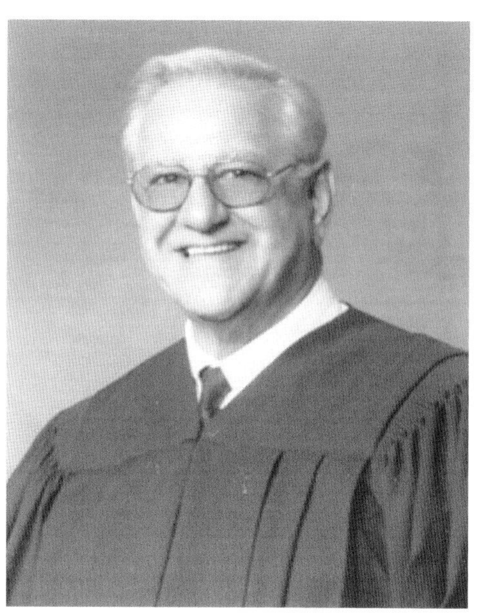

Judge James R. Vosburgh
For more than 20 years, James R. Vosburgh had a law practice in Washington with law partner John A. Wilkerson. During that time, he became involved in politics. In 1985, Gov. Jim Martin chose him for a project to recognize the legal department in the Employment Security Commission of North Carolina. After successful completion of this project, Vosburgh returned to Washington and opened a new private law practice, where he worked until Gov. Jim Hunt appointed him to the Office of Special Superior Court Judge in 1997. He served in that capacity through 2002. He is remembered as an active member of the First United Methodist Church and a volunteer with community youth programs for children. (Courtesy of *Washington Daily News*.)

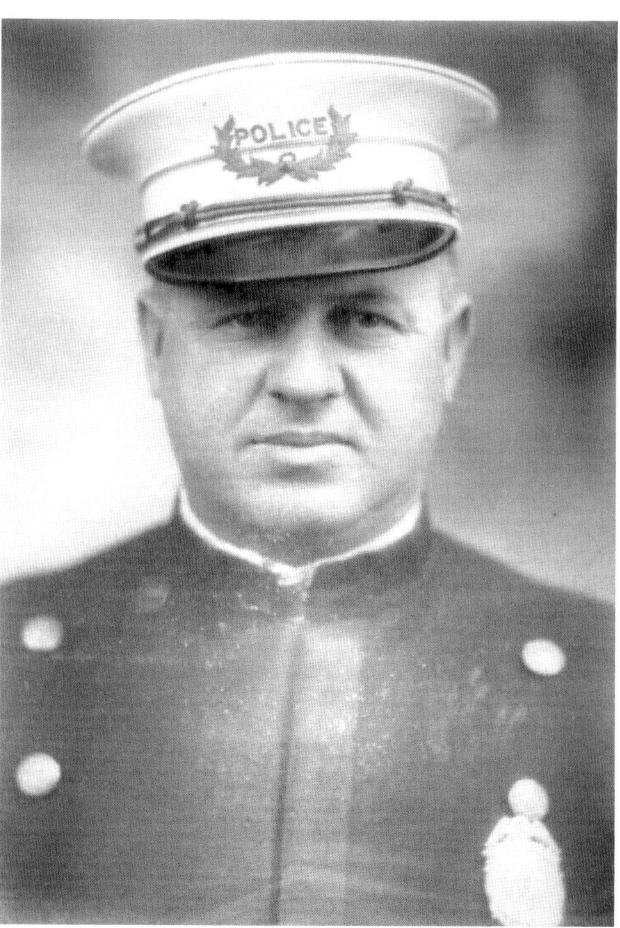

Chief Harvey Lee Dellinger
Responding to a report of an attempted breaking and entering, 36-year-old Harvey Lee Dellinger arrived at the East Second Street home. As he stepped from his car, shots rang out from a handgun. Three bullets hit Dellinger in the head, killing him immediately. The gunman then grabbed Dellinger's pistol and committed suicide just moments after the homicide. Dellinger's 1926 death is the only recorded incident of a Washington policeman dying in the line of duty. (Courtesy of Avis Dellinger.)

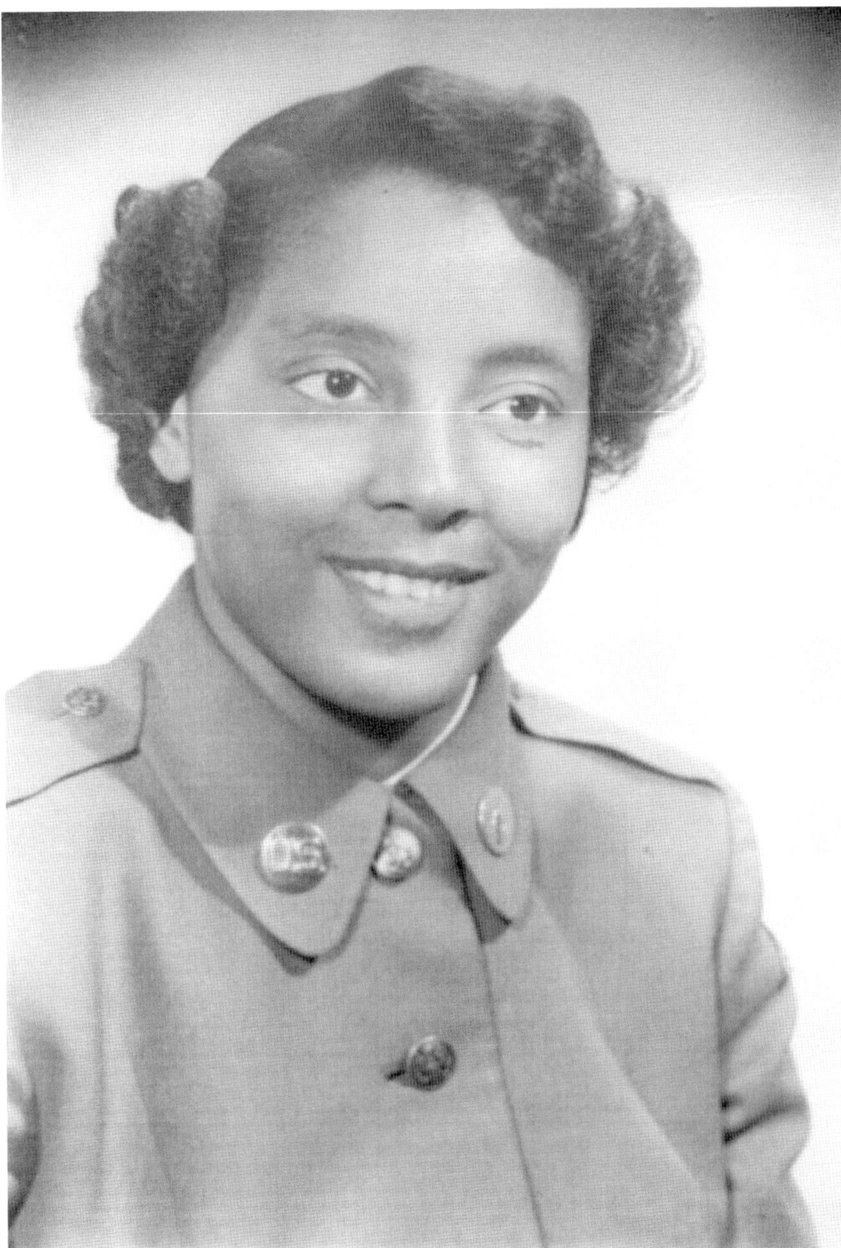

Sarah Keys
As a private in the US Army, Sarah Keys was on her way home to Washington when she walked into civil rights history. When the bus she was taking from New Jersey made a stop in Roanoke Rapids, North Carolina, the ticket collector suggested she change her seat on the bus. This was 1952. Segregation on interstate buses was illegal and had been for nearly a decade, so she ignored the suggestion and stayed in her seat. As a result, she was arrested for disorderly conduct. By her father's suggestion, Keys sought legal recourse to prevent these situations from happening again. Just a month prior to Rosa Parks's famous bus ordeal, the Interstate Commerce Commission ruled in the Keys case that such racial discrimination was illegal. (Courtesy of Sarah Keys.)

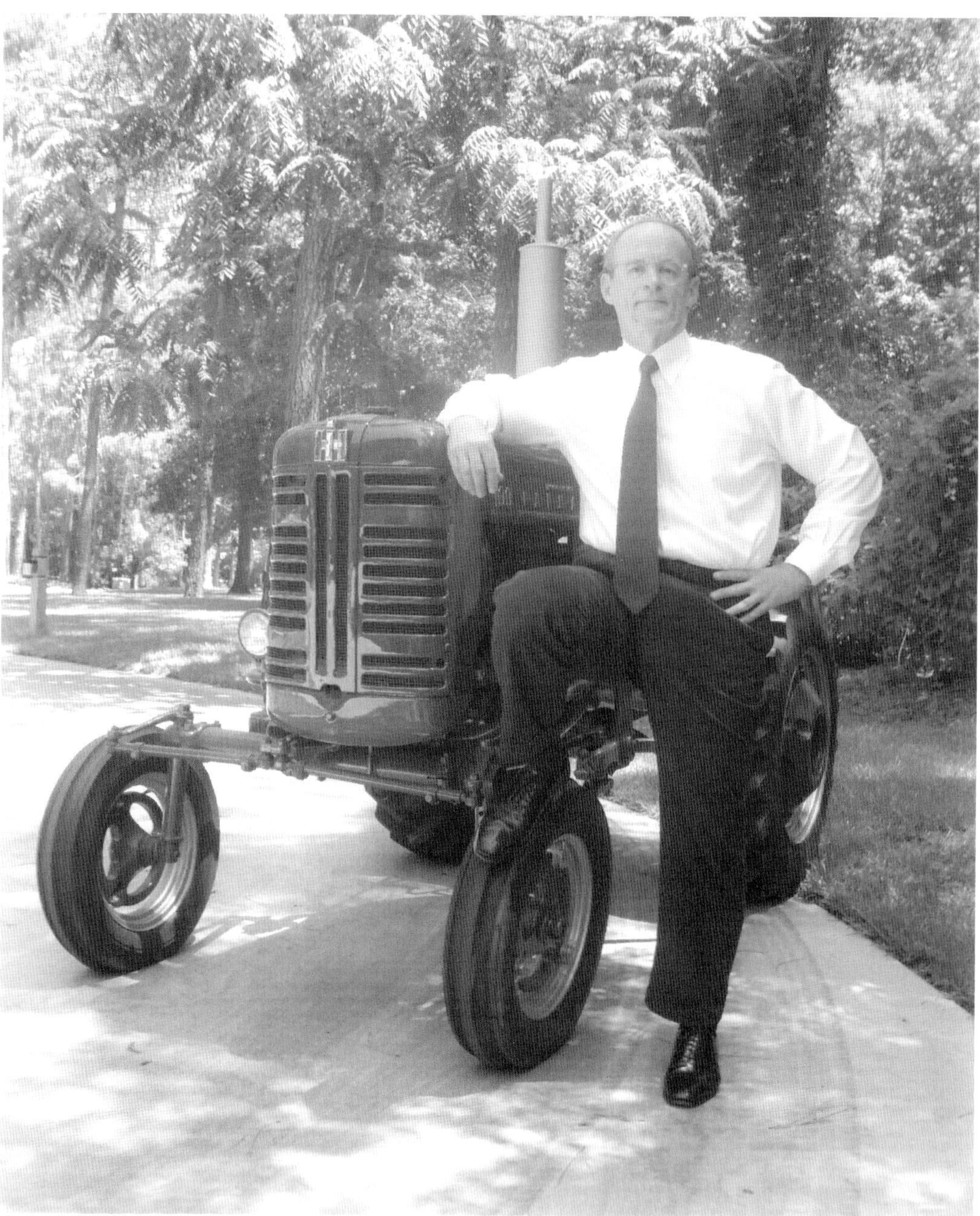

Herman Gaskins

Anyone from Washington, Greenville, and the surrounding areas knows Herman Gaskins from his television commercials featuring his father's old Farmall tractor. Gaskins had the tractor, once rusting, restored at the bequest of his clients and friends. Today, it stands as a symbol of the Gaskins firm, whose motto is "A Strong Voice for the Injured." An Eagle Scout, Gaskins says he uses the Boy Scout motto and law as a compass for his life and his work for his clients. Gaskins & Gaskins, located in the historic Myers house on Water Street, is a family business; his law partner is his wife, Debra, and his sons also work with the firm. (Courtesy of Herman Gaskins.)

CHAPTER SEVEN

Businesspeople, Innovators, and Professionals

The Washington waterfront has been a hub of activity since the town was first founded. Early settlers in the area took advantage of the location, and it was not long before wharfs were founded on the river's banks. Thus began the shipping industry in Washington. Family names like Moss, Myers, and Havens adorned the many warehouses nestled along the waterline. In other industry, the Bonners and Blounts ran mercantiles, and the Blount name became known well beyond the town as the shipping industry grew. Likewise, the Mosses were drawn to Washington's lumber industry. Many of these family names still adorn businesses in the downtown area, but these days, they are more often found on the doors of professional offices on the town's main streets rather than the shoreline.

In the 20th century, the Hackney family found a niche in Washington that allowed its small beverage delivery truck assembly business to become a part of the international consumer market. Other families, like the Stewarts, have made a mark through their steadfast presence in the downtown business district.

Many of these businessmen contributed to the growth of Washington, either by representing the area's residents in local governments or by partnering with the local civic organizations of their day. Each has left a significant mark on the history of Washington, and without these men, Washington would not have the character that makes it unique.

Other professionals, such as the decorated military men who called Washington home, are also part of the unique fabric of the town. Col. James Bonner and many members of the founding families served in the military in some capacity, reaching significant ranks before retirement. In the more modern era, men like D.C. Cooper did not set out to make a difference, but his role in the Navy helped pave the way for others like him to serve as officers.

The tapestry of Washington is weaved with many facets, and the businesspeople and professionals in town contribute to the diversity it enjoys today.

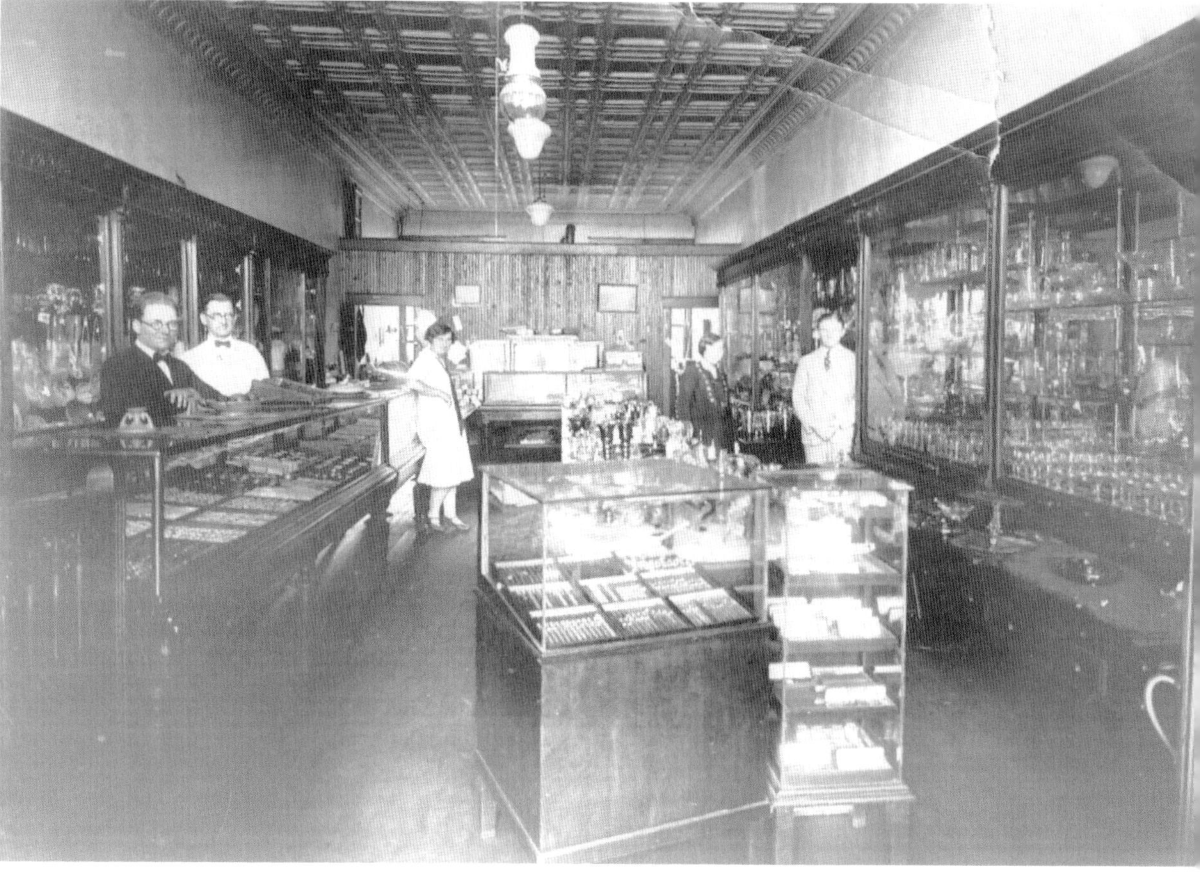

The Stewart Family

In downtown Washington, there is a business that has stood for more than 100 years. Stewart's Jewelry was started by R.L. Stewart in 1908. He soon built his own shop at 121 Market Street, where under a blue awning, customers can still purchase jewelry from the business today. The Stewarts were not only interested in their business, however. Three Stewarts have served as Washington's mayor. Along with R.L. Stewart, both his father E.T. Stewart and his son Thomas Stewart were elected mayor. During Thomas's term in office, urban renewal came to downtown Washington. In fact, the city street next to the Pamlico River was named Stewart Parkway for his support during these upgrades and changes.

While Thomas forayed into politics, his wife, Virgil, started working at the jewelry store more often. Opposite, Thomas and Virgil are pictured with their granddaughter Mary Elizabeth Robertson. Also pictured is the November 11, 1971, ribbon-cutting ceremony at Stewart's Jewelry after the building was remodeled. From left to right are Thelma Alligood, Neva Pearl Latham, Clara Bradly, Lilly Darracott, Louise Whitgood, Mayor Max Roebuck, Eddie Buchman, Virgil Stewart, Thomas Stewart, Julia Litchfill, Sal Mills, Debra Roebuck, Edna Spruill, and Mrs. Pinkham. (All, courtesy of Betty Stewart.)

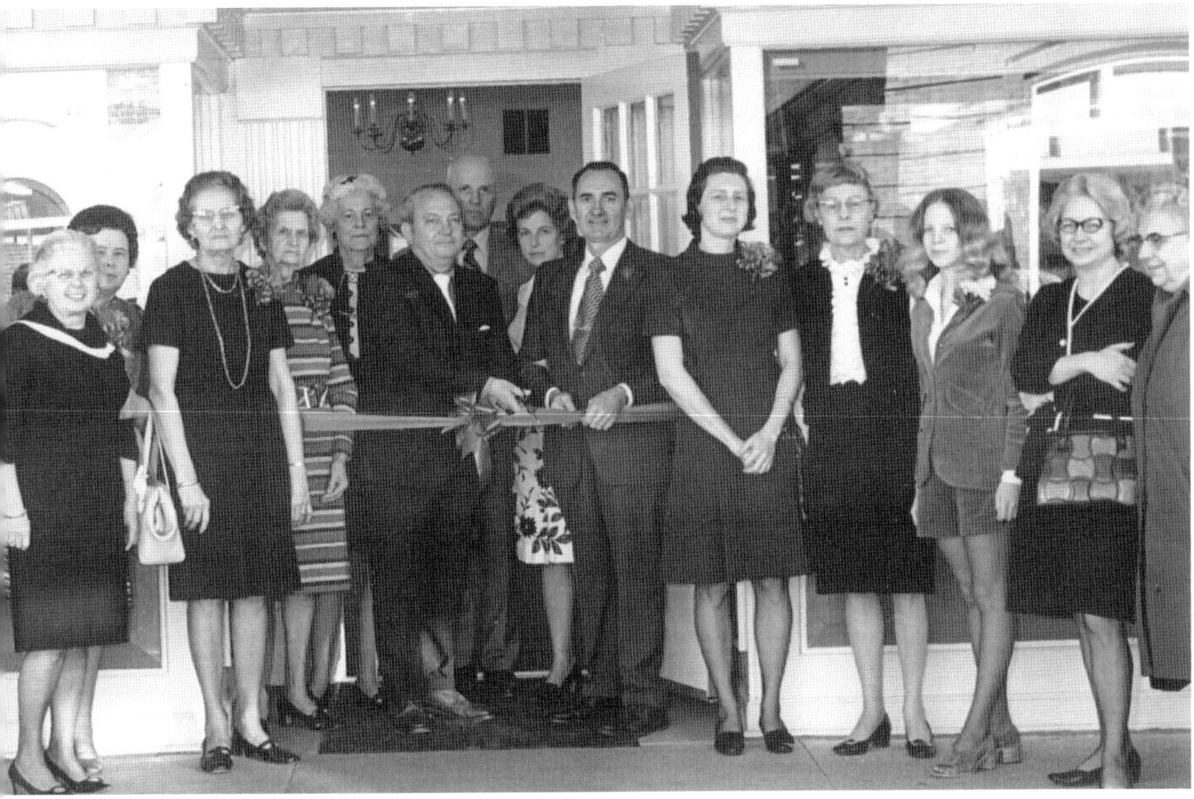

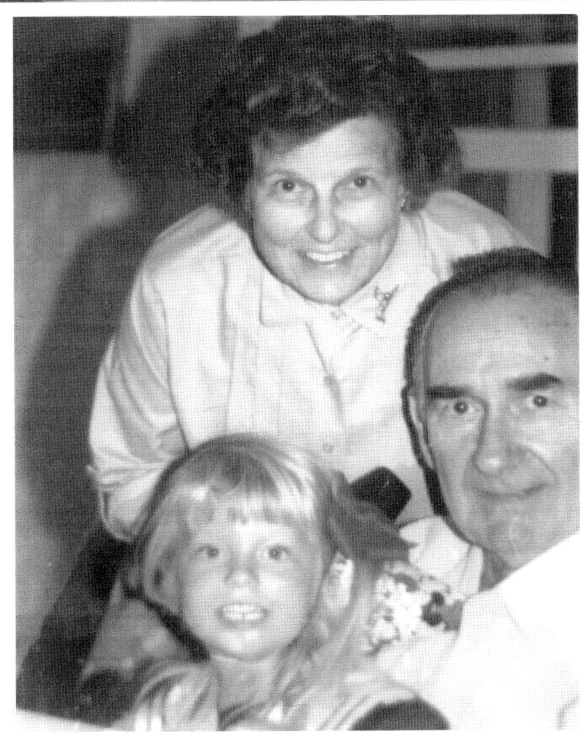

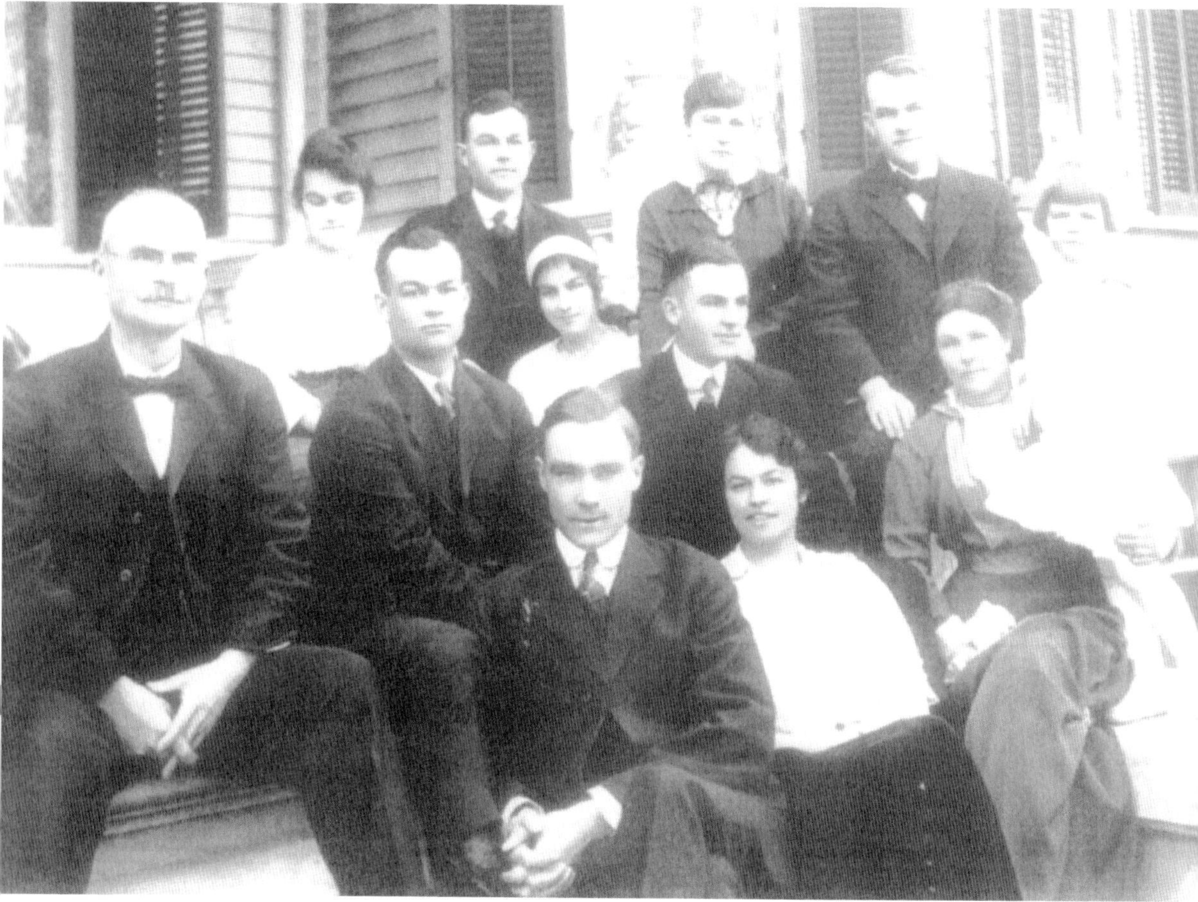

The Hackneys

The Hackney family is unique in that they can trace their basic occupation all the way back to 1600s England. Descended from wheelwrights, the family immigrated to America, finally settling in North Carolina in the 1800s. Willis N. Hackney started Hackney Brothers, a carriage-building outfit in Wilson, and by the early 1900s, business was booming. With the boom came expansion into many areas, including the start of the Washington Buggy Company by Willis's grandsons George Jr. and Jim. However, the Hackneys scaled back their many expansions after demand for wagons and the like had decreased following the First World War, and the buggy company folded in 1923.

Luckily, the Hackneys were savvy businessmen, keeping their businesses separate to allow for growth and expansion in specific areas. Around that time, the Wilson business had moved toward constructing motorized vehicles for transporting goods, and in 1946, the Hackneys once again tried a business in Washington. This time, Jim took the helm and started an electrical contracting business with his father as a partner. Soon, the Washington Hackneys moved back into the vehicle business, and after constructing some beverage delivery trucks for the local Dr. Pepper company, word got out about their innovative vehicle designs. Jim's sons Jim Jr. and Hodges joined the company in the 1960s and moved the company into the national level of production. It was not long before the company was making innovations in vehicle designs for beverage companies, emergency vehicles, and the like.

The Hackney family is pictured here around 1917. From left to right are (first row) William Dennis Adams and Bess Hackney Adams; (second row) George Hackney, James N. Hackney, John. N. Hackney, Bessie N. Hackney, and Eva Hackney; (third row) Ella Hackney, Thomas J. Hackney, Eva B. Hackney, and George Hackney Jr. (Courtesy of Hodges Hackney.)

The Hackneys Today

The Hackneys became pioneers in using all-aluminum bodies on their vehicles, and in the process, they developed many unique features to better serve their customers. "We're all engineering graduates," Hodges Hackney said. "We liked designing the best product."

In the 1990s, the family sold off the company, now called VT Hackney, but Hodges stayed on to build the Hackneys' international presence. He retired in 2015 after more than 50 years with the company.

Today, the Hackney brand is found on garbage trucks, refrigerated trailers, emergency vehicles, and more. Hackney trucks are sold to countries all around the world. Pictured here are Jim Hackney and his children. (Courtesy of Hodges Hackney.)

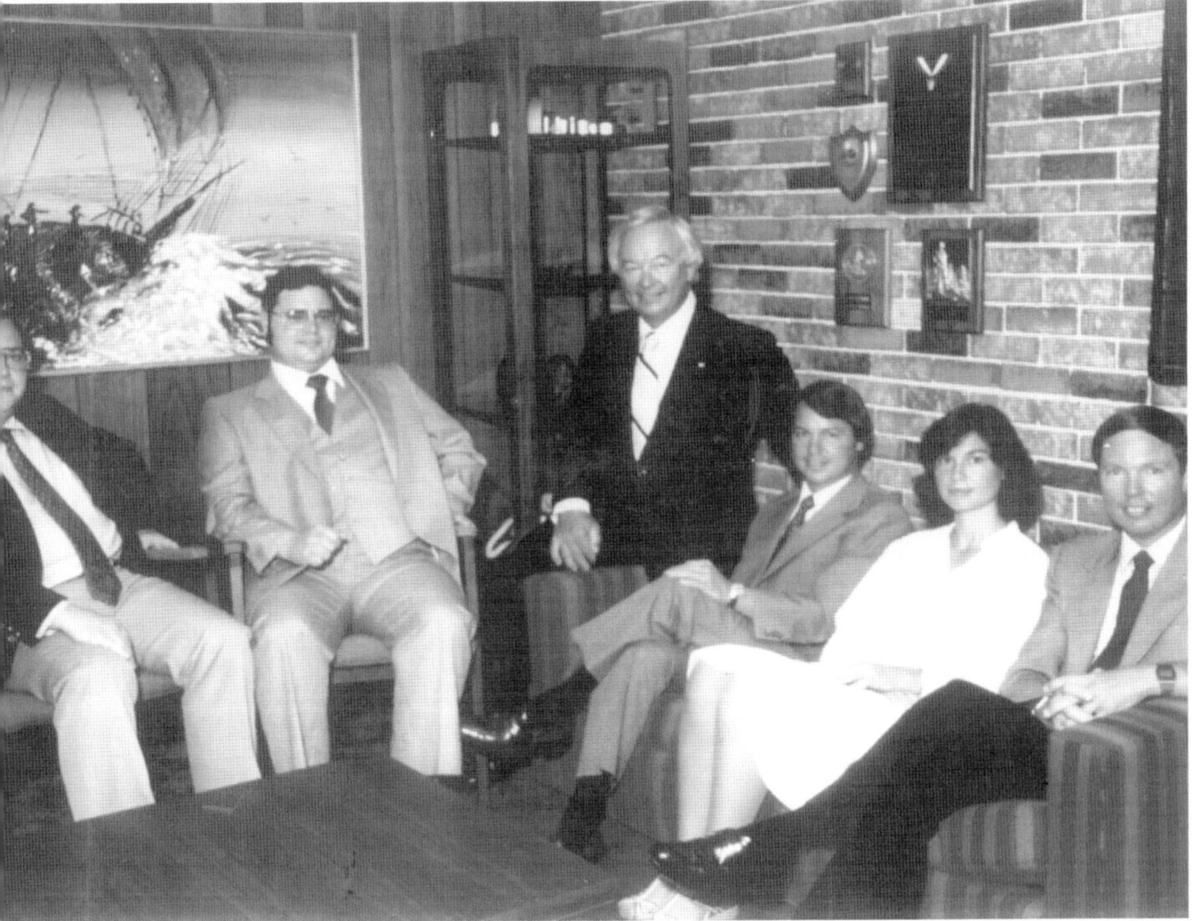

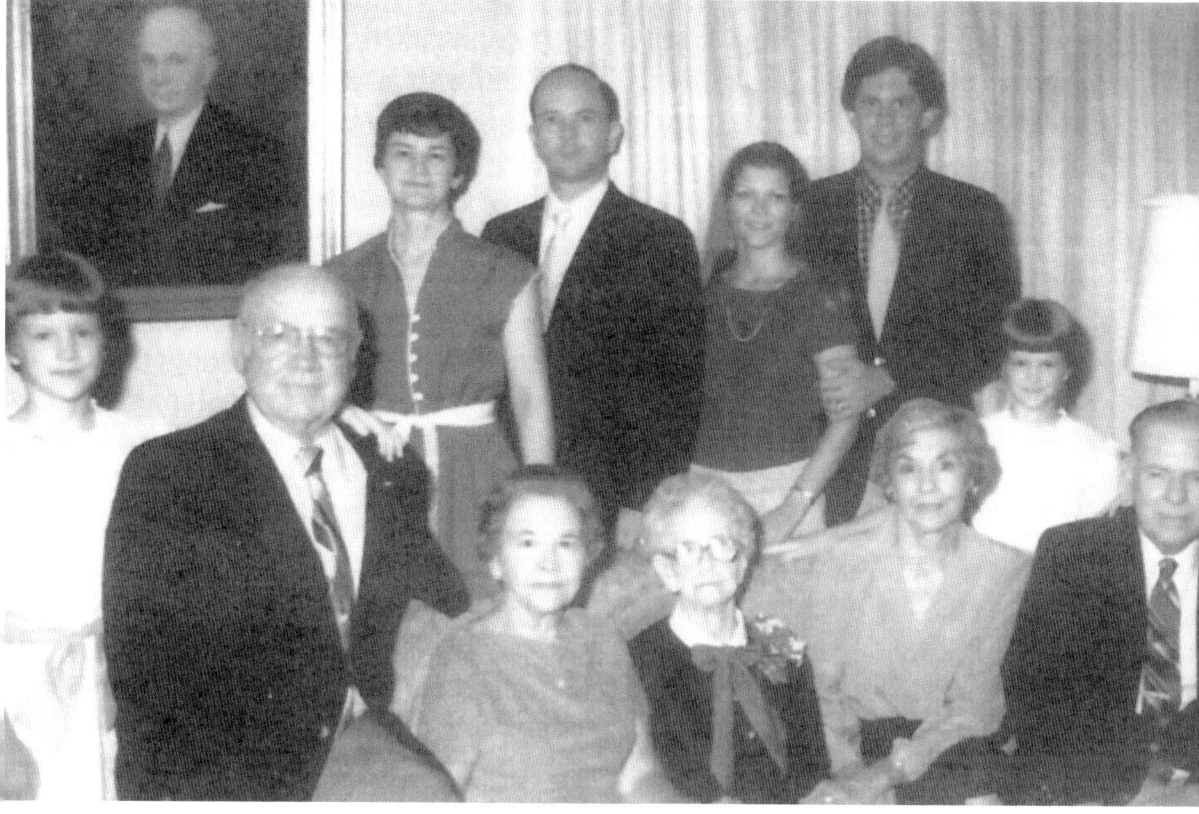

The Newspaper Family

Ashley Futrell purchased the *Washington Daily News* in 1949. His determination to create a community-centric news source gave the newspaper the push it needed to grow in popularity in the Washington area. Pictured here from left to right are (first row) Glen Neal Titus, Cleo Fox Titus, Effie Brooks Fox, Rachel Fox Futrell, and Ashley Brown Futrell; (second row) Stephanie Carol Titus, Linda Hamlin Titus, Glen Neal Titus Jr., Susan Boyette Futrell, Ashley Brown Futrell Jr., and Emily Pattrice Titus. George Martin Fox Jr. is shown in the portrait on the wall. (Courtesy of *Washington Daily News*.)

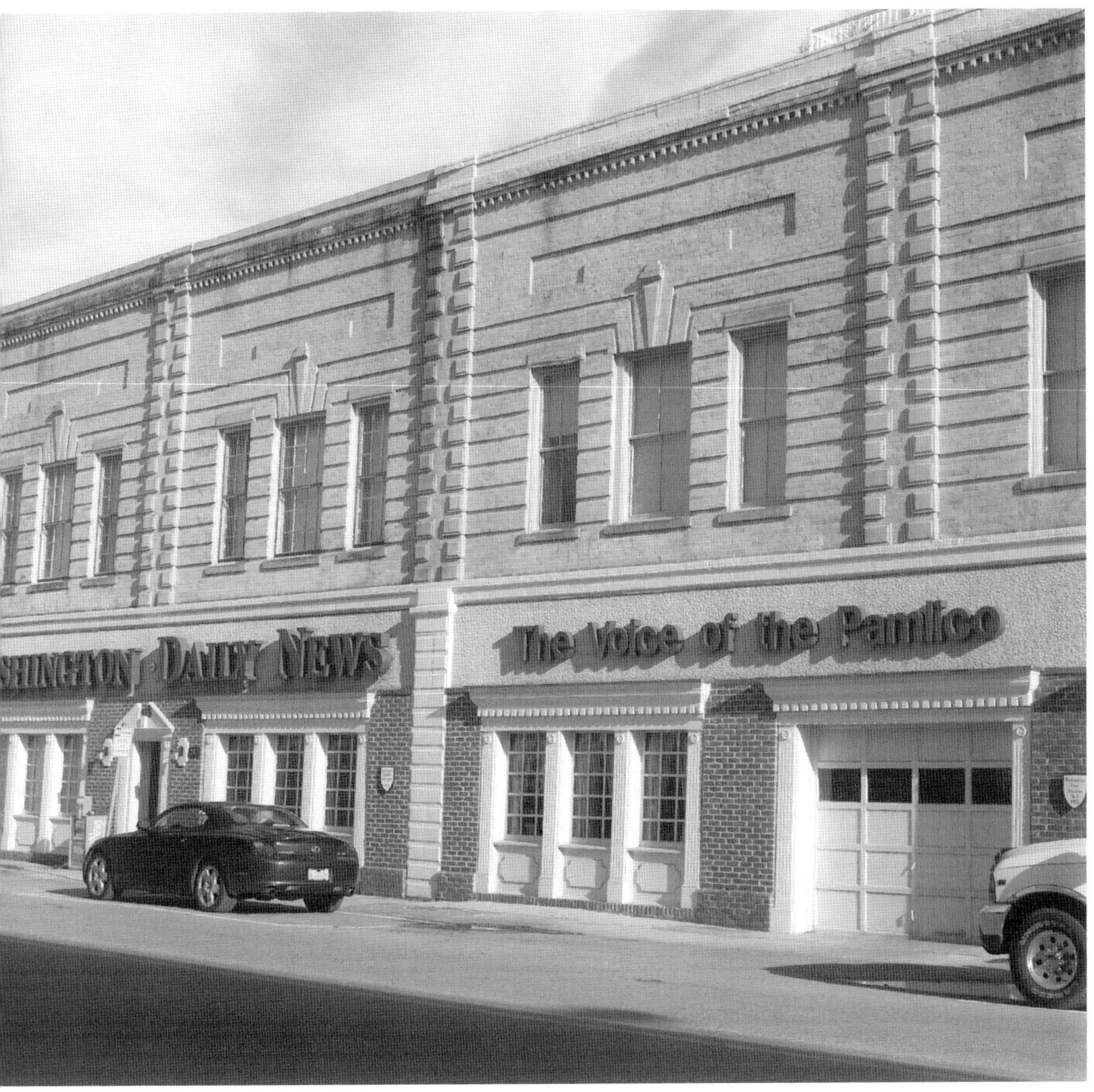

Washington Daily News

Ashley Futrell took a detour from the news industry for a few years to serve as a state senator, at which time his wife, Rachel, took an active role in the business during his absence. In 1978, their son Brownie Futrell came into the family business as publisher after finishing college to assist his father, whose health was failing. However, Ashley remained active in the business and continued to write articles and editorials for the paper until his death in 2005. In 2010, the *Washington Daily News* was sold to Boone Newspapers. Since then, Brownie, like his parents, has remained active in the community by serving with many organizations. (Author's collection.)

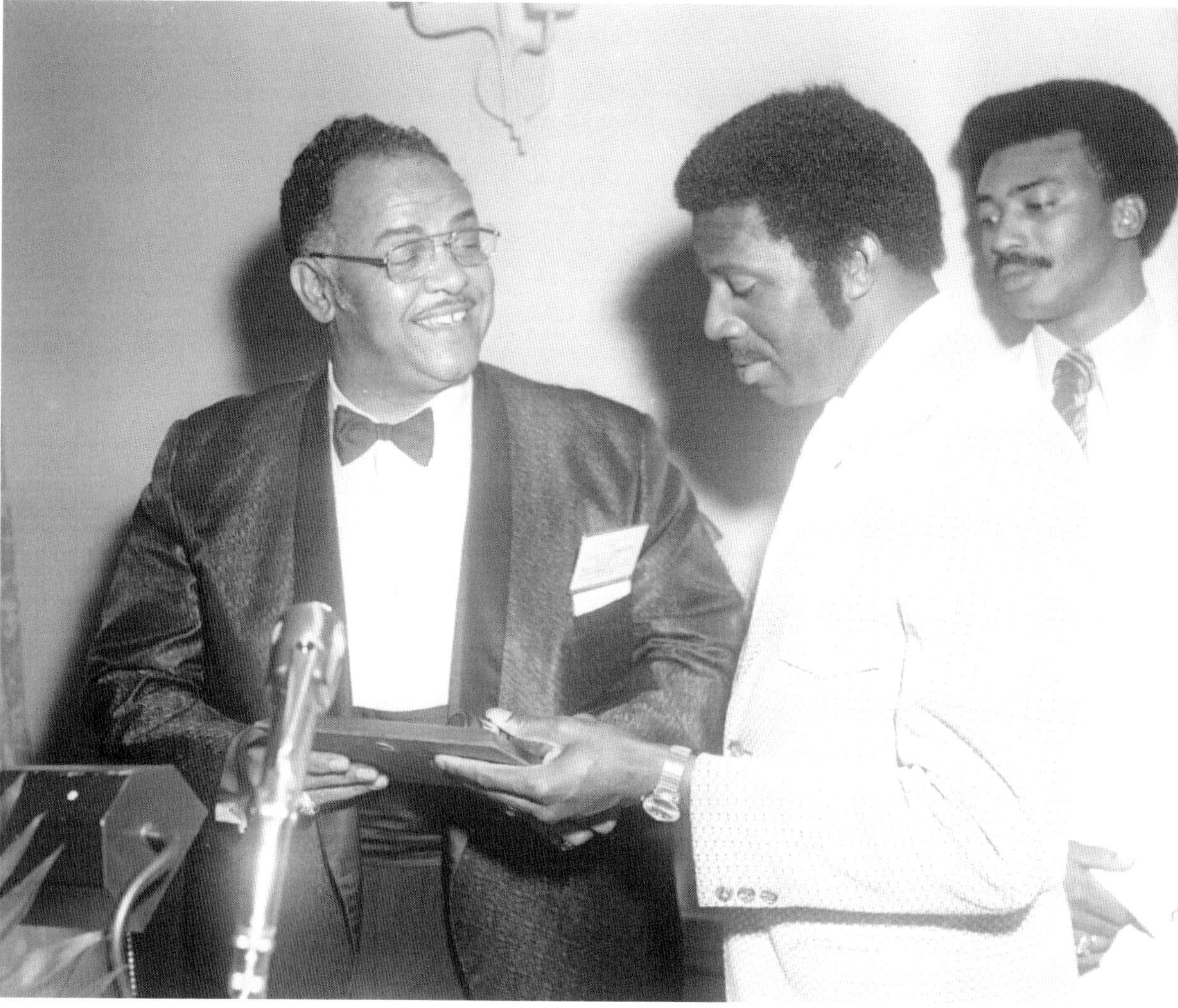

Louis Randolf Jr.

A native of Washington, Louis Randolf Jr. owned and operated Randolf Funeral Home until his retirement in 1989. His original intention was to become a doctor. Later, he turned his attention to athletics, but in 1951, he returned home to take over the family funeral home for his ill father. Having worked with his father since he was a boy, Randolf already had experience, and he was determined to excel in the business. Over the years, he served on many mortuary boards, including a turn as president of the Funeral Directors and Morticians Association of North Carolina, an organization that also named him Man of the Year in 1975. Although he was a businessman, he also contributed time to his community. Randolf served on many local councils and boards, including three terms on the Washington Town Council. Above, Randolf (left) receives one of many awards for his service in the funeral industry. At right, Randolf (right) speaks during a national funeral convention. (Both, courtesy of Betty Randolf.)

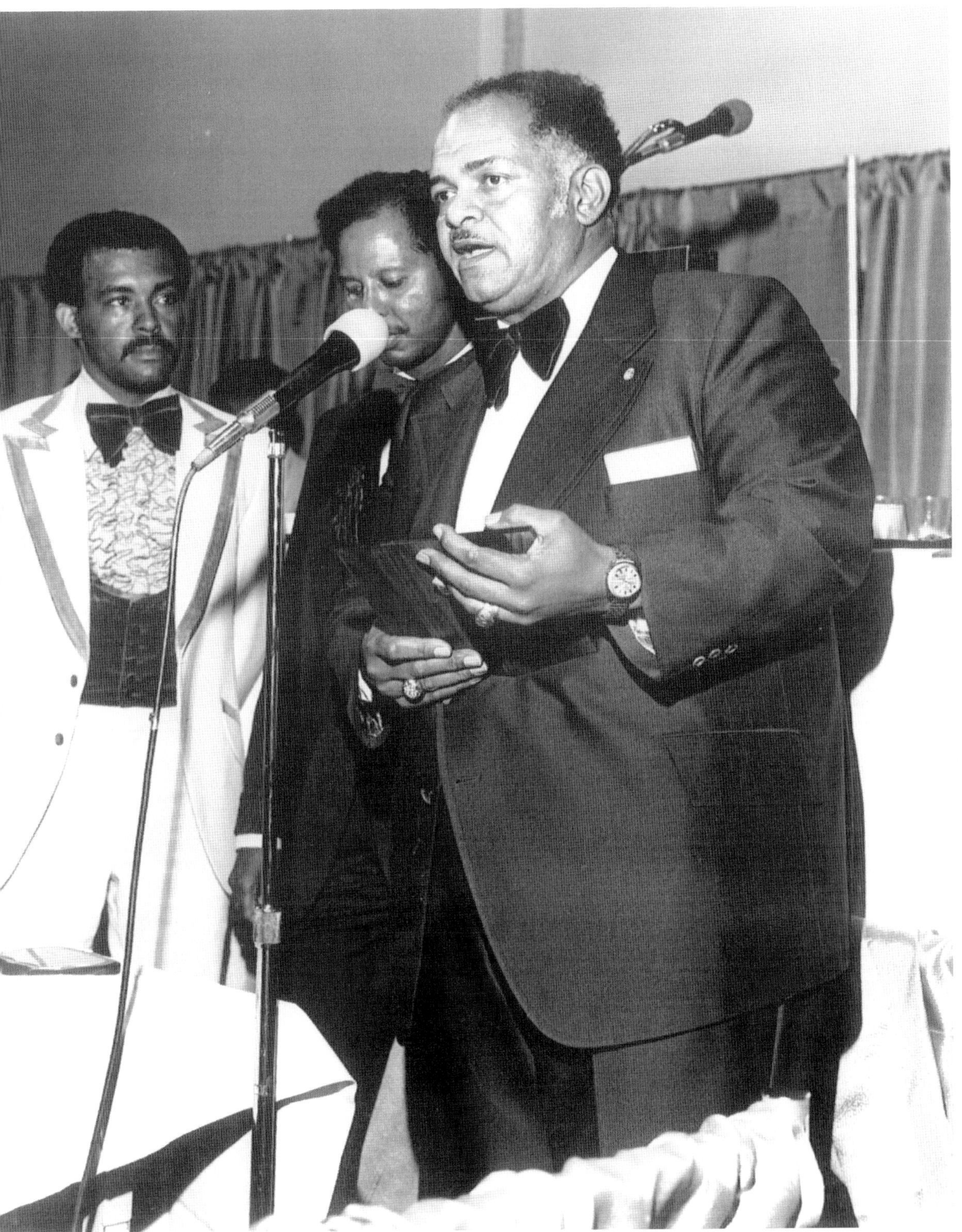

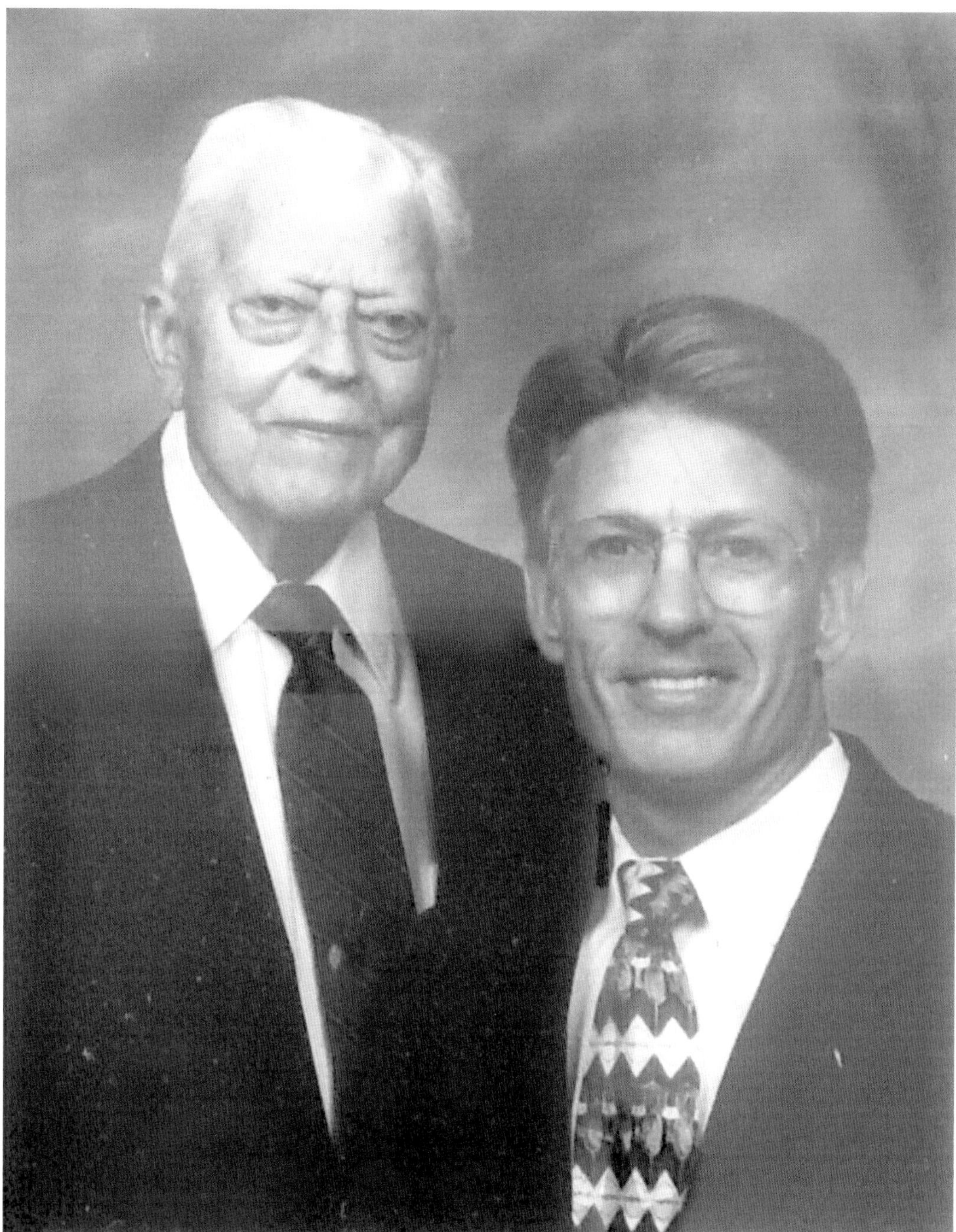

F. Ray Moore

F. Ray Moore owned his self-named oil company for 55 years. Moore hired his son to help expand the company, the smallest of its kind in the area for many years. He played a more minor role in the company during the last 20 years of his life, allowing time for more civic and personal pleasures. He officially retired in 1998, but the F. Ray Moore Oil Company continued business under his son's leadership until 2015. (Courtesy of F. Ray Moore Jr.)

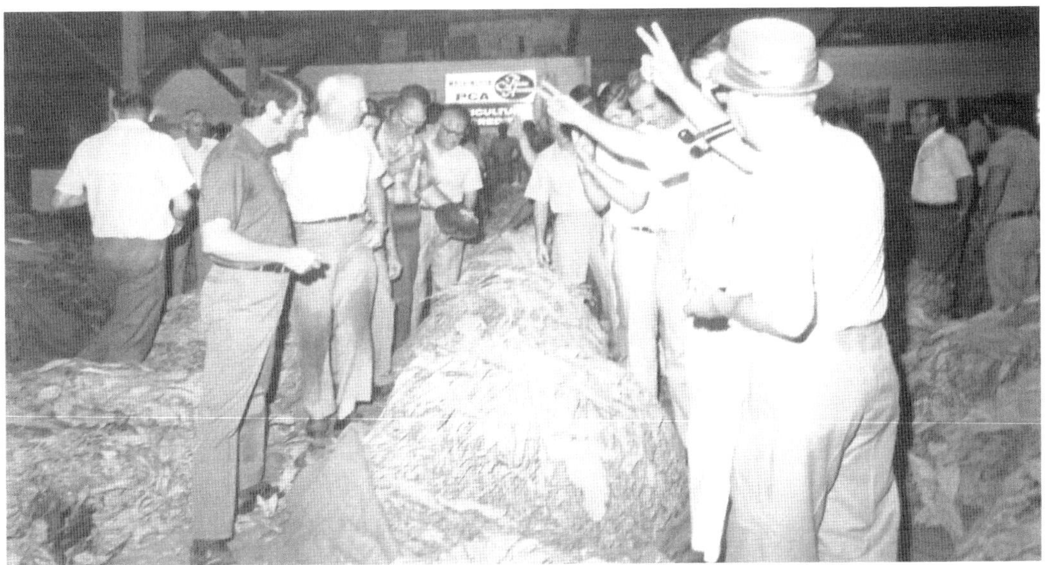

Wayland Sermons

Tobacco brought Wayland Sermons to Washington, where he worked in tobacco houses from here to Florida. "In the tobacco business, you have to be very personable and outgoing . . . and he was both of these," according to his son, Wayland Jr. "He was one of those people who did a little bit of everything." Sermons worked with several business ventures, but he also liked to have fun as a pilot. He was involved with many organizations, including the chamber of commerce and the Jaycees. He also represented Beaufort County in the North Carolina General Assembly for 15 years. From left to right below are Sermons and governors Terry Sanford, Dan Moore, and Luther Hodges. (Above, courtesy of Brown Library; below, courtesy of Wayland Sermons Jr.)

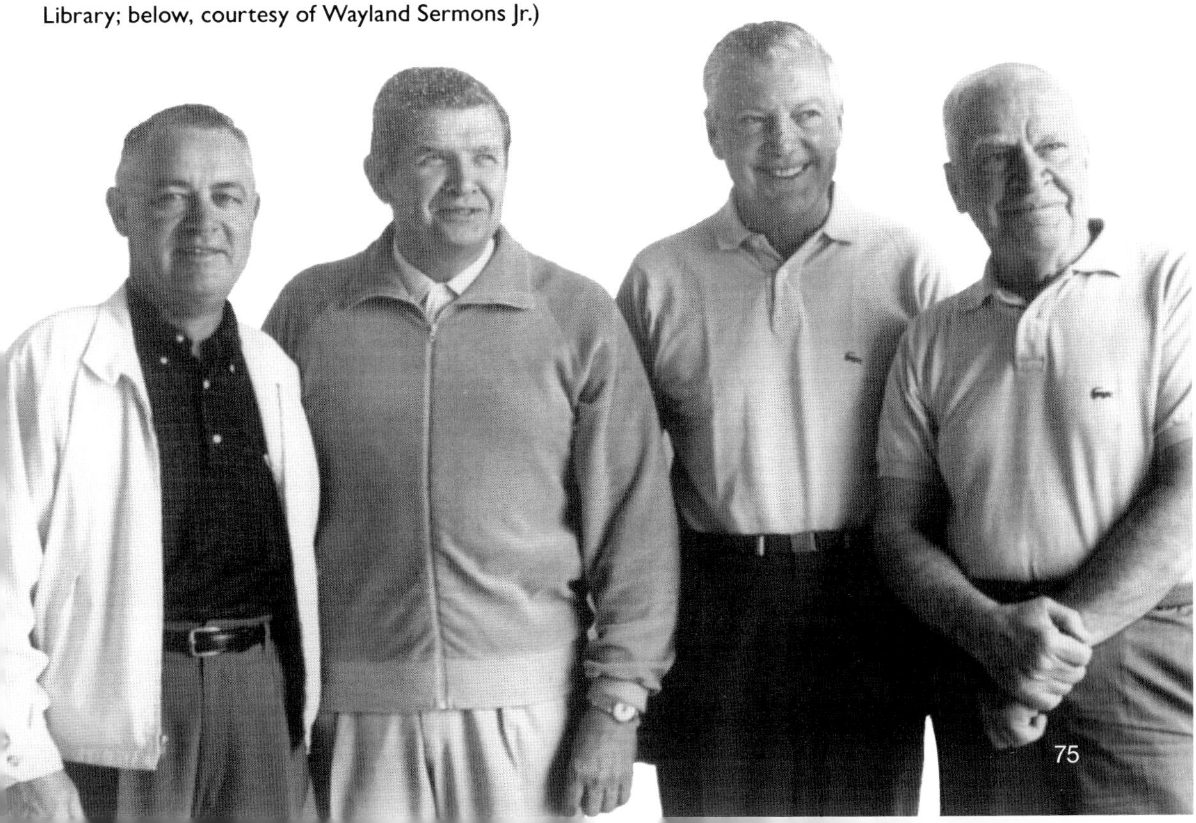

Dr. S.T. Nicholson

Samuel Timothy, or "Sam Tim," as his family referred to him, built the first tobacco warehouse in town. To pay for his medical school, he hauled cotton all the way to Baltimore. Dr. Nicholson returned to his community following medical school and became an esteemed physician. He and his brother Plummer "Plum" Nicholson were well respected as medical professionals in the community. Samuel served the town as mayor and participated in many civic and social activities in and around Washington. Along with many other doctors in town, he helped advocate for a community hospital, which became the S.R. Fowle Memorial Hospital. His son Dr. Jack Nicholson later served as chief of surgery at the hospital. (Author's collection.)

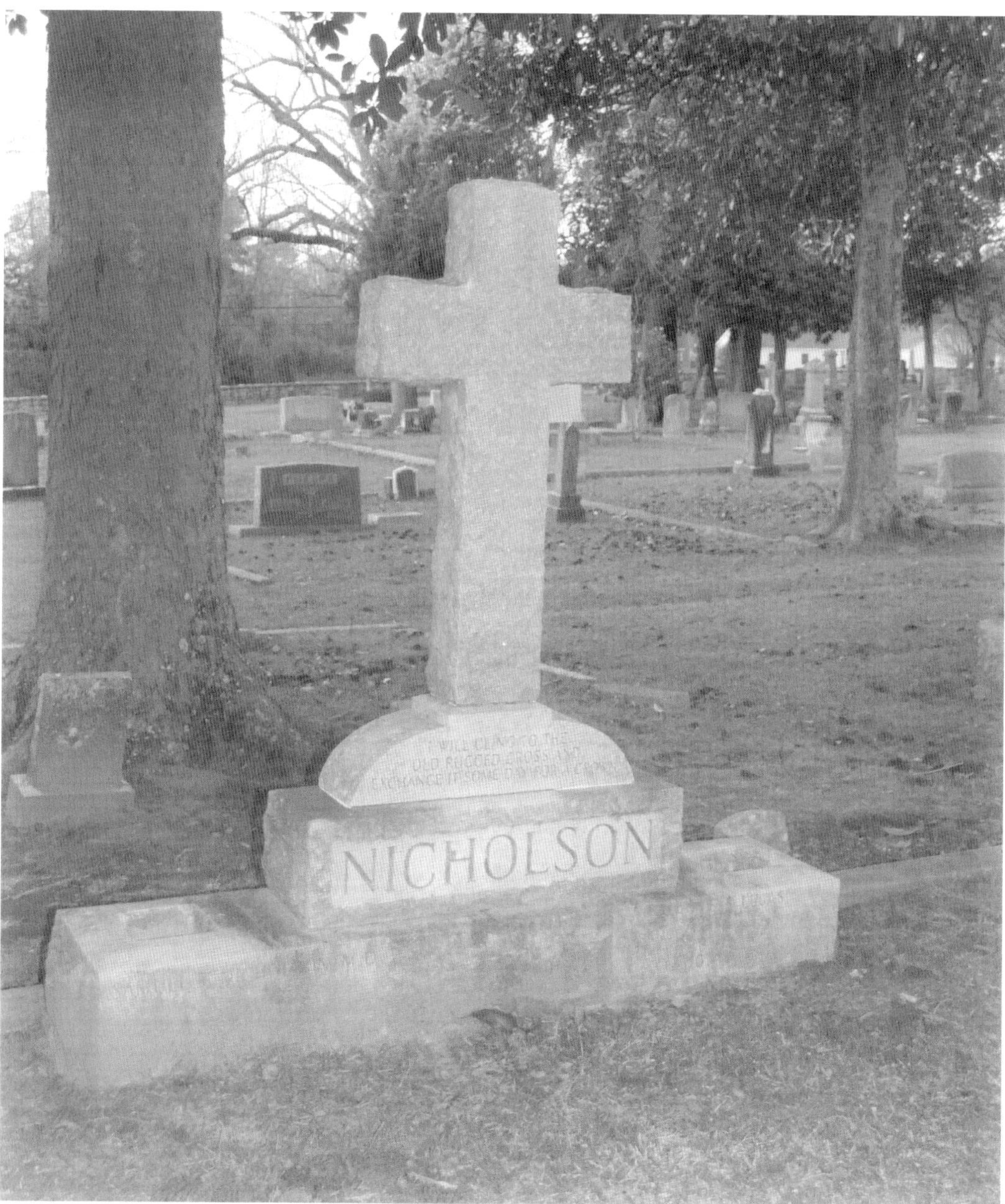

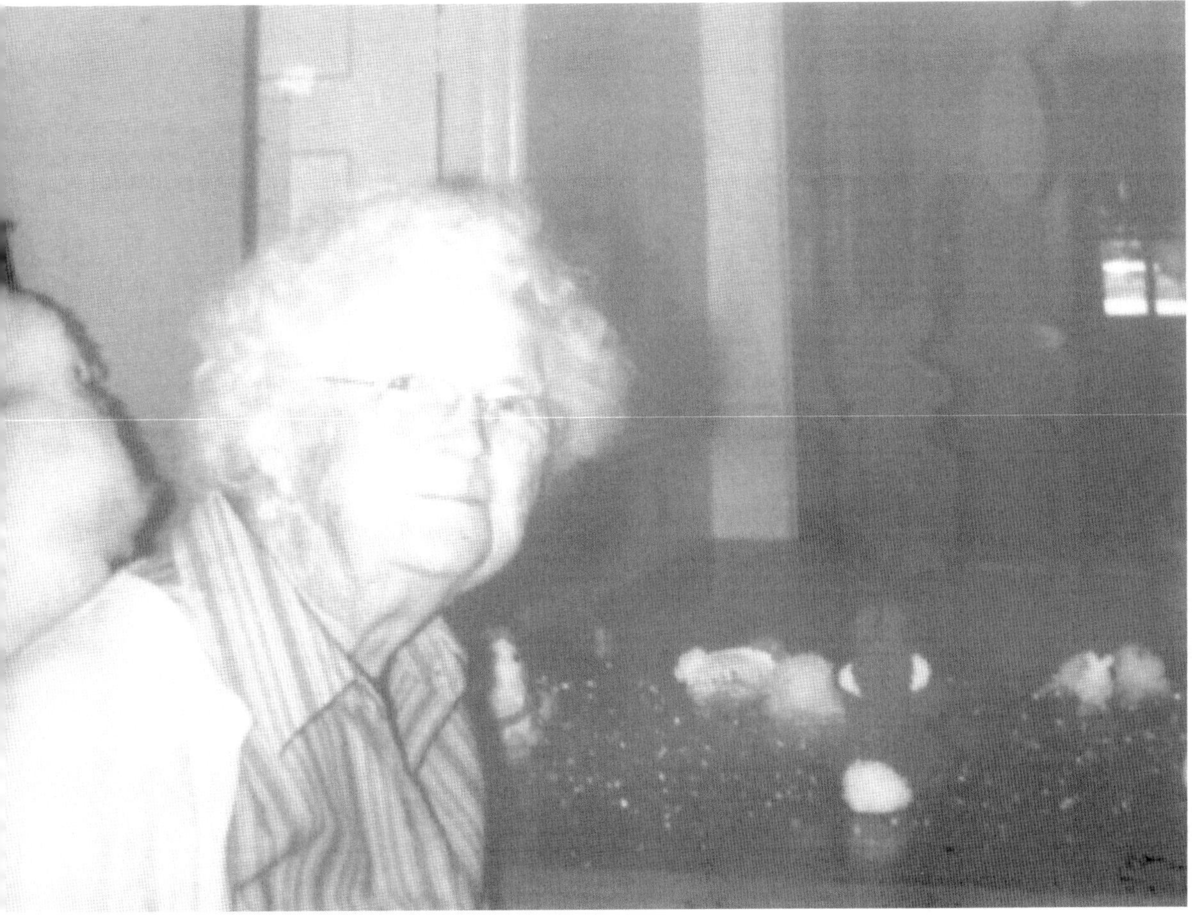

Lucretia Hughes

Lucretia Hughes was a lifelong resident of Washington. Born in 1890, she attended East Carolina Teachers Training School and became a teacher in the Washington Public Schools, where she worked for about a decade. She also taught Sunday school as an active member of St. Peter's Episcopal Church. In her 70s, she started personally maintaining the cemetery for Trinity Episcopal Church in Chocowinity—a task she kept up until she was 90. Eventually, she helped establish a fund to maintain the cemetery. With a passion for history, she spent years conducting historical research in her community. Her work with the local historical society has helped document many years of the area's history, of which she had a vast knowledge. She lived to be more than 100 years old, and much of her research has been preserved at the Brown Library. (Courtesy of the Brown Library.)

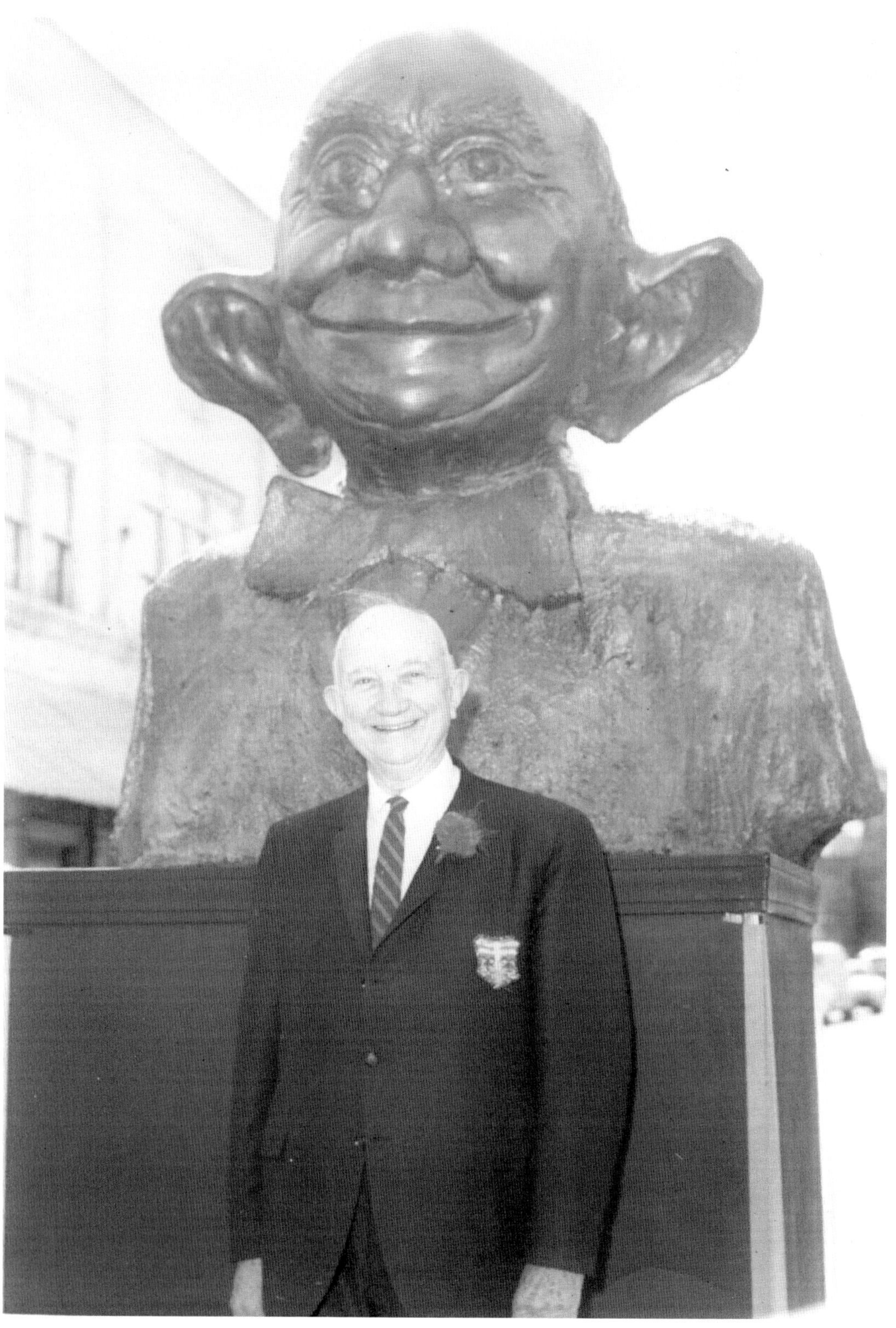

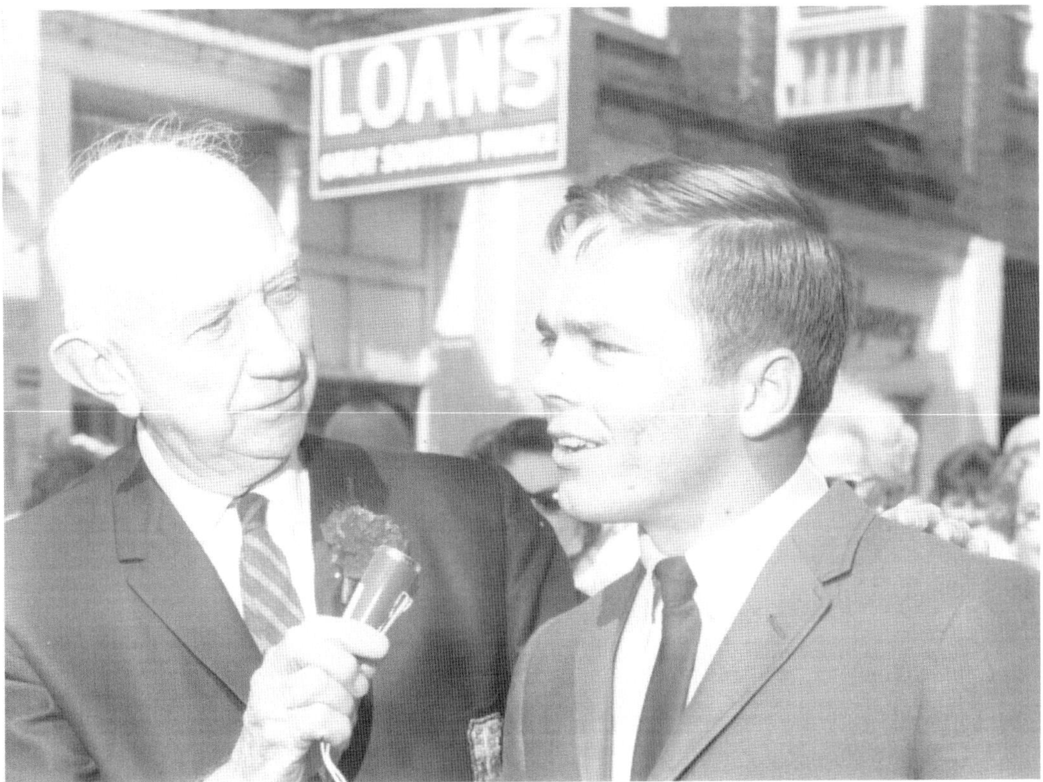

"North Carolina's Ambassador of Goodwill"

Edmund H. Harding was a man who found a talent for public speaking at a young age, excelling at showmanship and resourcefulness. A devoutly religious family man, Harding's humor and storytelling were the cornerstones of his popularity.

Close friend Ashley Futrell wrote, "As a storyteller and humorist, he was truly one of America's greatest. He made heroes out of everyday people, and he loved every one of them and every minute of the experience. If ever a man lived life to the fullest—every hour of it—Edmund Harding was that man."

An excellent salesman, Harding worked several retail jobs, starting with Brook's Shoe Store and the Washington Horse Exchange. He later took over his father-in-law's business, Bragraw & Co. For 30 years, he was the sales supervisor for the Washington Tobacco Market, and under his guard, Washington's tobacco prices soared.

Not one to idle away his free time, he spent time with his extended family and the people in the community. He also found time for many community projects, including the rebuilding of St. Peter's parish and the restoration of historic Bath.

Possessing a quick sense of humor and a surplus of anecdotes, Harding became well known as an after-dinner speaker, scheduling engagements several times a week across the country. His schedule kept him on the road, but he always found time between engagements to visit hospitals, nursing homes, and schools to share his humor and goodwill.

His civic-minded nature led him to join many local clubs, including the Masons, Rotarians, and Shriners, and he had been awarded honorary membership in nearly every civic club in town by the time of his passing. He organized community performances and celebrations, often incorporating his love for the history of his hometown into the events. For his works in the community, he became known as "North Carolina's Ambassador of Good Will."

To commemorate his dedication to the community, the county and the city honored him with the creation of Edmund Harding Day in May 1966. (Both, courtesy of Whiting Toler.)

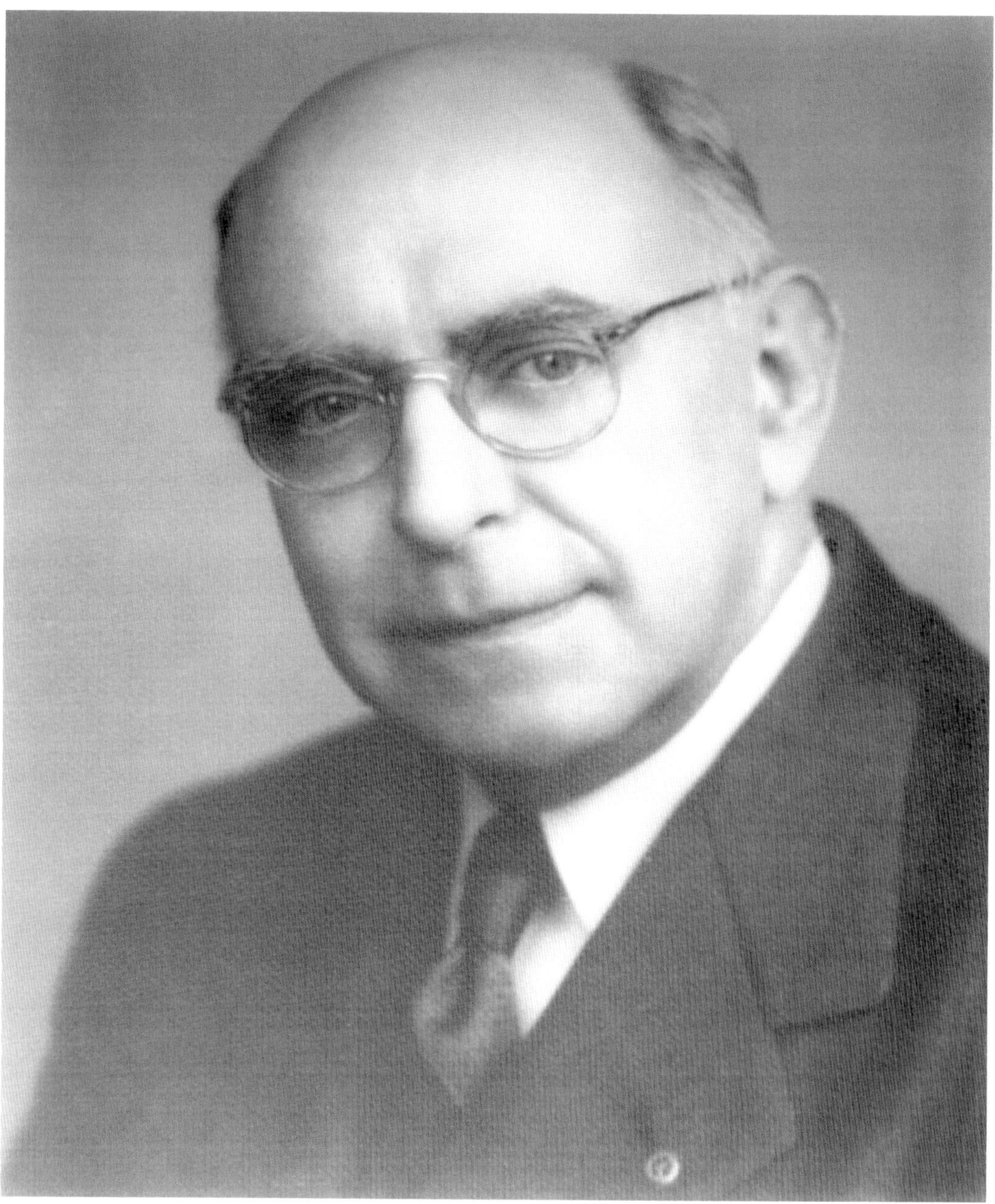

John Bragaw

Working at Bragaw & Co. Insurance for many years, John Bragaw had business savvy. In 1902, he helped establish Washington's first Home Building and Loan Association. Bragaw was also a writer, and he contributed to *Our State Magazine*, writing a column called "Regular Shots." For more than 30 years, he was a regular columnist for the *Washington Daily News*, where his column "Now and Then" was very popular. It is oft quoted that he was "the most beloved man in Beaufort County" for his work in the community and at St. Peter's Episcopal Church, where he taught Sunday school for over 50 years. His roles in the community were vast. He also served as a town alderman and as chair of the Beaufort County Board of Elections. (Courtesy of Walker Lynch.)

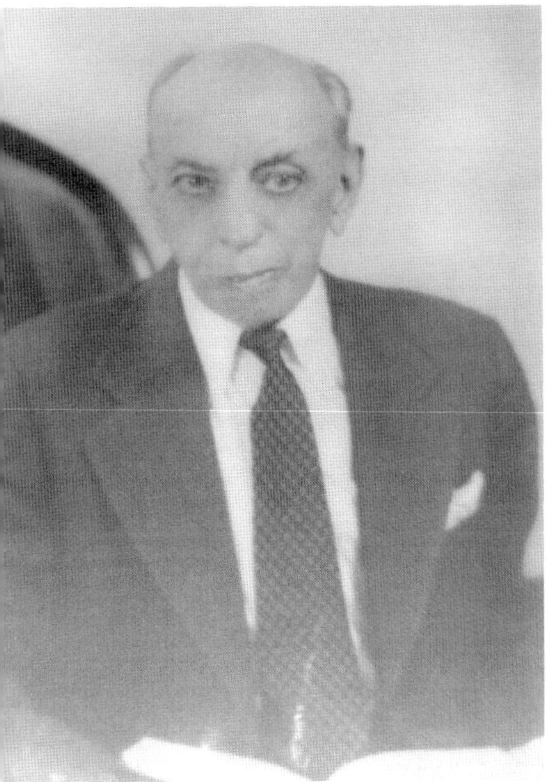

William Bragaw

In 1888, William Bragaw started an insurance agency in downtown Washington. Both John Bragaw and William H. Harding, talented businessmen and well-known local personalities, worked for the growing family business. Today, Bragaw & Co. is the oldest continuously operating insurance agency in the state. In fact, when Bragaw passed away in 1953, he was the oldest insurance agent in the state, both in terms of age and time of service. (Courtesy of Walker Lynch.)

Nathan Keais

Following his service as a captain in the Continental army, Keais settled in Washington, where he served as the collector for the port of Bath. He attended the North Carolina Convention in 1788 to represent Beaufort County, and served as a member of Washington's first town board. His family's close connection to Bath may be most evident in his great-grandson Edmund Harding, who championed the restoration of historic Bath. (Author's collection.)

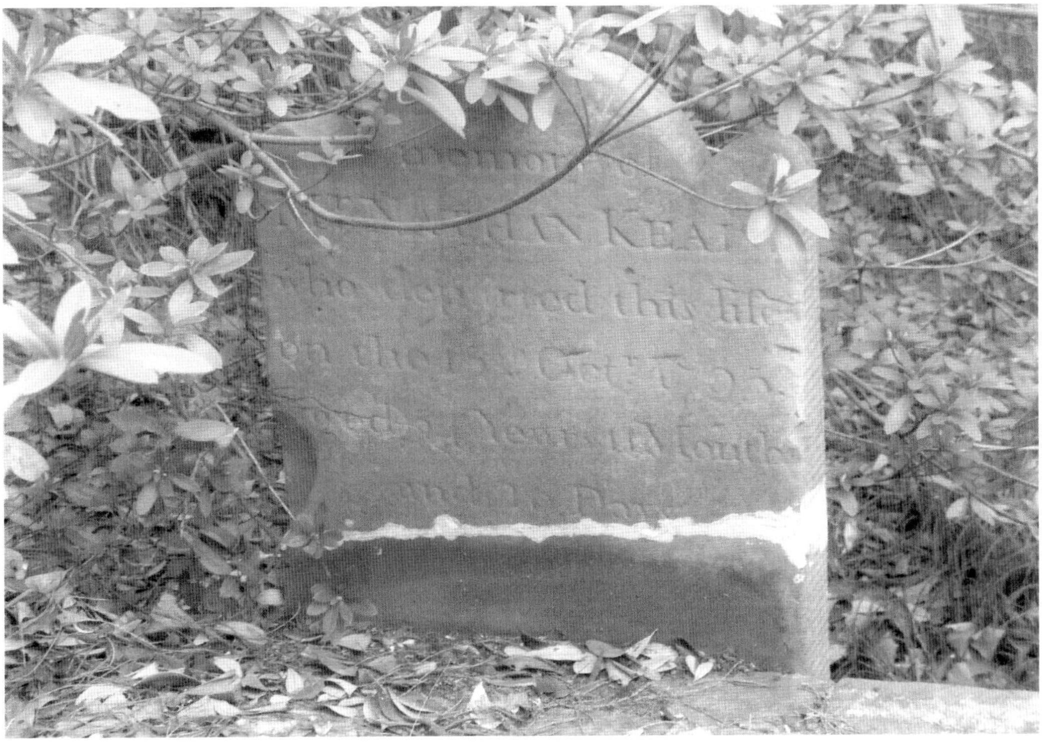

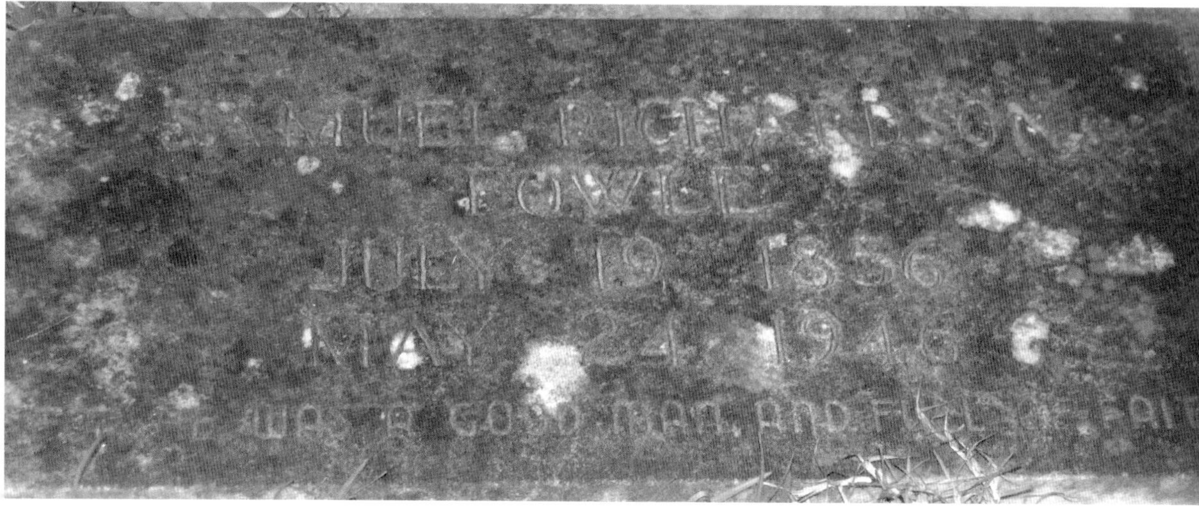

The Fowle Family

The Fowles came to Beaufort County from New England around the end of the War of 1812. S.R. Fowle was an entrepreneur, and he wasted no time setting up a mercantile in Washington. He was an upstanding member of the community who was involved in business and industry on the town's wharfs for many years. More members of the Fowle family came to town, including brothers Josiah and Luke, who established a shipbuilding business on Castle Island in the Pamlico River. Ships built and operated by S.R. Fowle & Sons made regular trips to the West Indies and Cuba to bring exotic fruits and spices to the Carolinas and New England states. (Author's collection.)

Fowle Memorial Hospital

After S.R. Fowle's death, his sons James L. and Dan Fowle (future governor of North Carolina), along with many local physicians, convinced an old business associate of S.R. Fowle's to contribute to a public hospital to honor his colleague's memory. With the community behind the idea, in 1902, the S.R. Fowle Memorial Hospital was established on the corner of Market and Fifth Streets (opposite). Today, Fire Station No. 1 stands in the location where the hospital once was. (Courtesy of Washington Fire Department.)

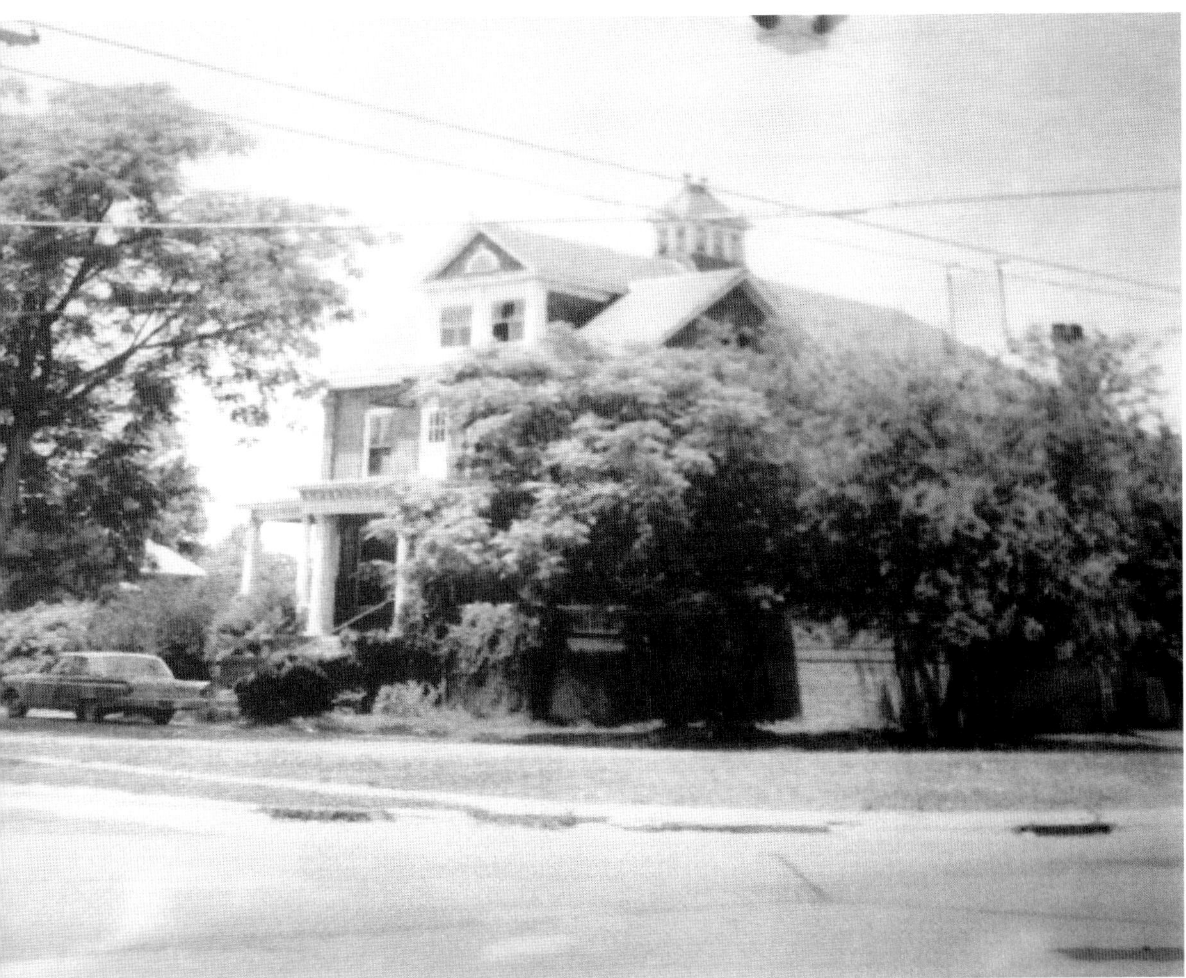

Beverly Turpin Moss

The Moss family moved to Washington to establish a lumber business. Moss Lumber Mill was the first officially incorporated business in town. The company thrived on the banks of the Pamlico River until Moss's tragic death five years later. The company then closed, but his son, Beverly G. Moss, went on to establish Moss Planing Mill. (Courtesy of Blount Rumley.)

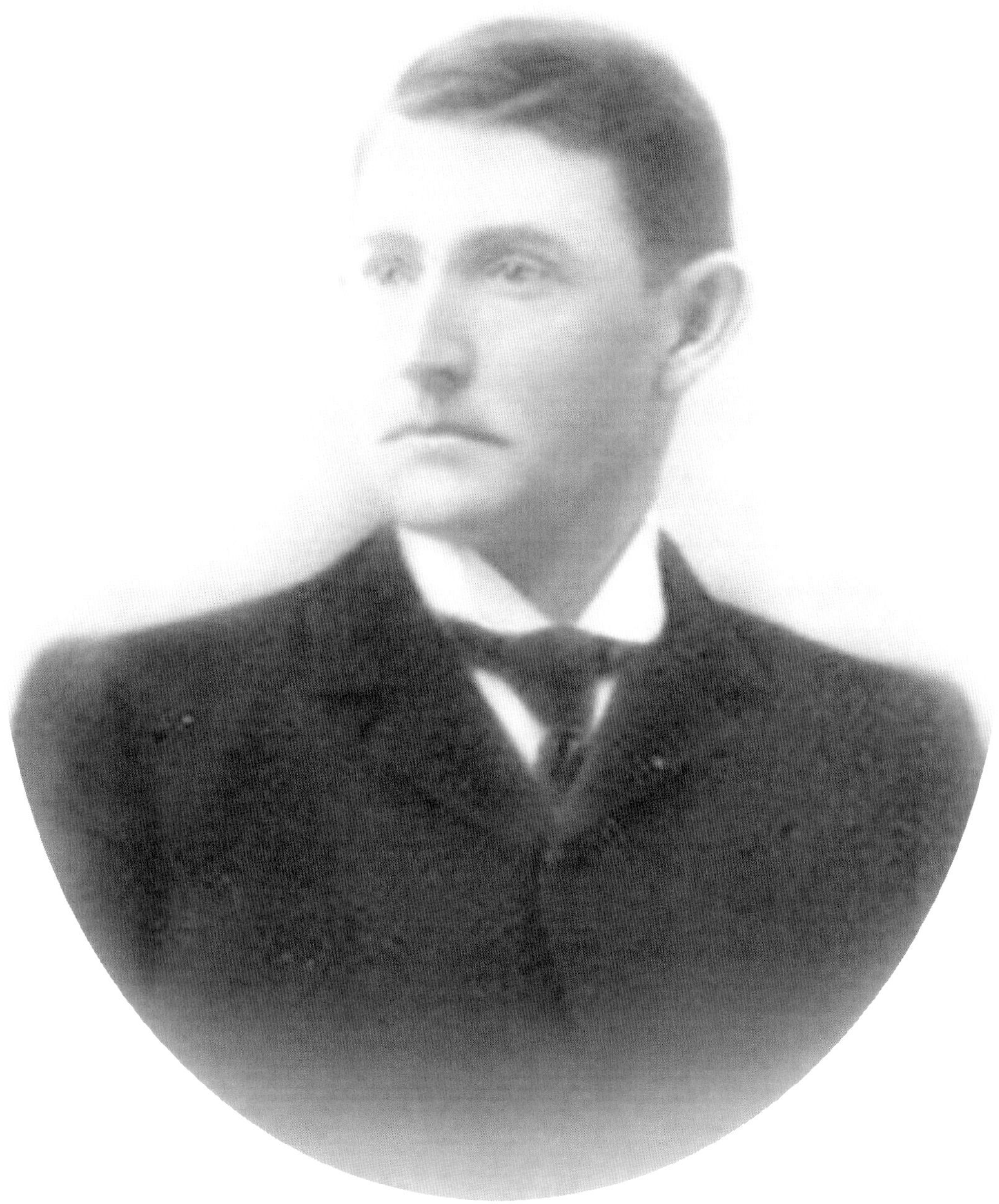

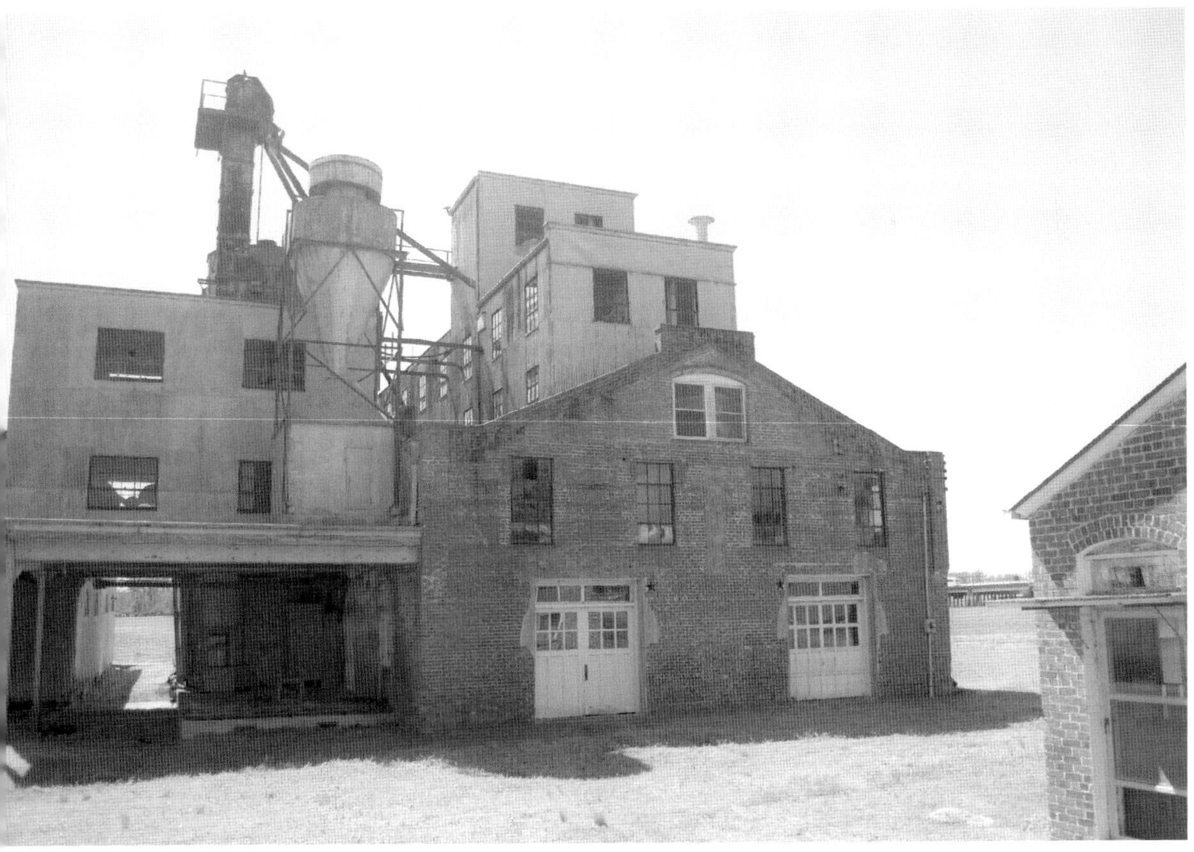

John Havens Moss

John Havens Moss was the owner of John Havens Moss Industries. His business ventured into many areas including a flour mill and a sawmill. His mill on the Washington waterfront was one of only a few that continuously provided employment through the Great Depression. Not just a savvy businessman, Moss was involved in many elements of growth in the town, including being a part of the building committee for the Bank of Washington. (Author's collection.)

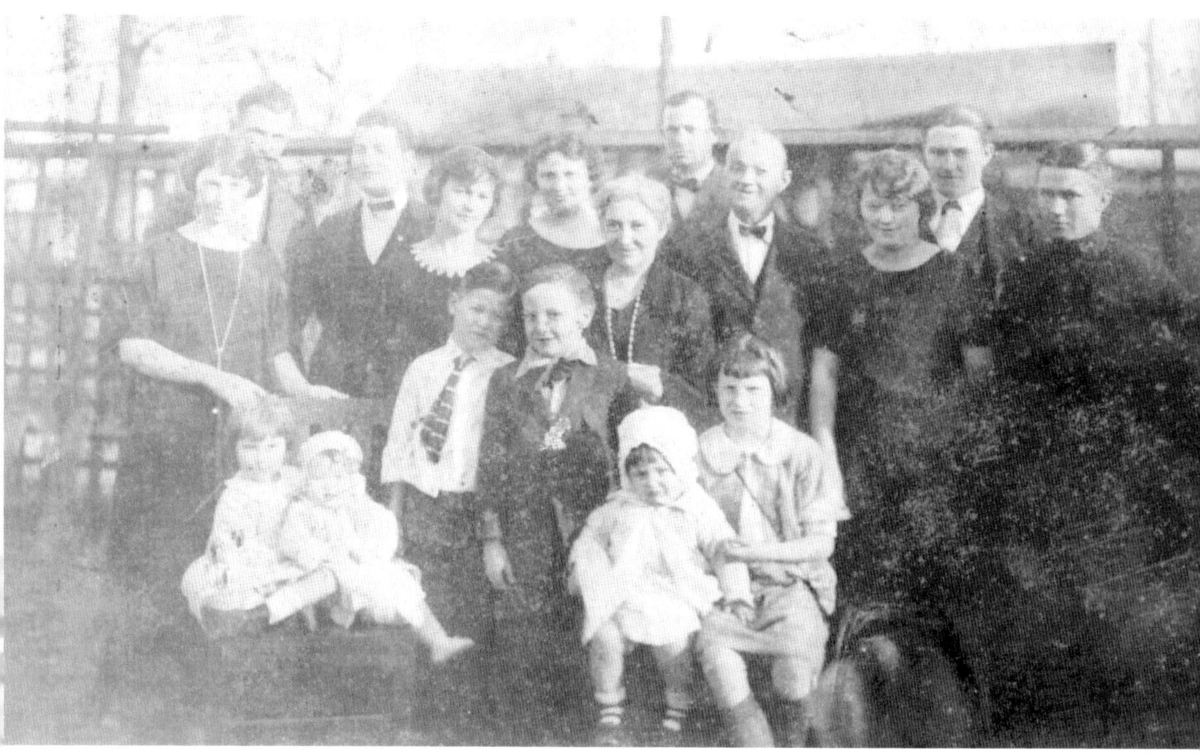

Adm. Harry H. McIlhenny

The McIlhenny family of Washington believed in serving its country, so it was no surprise when Harry H. McIlhenny joined the US Navy after finishing school. In World War II, he commanded counterattacks against Japanese submarines in the Pacific, and for his efforts, he was awarded the Navy Cross, Silver Star, and Legion of Merit. He retired in 1957 as a rear admiral. Here, he is pictured as a teenager (back left) with the rest of his family. (Courtesy of Whiting Toler.)

One of Thirteen

George C. Cooper did not set out to change history, but with a stroke of luck, that is exactly what he did. One of 11 children, Cooper was enlisted in the Navy at the onset of World War II. He was chosen as one of the men who later became known as the "Golden Thirteen," the first 13 black men to become officers in the US Navy in 1944. Chosen by chance, Cooper (front row, center) and his fellow officers paved the way for future generations of black officers in the military. (Courtesy of the US Naval Historical Center.)

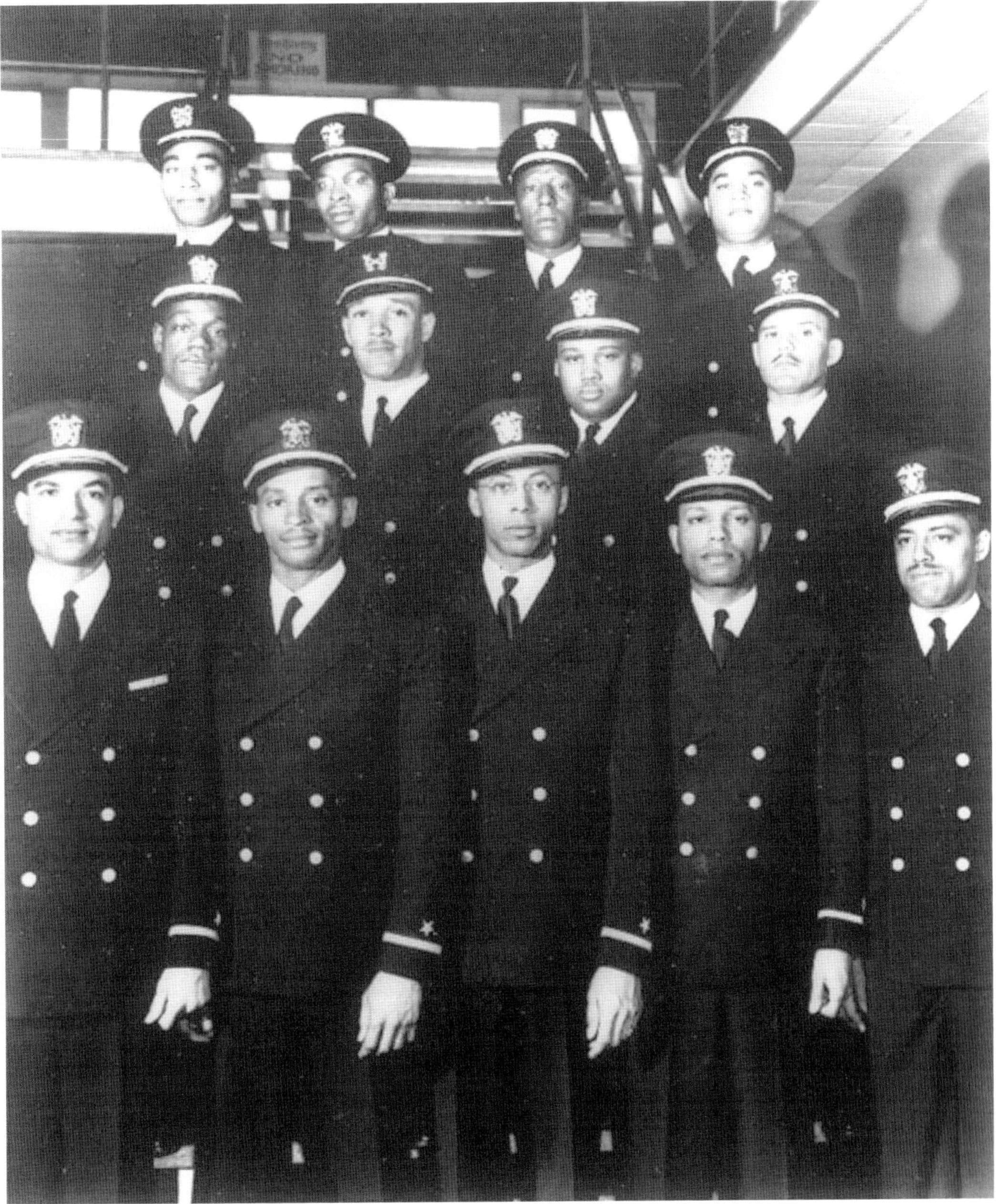

John Myers

A successful businessman, John Myers opened a mercantile in Washington in 1825. He purchased his home on the waterfront (pictured) in 1826. It still stands as one of the oldest surviving homes in town. Currently, the building houses Gaskins & Gaskins law firm.

Over the years, the Myers family's business interests grew, and soon Myers & Co. constructed everything from railroads to sailing vessels. When the Civil War began, Myers joined the Confederate army as a quartermaster.

Following his death, his sons reorganized the company as John Myers' Sons. No ships were built for 10 years after the Civil War, and the first ship to be built, the *Pitt*, was entrusted to the company. (Author's collection.)

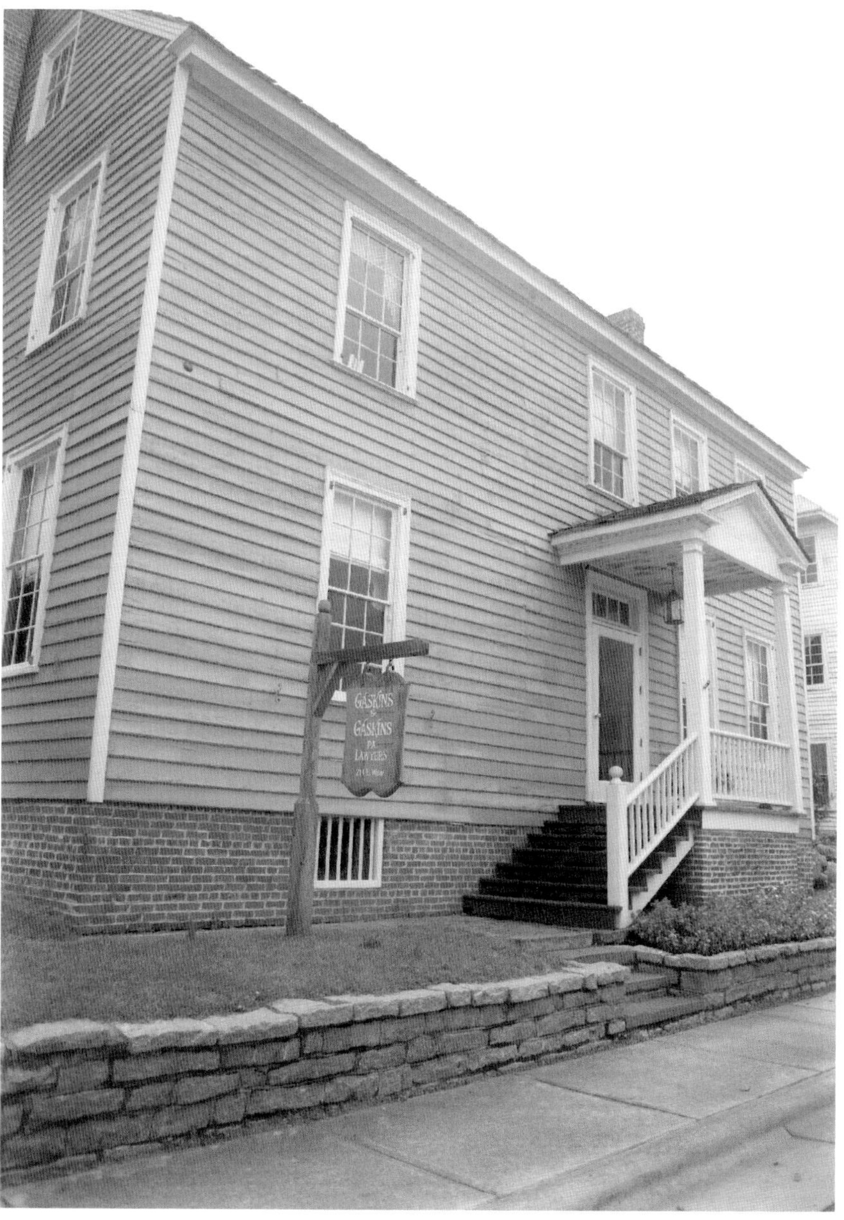

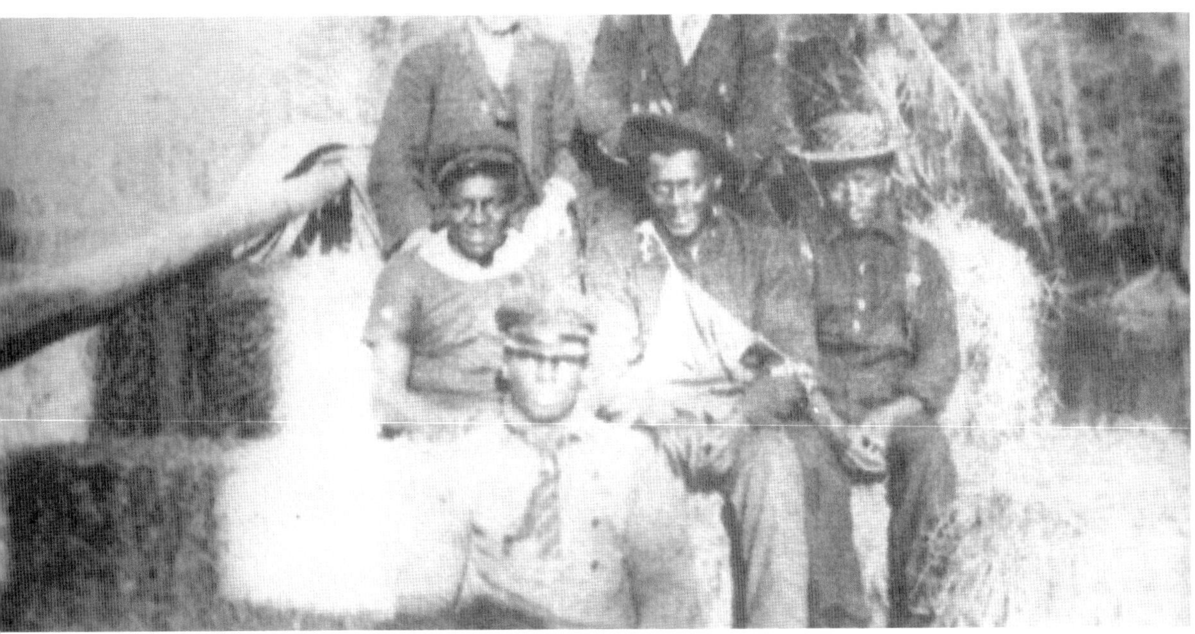

R.L. Myers II Crew

Pictured here are a few men thought to be from the *R.L Myers II*, a steamboat under John Myers' Sons agents. The steamboat was built in 1885 to replace the original *R.L. Myers*, which burned. The *R.L. Myers II* was a constant presence on the Tar and Pamlico Rivers until it was put out of service in 1907. (Courtesy of Historic Port of Washington.)

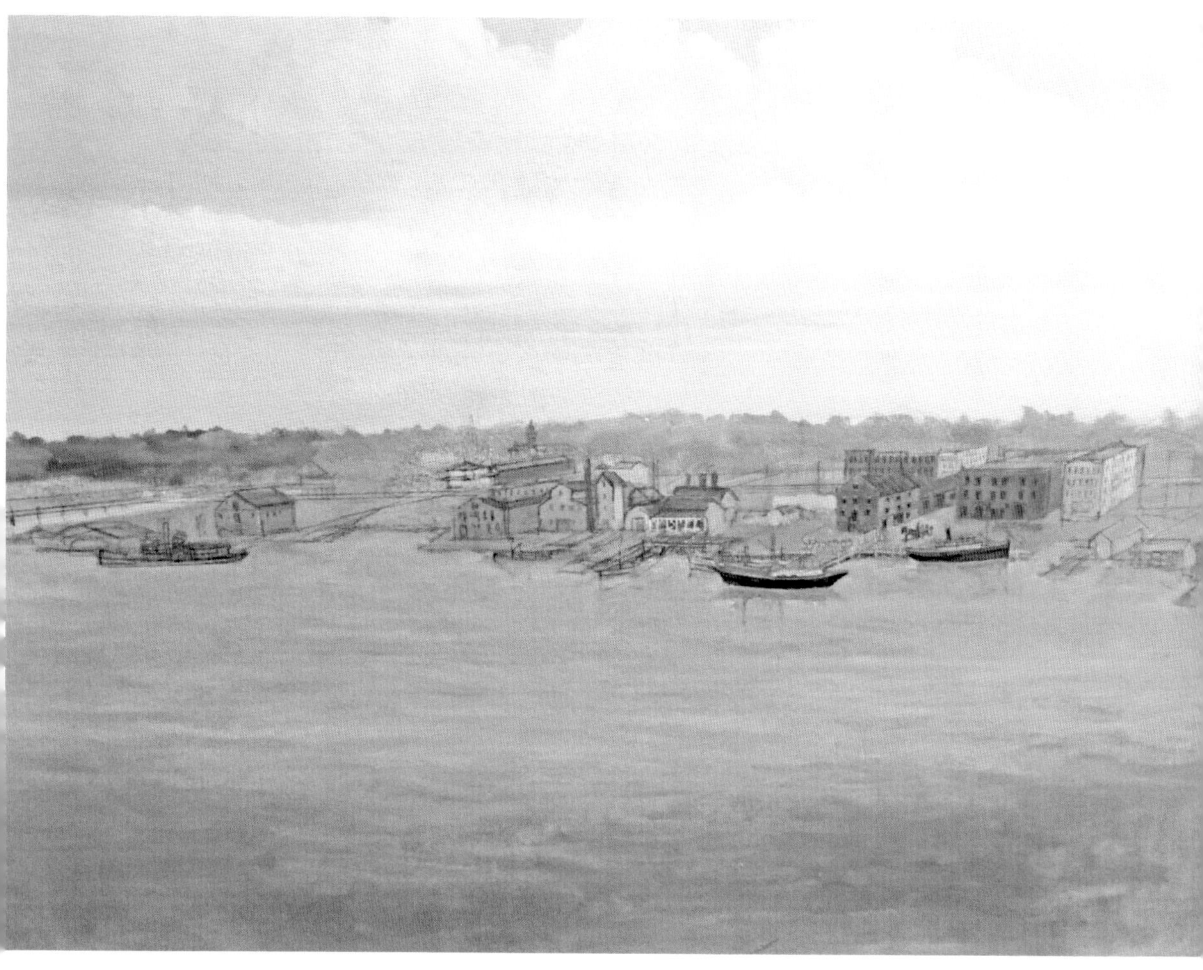

Hull Anderson

Hull Anderson was born a slave in 1784; however, in 1828, he was bequeathed his freedom in the will of his owner, Sally Anderson. He had to pay fees totaling $350 for the privilege, but he became a freeman.

Anderson was employed as a shipwright in a downtown shipyard, and it is assumed that his first name was derived from his profession. He did, however, keep the Anderson family name. Anderson built a home and married Cherry, a slave nine years his junior. He built a life and, eventually, a business. In 1840, he opened the first African American–owned shipyard on the Washington waterfront. This was a major accomplishment in a time when only 10 percent of the black population lived as free people.

Alas, fortunes in his hometown did not last. Laws were being implemented to suppress free African Americans.

A less ambitious man might have tucked tail and accepted defeat, but Anderson instead developed a radical idea. He decided he would relocate to Africa, where his family could live in a more accepting society. This, along with some quirky habits, helped Anderson gain a reputation around Washington, a town he could not let go even after he and his family had sailed for the African shore.

In Liberia, he purchased 100 acres of land where he grew coffee. As the business grew, he started to trade internationally, his product even being shipped to his hometown of Washington.

Anderson died in 1852, leaving his farmland to his grandchildren and dictating that the land in Monrovia remain in the family as long as there were heirs to take it. His heirs still owned property in Washington for many years following his death.

Opposite is a portion of artist Douglas Alvord's panoramic view of the Washington waterfront in the 1800s, where Hull Anderson's shipyard was located. (Both, courtesy of the Historic Port of Washington.)

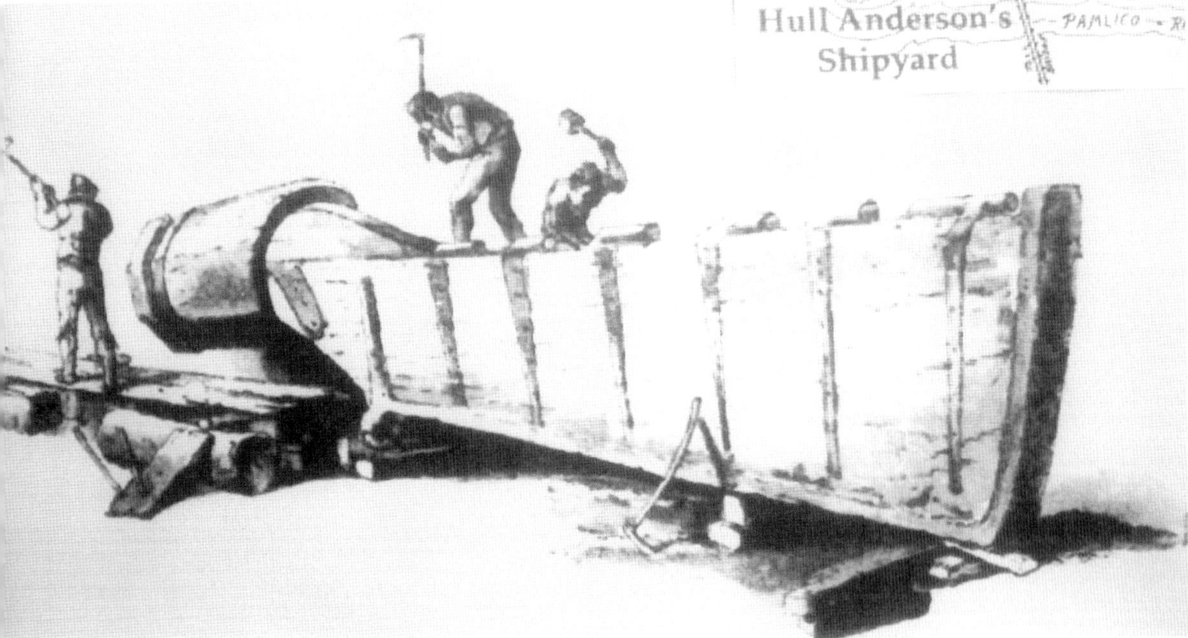

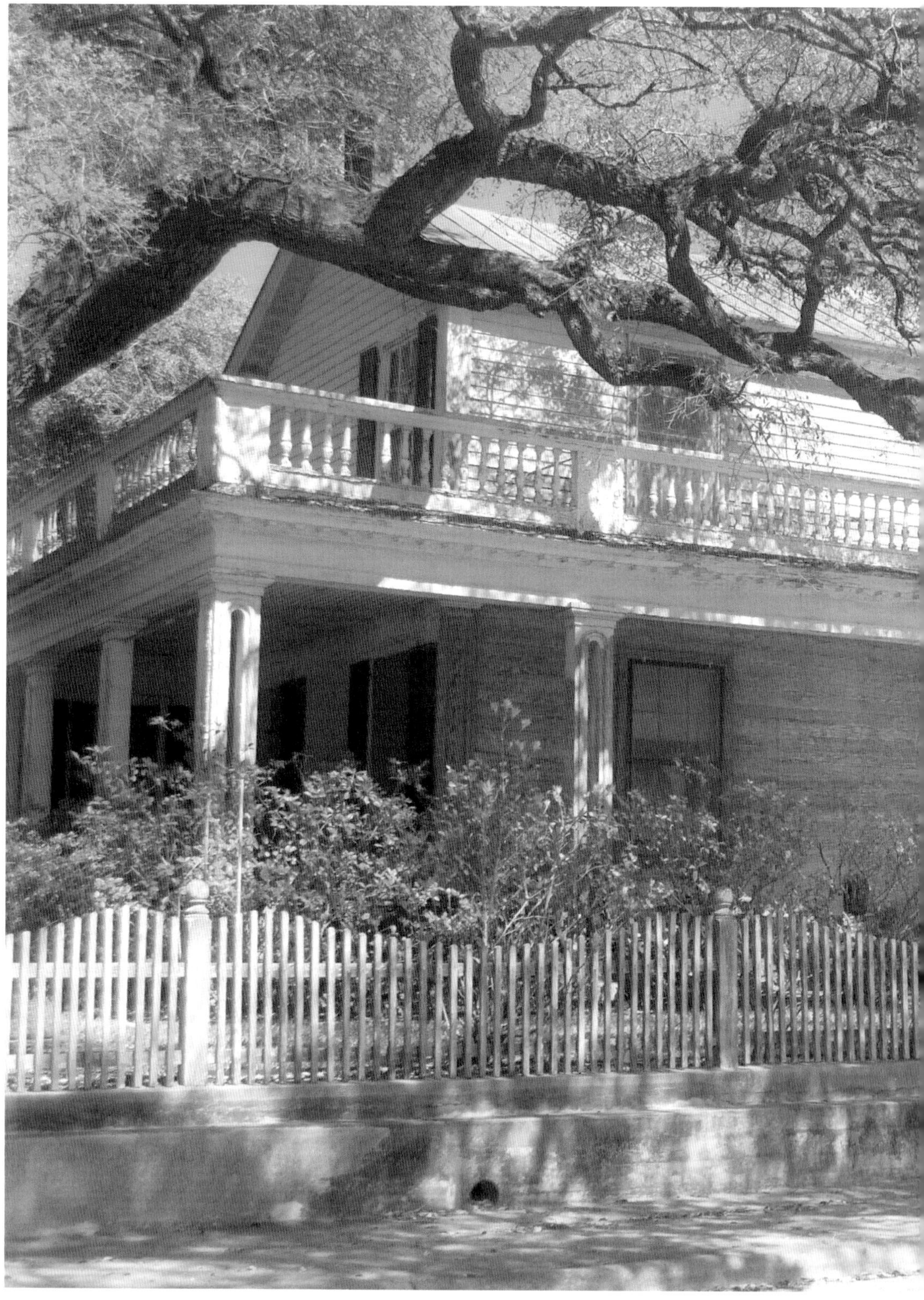

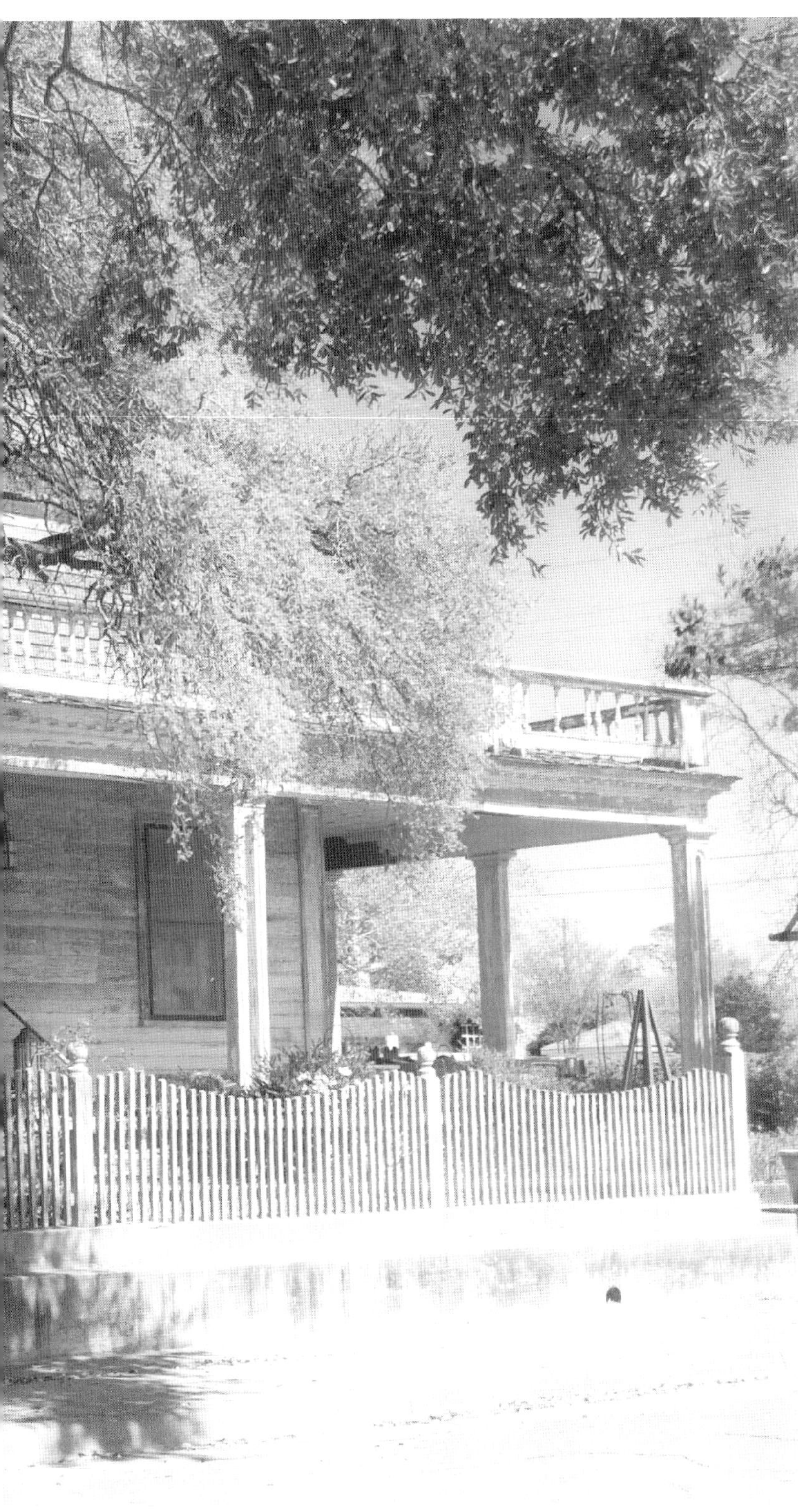

John Havens
John Havens was a successful businessman and was well known about town. In 1885, he and John Small created the Halcyon Club for the who's-who in town. The Havens family lived right by the waterfront, just across the street from the still-standing Havens' wharf building. Havens ran a cotton gin, a feed mill, and a gristmill, but he also served as president of the Bank of Washington, among other roles. On April 30, 1864, Union officers started a fire at Havens' wharf while on their retreat from town. This caused a major fire that engulfed most of downtown Washington. (Author's collection.)

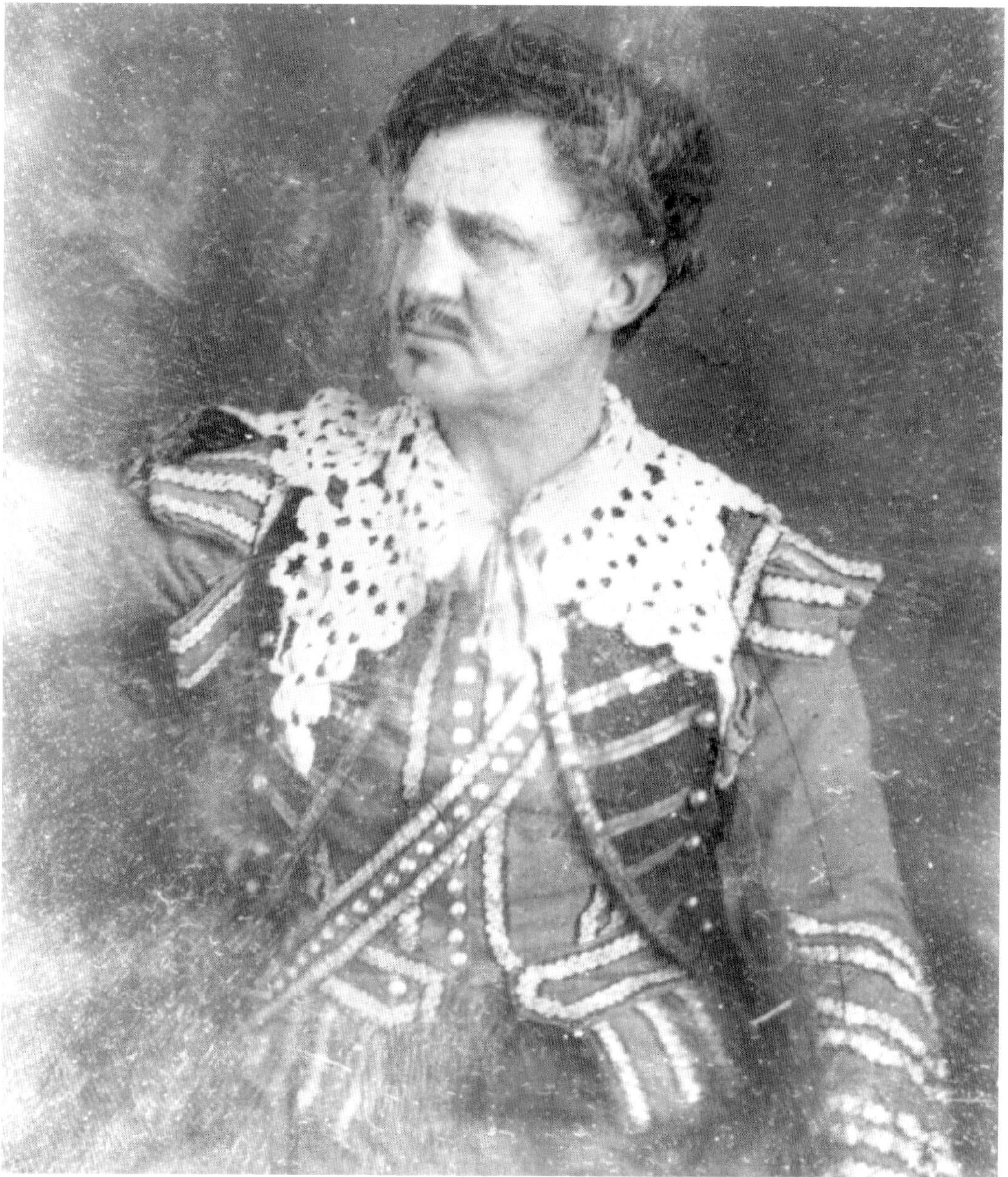

Thomas Harvey Blount

Much like the other men in his family, Thomas Harvey Blount was immersed in the shipping business, but he also served as the collector of customs for the Washington Port. Part of his job was to administer the lighthouses at Pamlico Point and Cape Hatteras. While sailing near North Carolina, Blount had a chance encounter with Junius Brutus Booth (father of John Wilkes Booth), a famous actor at the time (pictured). During the conversation, Booth lamented his fame and offhandedly mentioned that it might be better to retire from acting and pursue a career out of the limelight, such as manning a lighthouse. Blount attempted to get Booth the position at the Cape Hatteras Lighthouse (opposite above), but Booth's application was denied, possibly because his agents did not want to lose such a high-profile client. (Above, courtesy of Library of Congress; opposite, both author's collection.)

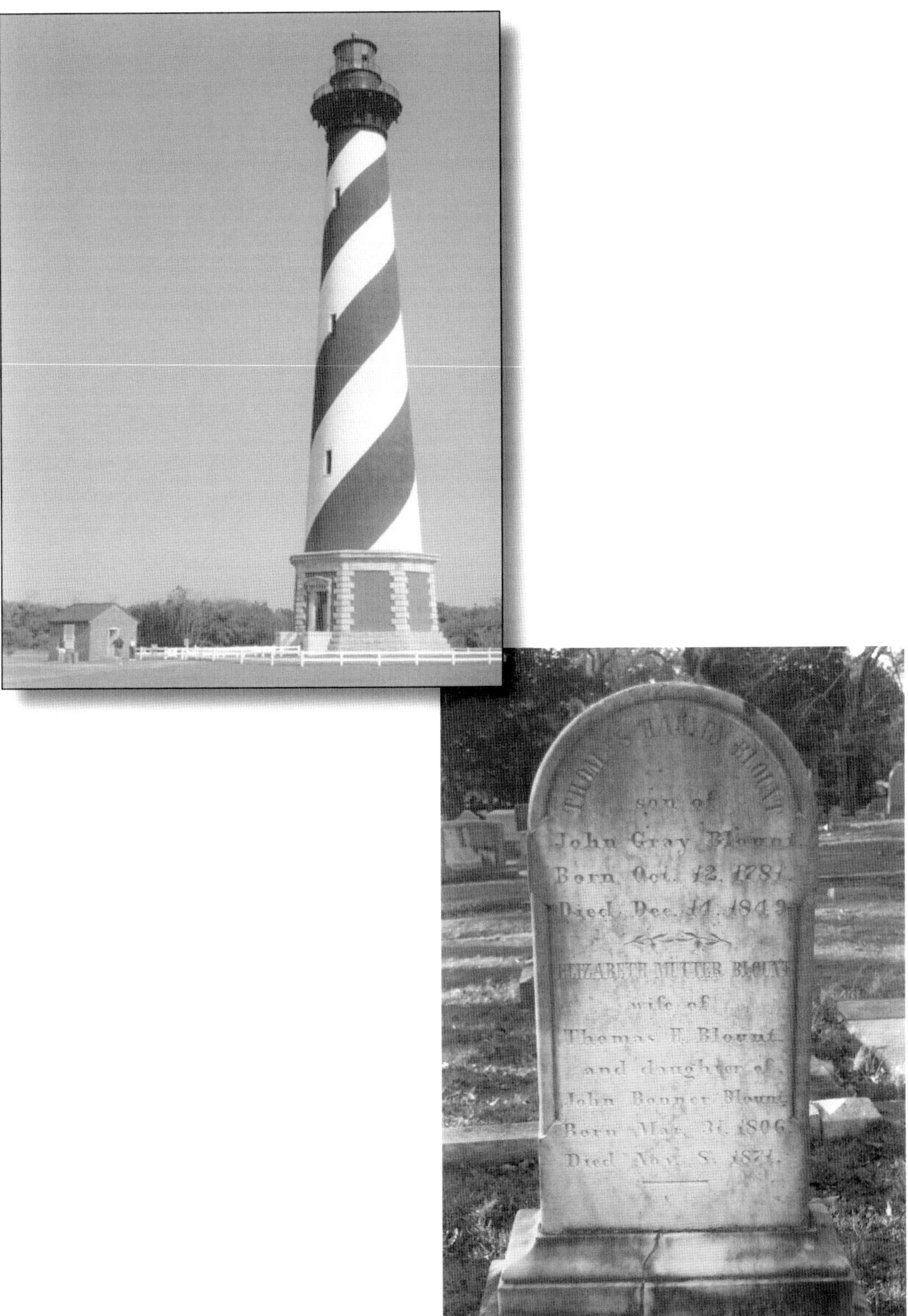
son of
John Gray Blount
Born Oct. 12, 1781
wife of
Thomas H. Blount
and daughter of
John Bonner Blount

Paul Funeral Home

Fenner T. Paul and two associates began a furniture and funeral business in 1926 (opposite). A few years later, the business split, with Paul taking over the funeral business exclusively. Fenner's nephew Bonner Paul joined the family business in 1934, and is well remembered as the longtime face of his family's business, serving for 73 years. Bonner was active in many local civic organizations and honored by many of them. A man with a keen mind for detail, he often shared his memories with locals who were seeking geographic information. (Courtesy of Beaufort County Community College.)

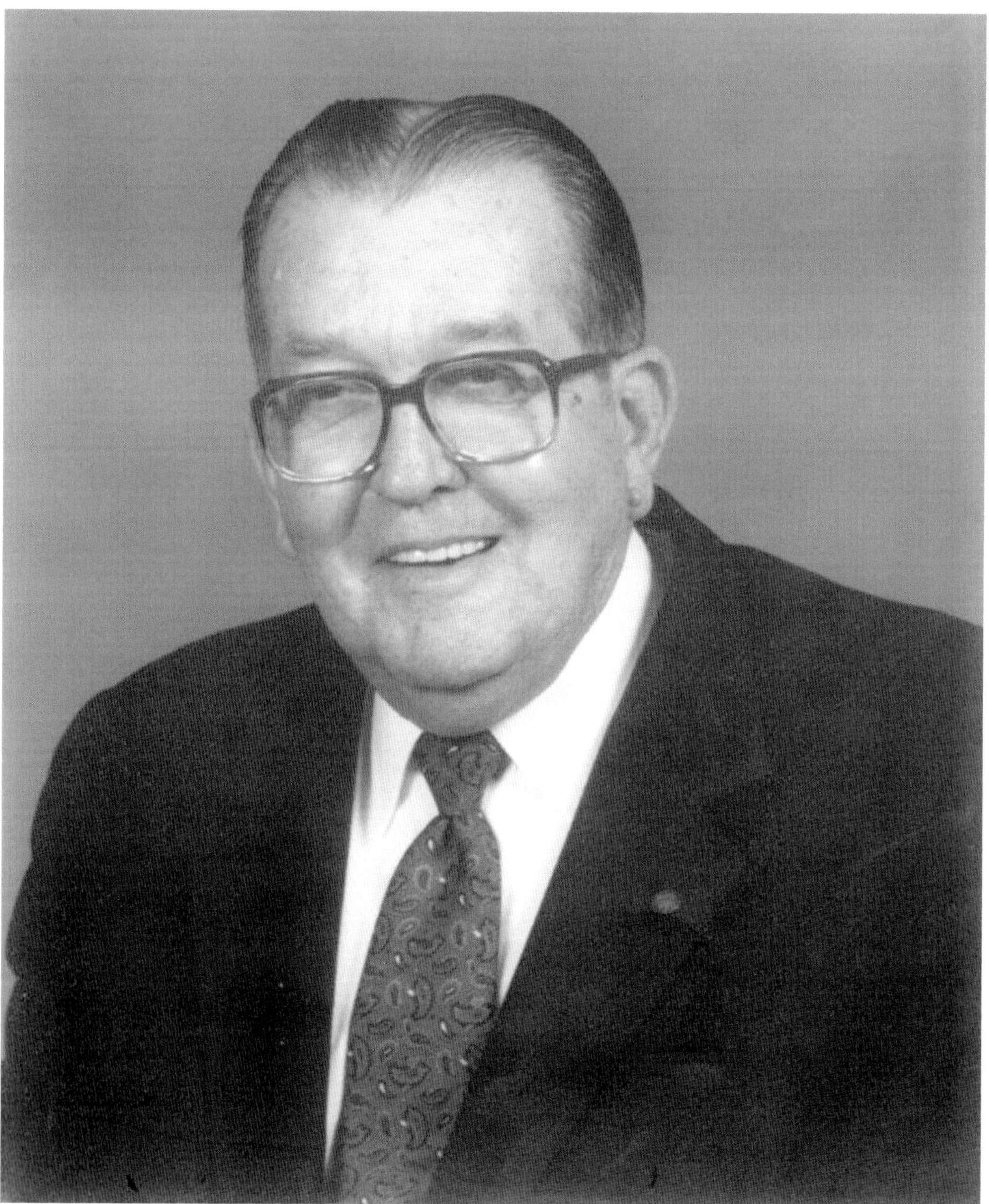

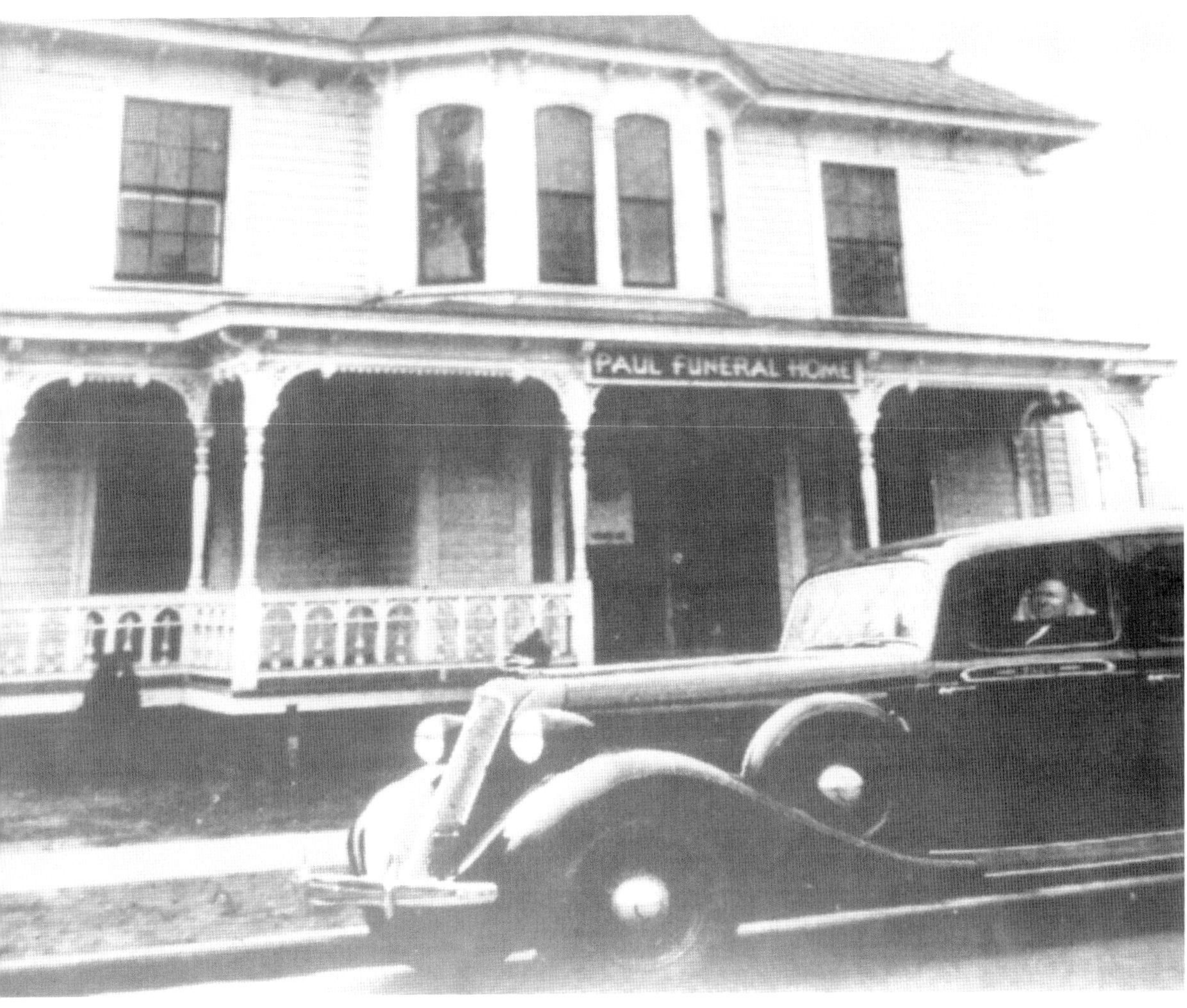
PAUL FUNERAL HOME

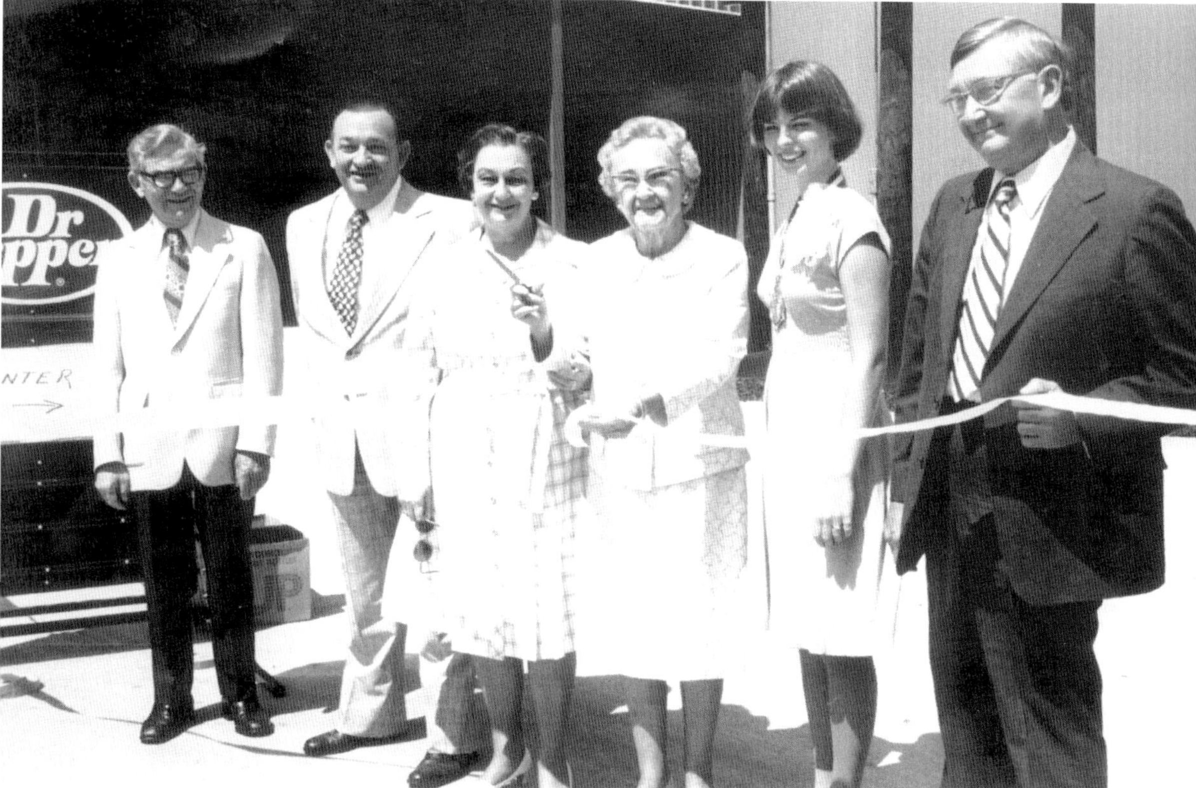

A Businessman and More

To say William "Bill" Riley Roberson Jr. played a significant role in the growth of Washington, eastern North Carolina, and even the entire state is an understatement for this man of many talents.

When Roberson started a small bottling operation in his backyard in 1946, he could not have foreseen that it would one day grow into Roberson Beverages, a company that operated several bottling plants in the East. He served on many soft drink boards, and was nominated to the Beverage World Hall of Fame in 1989.

In the 1940s, he ventured into media, founding two radio stations. However, Roberson is probably most remembered as the man behind the local television station WITN-TV, an NBC network that first aired in 1955 and remains a popular television station to this day. Roberson was a recipient of the North Carolina Broadcasters Hall of Fame award, and served on many media boards.

While his business savvy is well known, Roberson was also very civic-minded. He was a major contributor to the state art museum and a member of many civic organizations.

He served as a representative in the North Carolina General Assembly for 12 years, and his efforts in office helped establish the Goose Creek State Park, Swan Quarter–Ocracoke ferry, Beaufort County Community College, and Coastal Area Management Act. He was also active in helping to pass legislation that established the East Carolina School of Medicine.

Under Gov. Jim Hunt, he served several years as the secretary of transportation for North Carolina. Roberson passed away in 2009, leaving a business and civic legacy that will not be forgotten.

Pictured above is the 60th anniversary ribbon cutting at Roberson's Beverages Inc. on June 11, 1977. From left to right are Phil Roberson, Hannah Roberson Bagwell, Rosa Watson Roberson, Becky Reid (former Miss USA) and William Riley Roberson Jr., Opposite are, from left to right, engineer Dick Paul, Al Manning, and William Riley Roberson Jr., CEO of WITN-TV. (Both, courtesy of the Roberson family.)

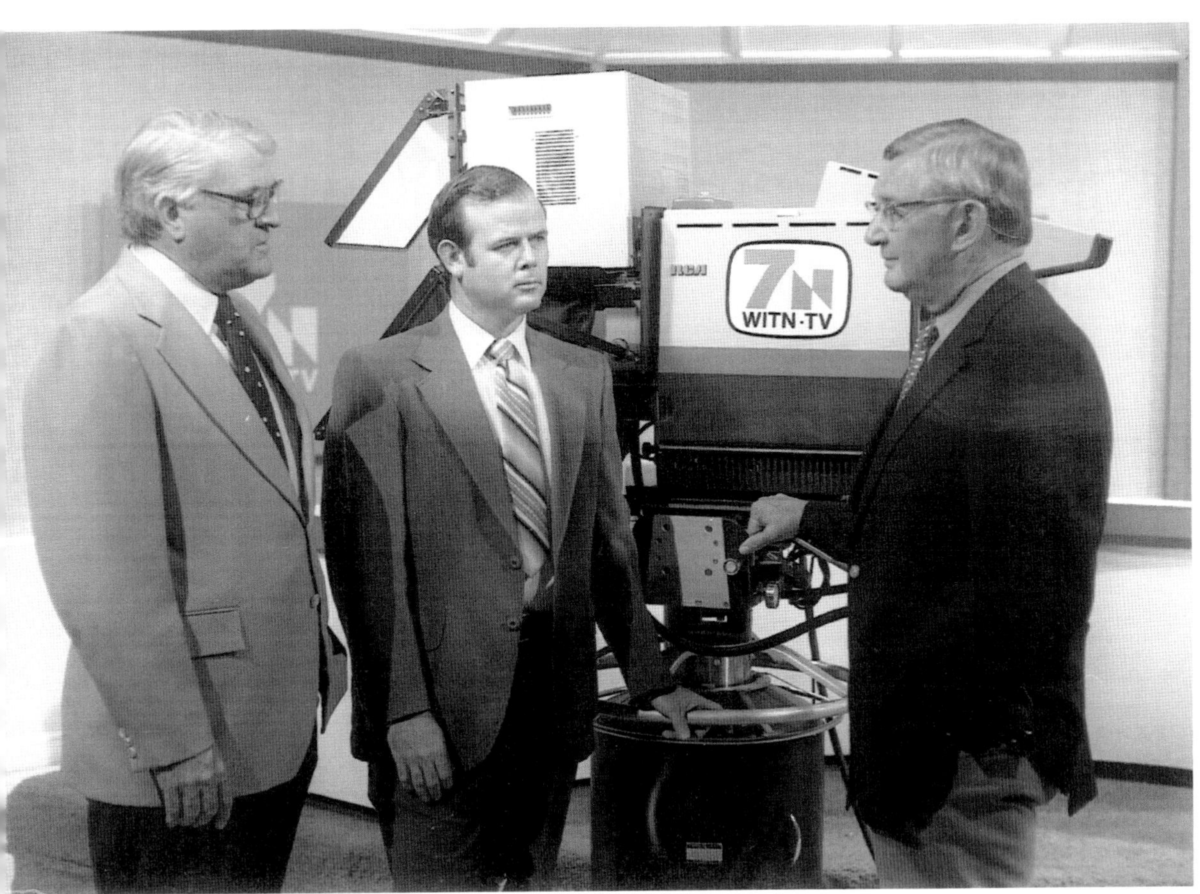
RCA
7N
WITN·TV

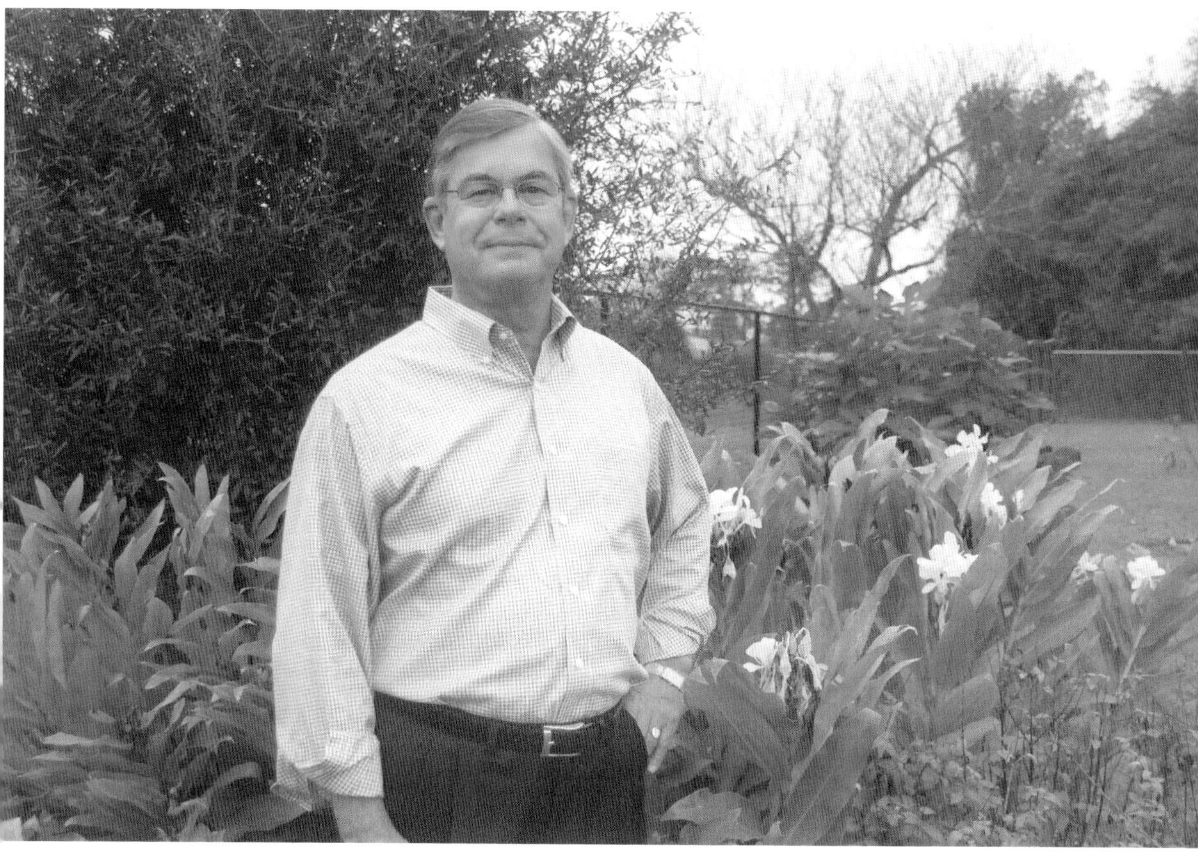

Tom Vann

After college and military service, Tom Vann applied at the Home Savings and Loan Company in Washington. Three years into his tenure, the death of a manager moved Vann into the position, making him the youngest manager of a savings and loan in the United States. For 37 years he worked at the business, overseeing its transition into First South Bank. Now retired, Vann spends much of his time gardening. (Author's collection.)

CHAPTER EIGHT

For the Arts

Washington is a town steeped in the arts. Many noteworthy artists, writers, musicians, and actors have called the small town on the Pamlico River home. The most famous may be the de Mille family, who owned the first brick house in town. The de Milles were playwrights, screenwriters, and directors. Cecil B. DeMille was a moviemaker, producing more than one film a year—an incredible accomplishment.

The arts are not limited to the most famous and the most recognized, however. Washington's citizenry advocates for the arts. A simple stroll downtown reveals several storefronts set up to sell and display local artwork. Venues come and go, but the River Walk Art Gallery has been a staple on Main Street for nearly 20 years. For several years, the Inner Banks Artisans' Center offered not only vendor spaces but also art studios where the public could watch the artists at work. The center also provided space for the Beaufort County Traditional Music Association, where banjos, guitars, and fiddles twanged everything from gospel to bluegrass. Unfortunately, this cultural center has closed, but several more art centers have sprung up in its place downtown. The dedication of the people to the arts is evident, not only in these many artisans' centers, but also in the massive revitalization of the Turnage Theater.

Acting is not just for the Washington novice. Murray Hamilton got his acting start on the stage at Washington High School, and later, he grew to fame in Hollywood.

Washington has a surprising amount of people who have gone on to make a difference. People like William Artis, one of the first widely recognized black sculptors, hailed from Washington. His works have inspired others like William O'Pharrow to pursue their own interests in art.

A vast majority of the artwork and artists stay here in Washington, and a variety of artwork is produced by locals and transplants alike. This focus on the arts just adds to the unique historical and educational atmosphere of Washington.

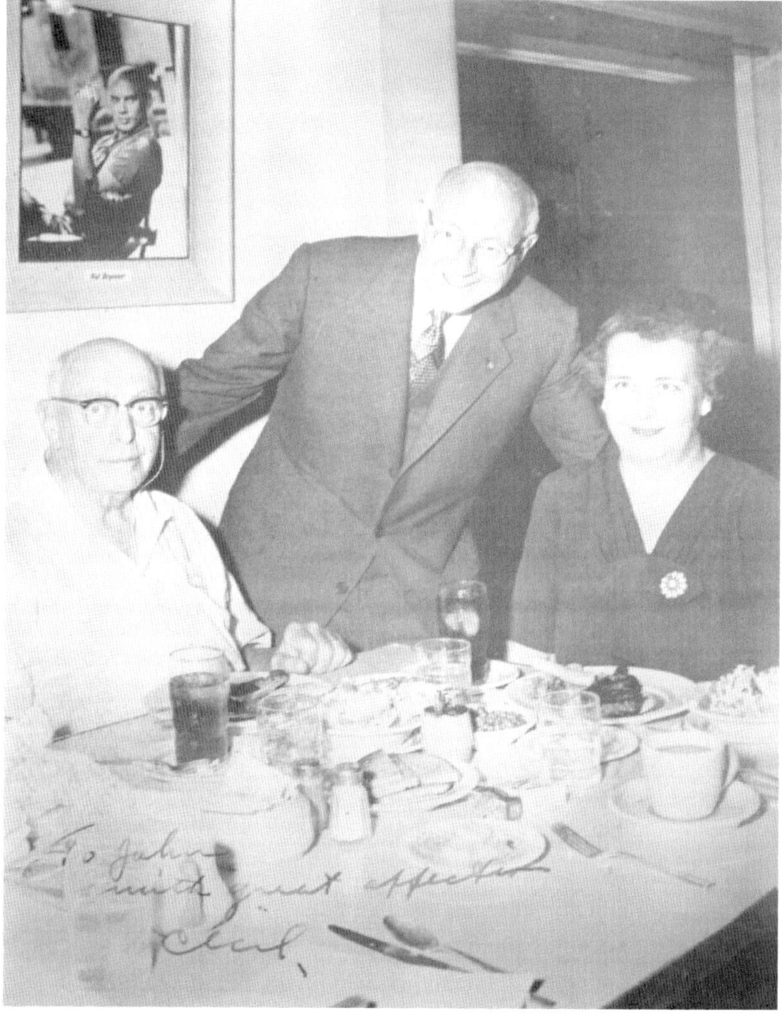

"All right, Mr. DeMille. I'm ready for my close up."

The de Mille family has been a fixture in Washington for a long time. William Edward de Mille is credited with adding the "e" to the end of "de Mill," which made the name sound more French than its Dutch origins. William owned the first brick house recorded in Washington.

His son Henry Churchill de Mille lived in Washington until he went to Columbia College. He first became a minister before getting involved in amateur theater. Years later, he became a well-known playwright, and his wife, Beatrice, wrote several screenplays.

William C. de Mille (opposite) and Cecil B. de Mille, their sons, also grew up in Washington. They left for New York to attend film school, and each one found his own way to fame.

William was a playwright and screenwriter. He directed films from the silent film era through the 1930s. Initially, he did not care for the direction his brother's career had taken, but William soon joined his brother to collaborate on film projects.

Cecil (center) was one of the most successful filmmakers of the early 20th century. He changed the spelling of his last name to DeMille for his professional career. Starting as a stage actor, Cecil's talents quickly shifted to behind the camera. He directed films throughout the silent film and talking motion picture eras. He ended his career following the 1954 film *The Ten Commandments*, for which he is probably best remembered. (Both, courtesy of the Brown Library.)

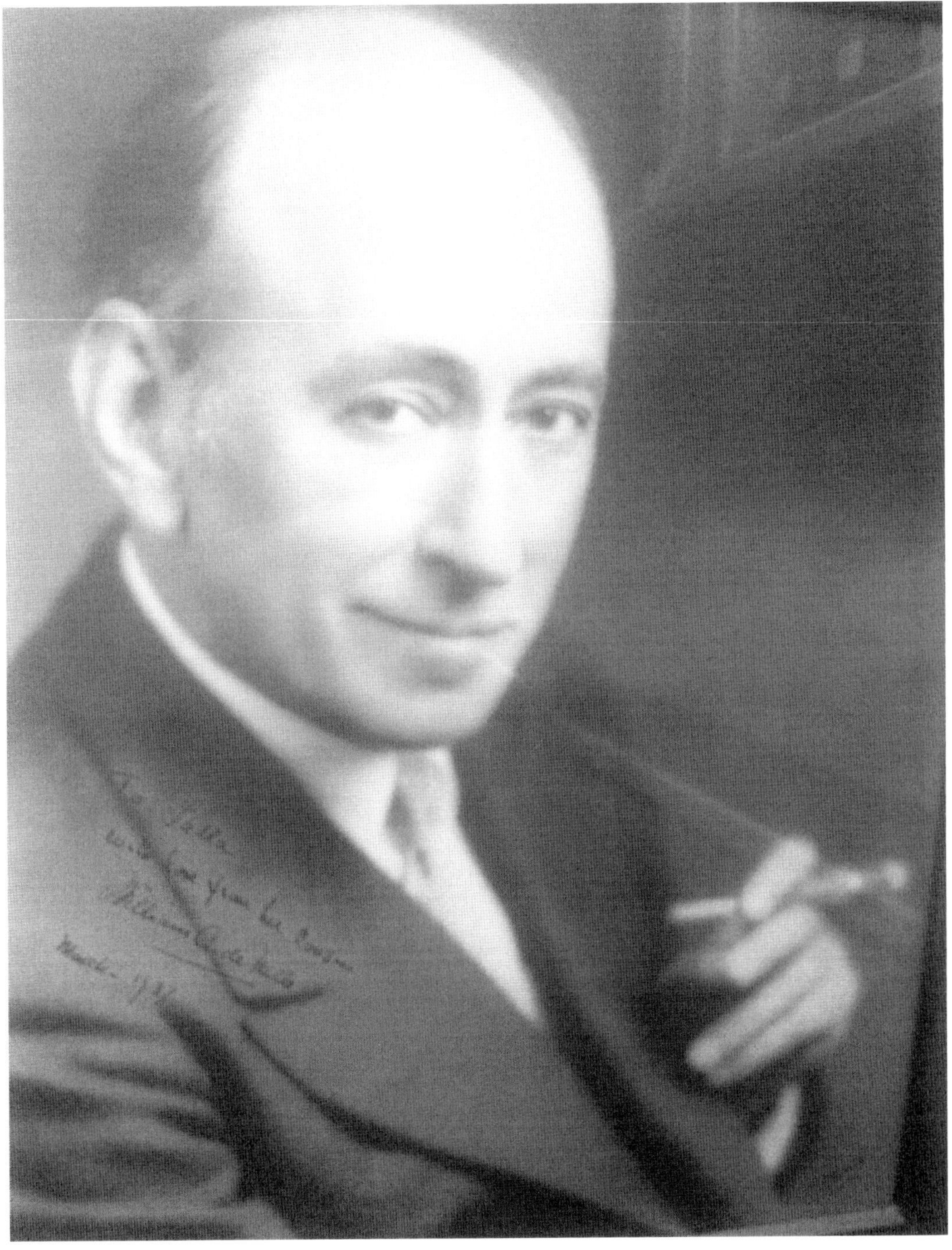

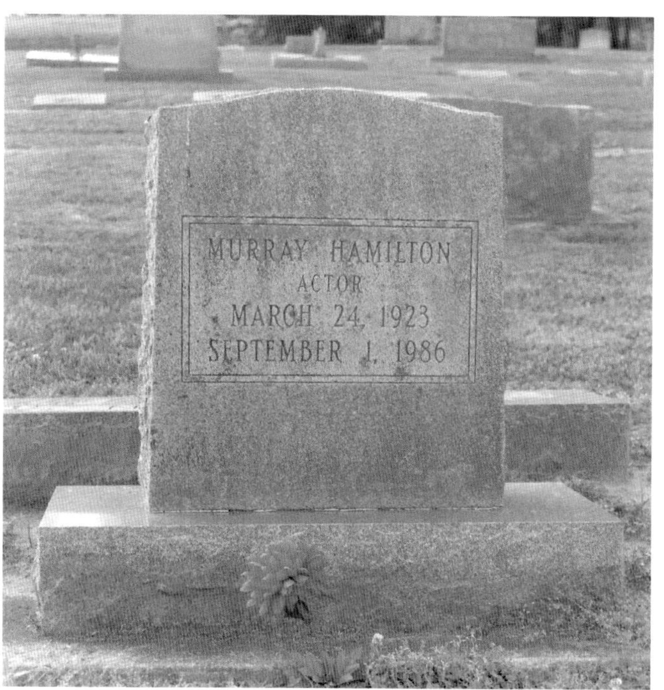

Murray Hamilton

Murray Hamilton found his niche on the stage at Washington High School. Unable to enlist during World War II because of hearing problems, he decided to move to New York City to pursue an acting career. He made his Broadway debut in 1945, but is most remembered for his appearances in minor film roles. One of his most recognizable roles is Mayor Larry Vaughn in the thriller *Jaws*. Throughout his film career, he acted in dramatic stage theater. He was married to singer Terri DeMarco of the DeMarco Sisters fame. Following his death, he was buried at Oakdale Cemetery in Washington. (Author's collection.)

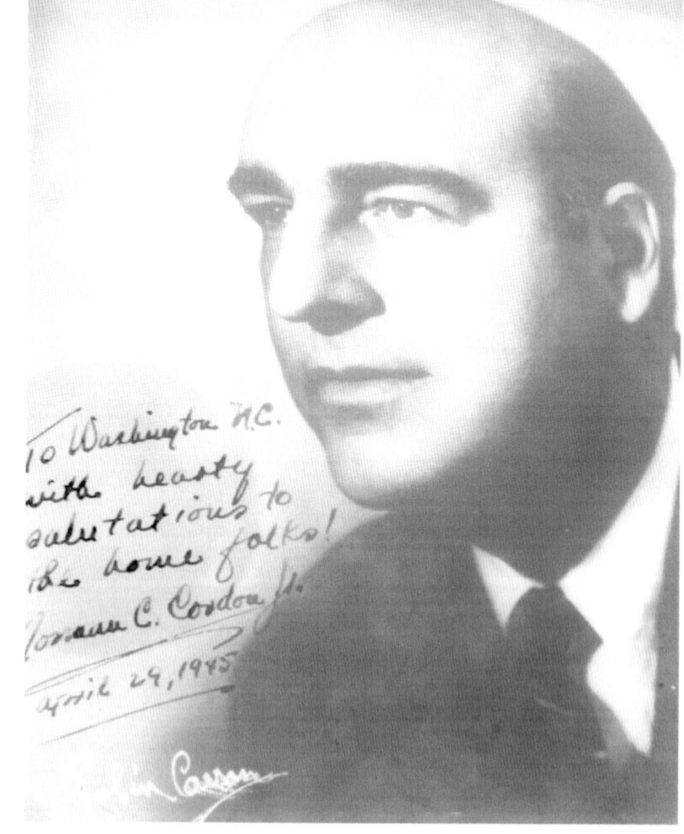

Norman Cordon

Washington native Norman Cordon lived locally until he was eight years old, but his family maintained a connection with the area. It is said that Cordon had a natural talent for music. As a member of the boys' choir at St. Peter's Episcopal Church in Charlotte, his interest in music grew as a singer. His abilities to perform in French, Italian, and German allowed him to star in a multitude of operas. For 12 years, he was a leading bass-baritone in the Metropolitan Opera Company in New York. His most famous role was Mephistopheles in *Faust*. In his later years, he returned to North Carolina to establish a statewide music program with an emphasis on opera. (Courtesy of the Brown Library.)

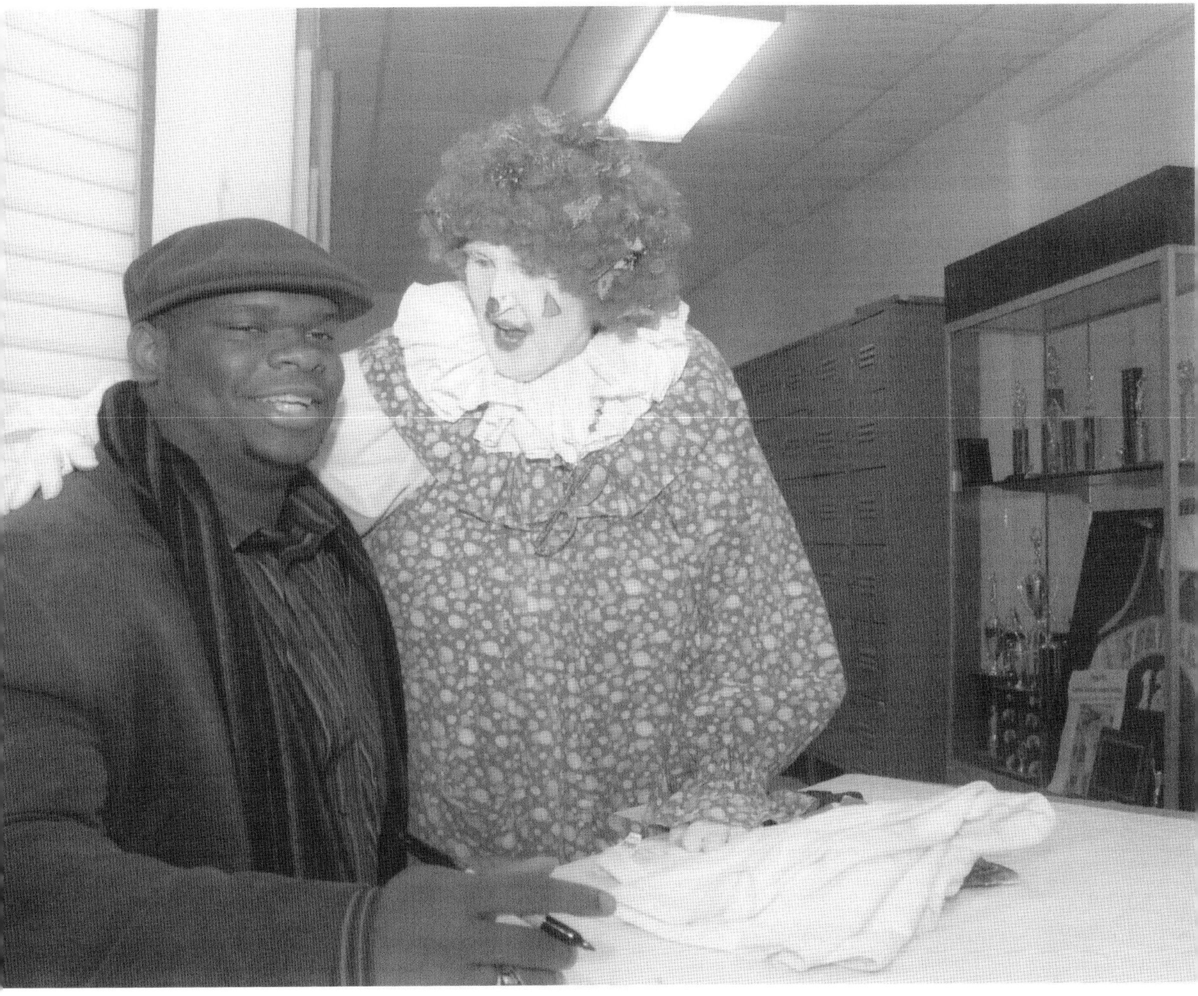

Bubbles the Clown

Fun is the name of the game with Martha Seighman. No stranger to working with children via her career as a music teacher and mother, she donned a clown costume one day to help children better understand the readings they attended at a library in Texas. Seighman's clown persona grew into "Bubbles the Clown," named for her bubbly attitude. Her smile and demeanor are contagious, and that is just the way she likes it. Since making her away to Washington, she has volunteered at many local events to inspire and delight children, and she is a queen of her local Red Hat Society chapter, Women of Whimsy. (Courtesy of Martha Seighman.)

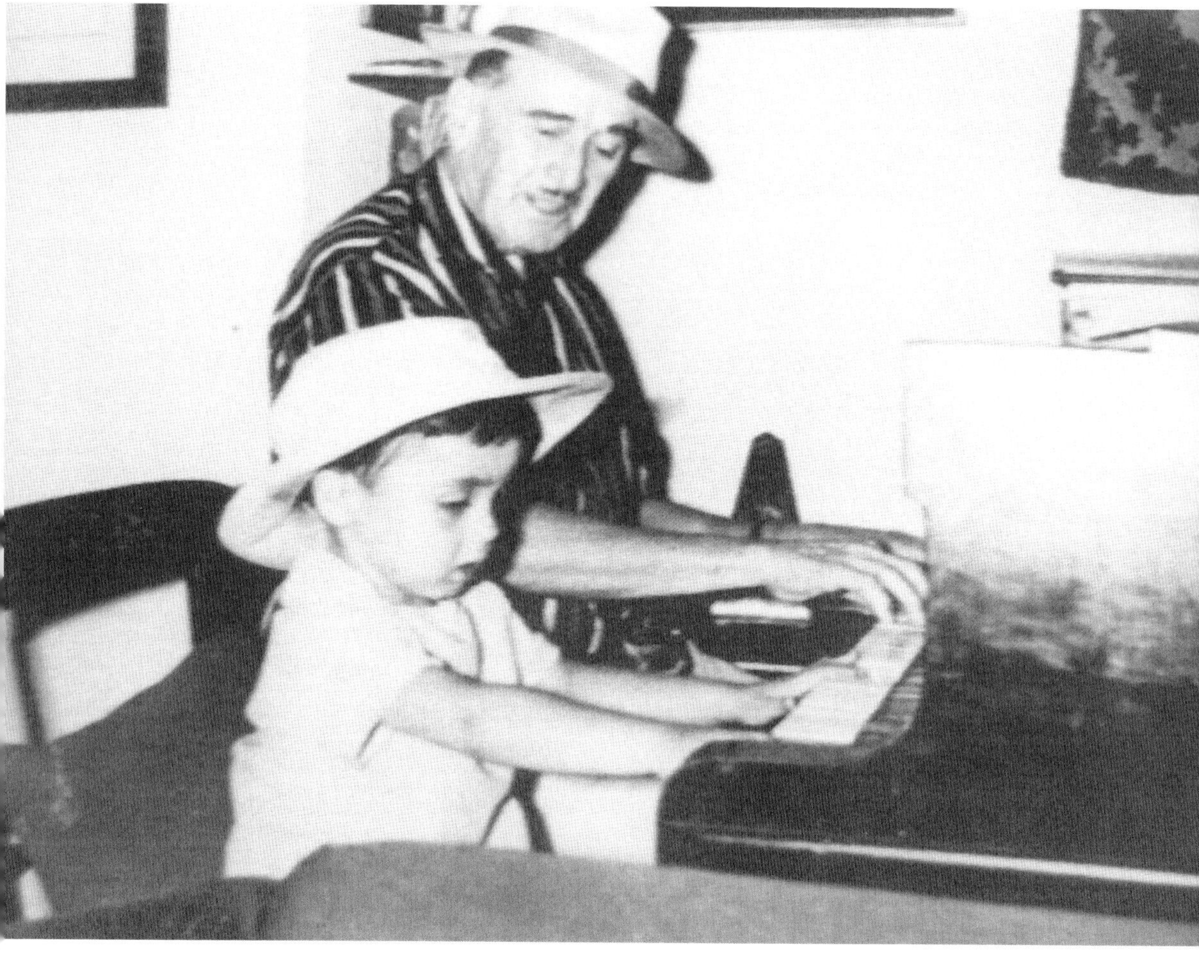

Eugene Bonner

Eugene Bonner spent eight years of his childhood in Washington, where his interest in music grew through the church. From his choirboy years, he grew into a composer of great merit. While he spent a majority of his adult life in Europe, Bonner maintained close ties to the people he knew locally. (Courtesy of Winthrop College.)

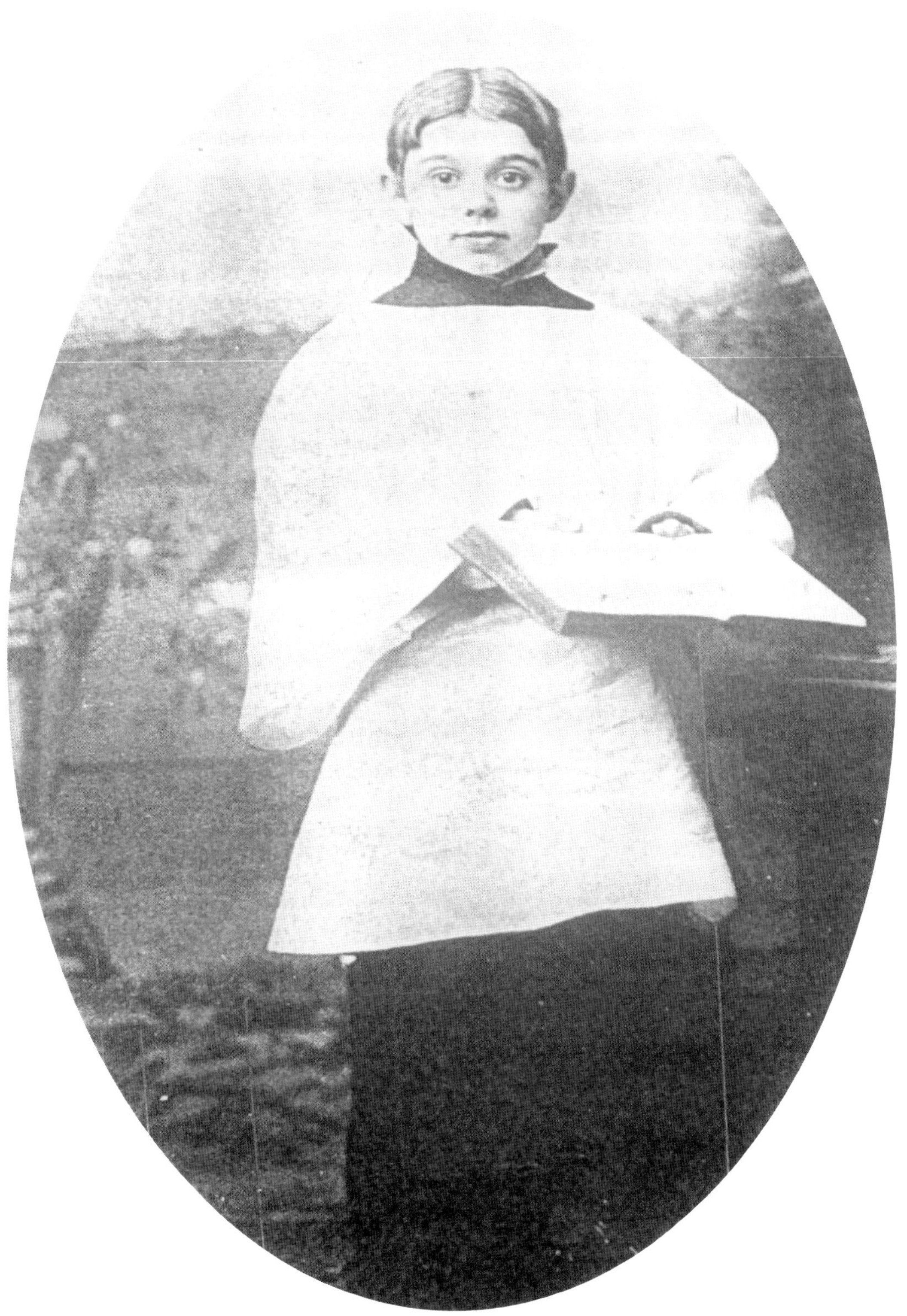

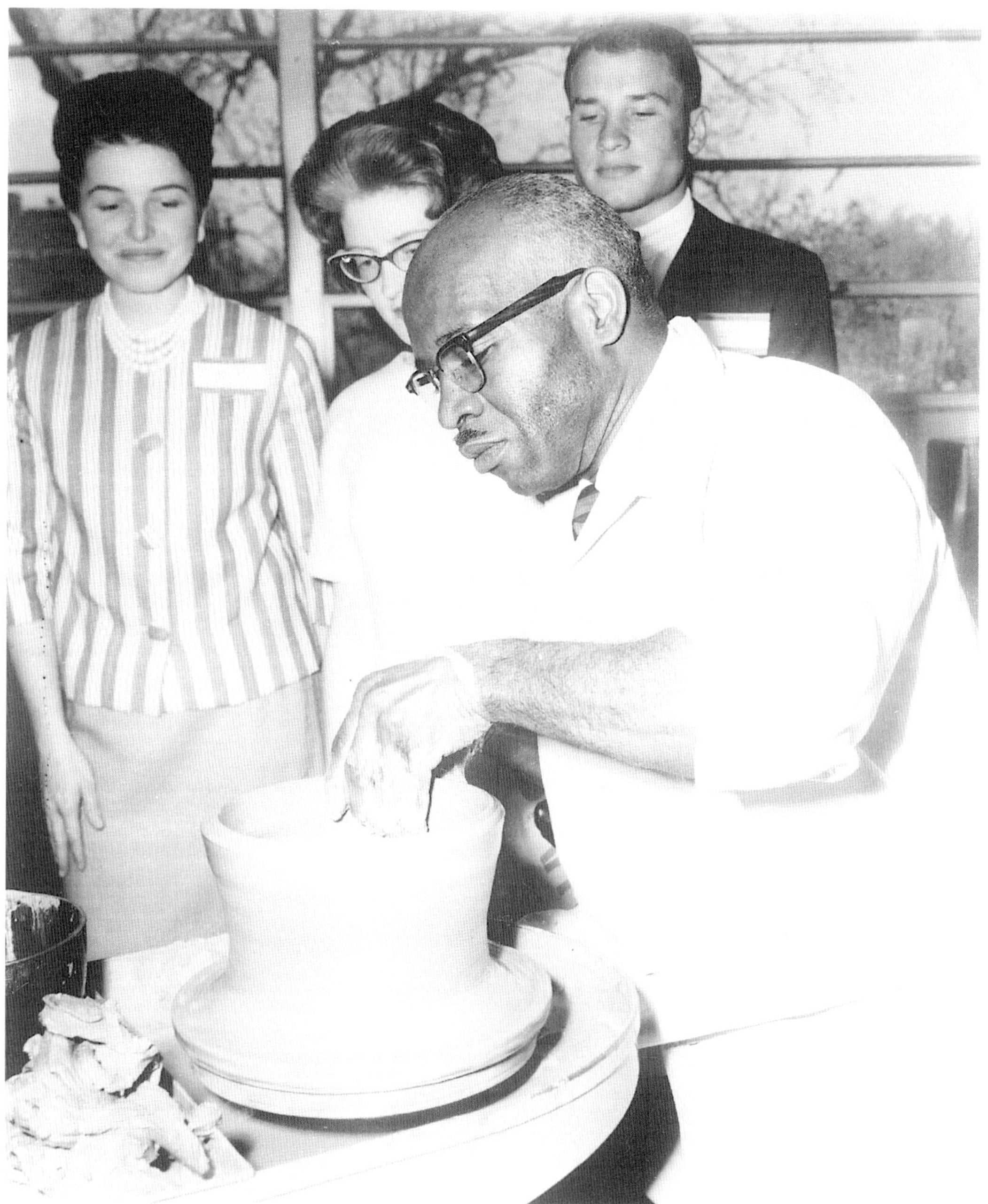

William Artis

Born in Washington, William Ellisworth Artis left for New York in 1927 to study sculpture and pottery. He was a major black artist during the 1930s, 1940s, and 1950s. Artis continued his art education in 1950, studying under sculptor Ivan Mestrovic, and started teaching art in 1956. Employed as an art professor at Chadron State University and later Mankato State College, he is primarily remembered for his work as a sculptor, though he also painted portraits, created mosaics, and dabbled in other art forms. His work is featured in many museums around the country, including Chadron University, which maintains a collection of his art to this day. (Courtesy of National Archives and Records Administration.)

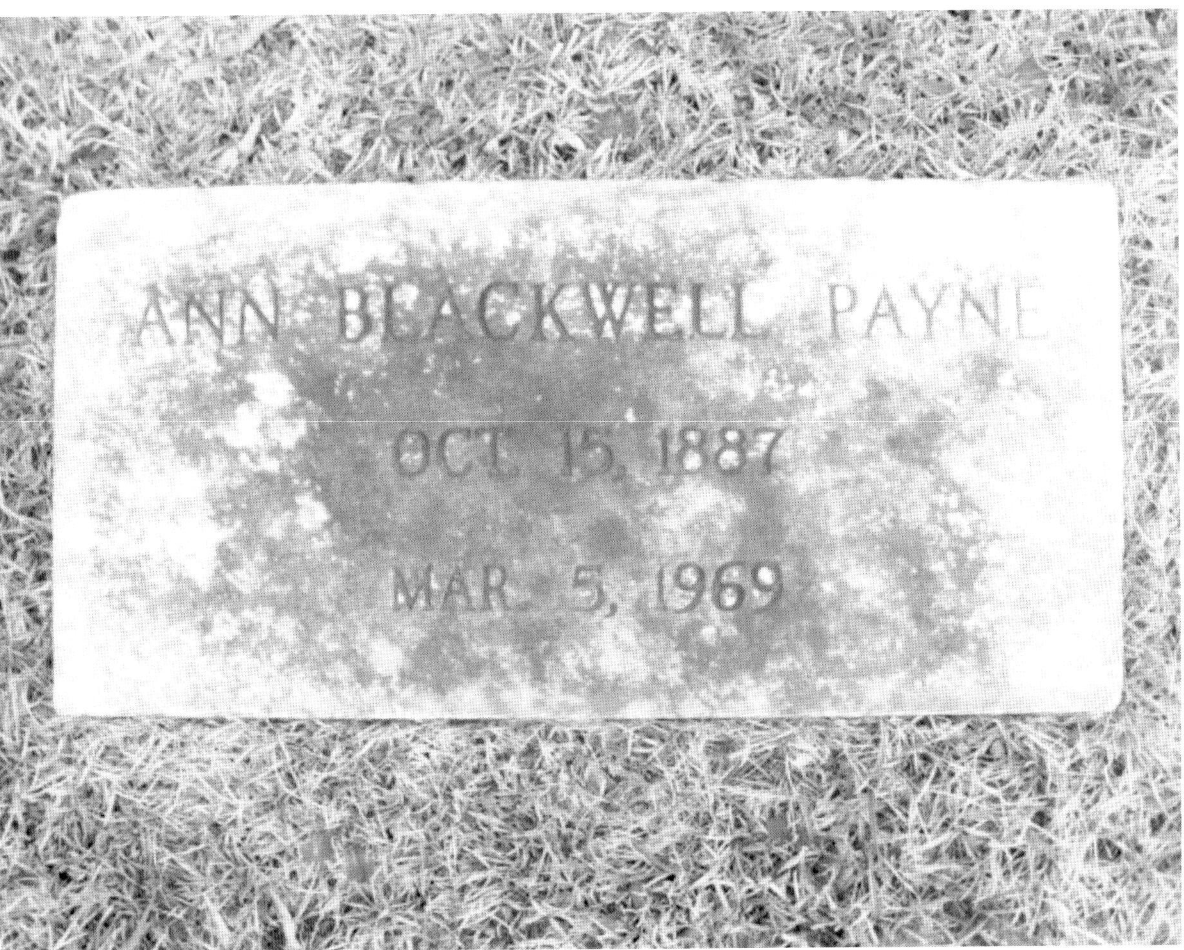

Anne Blackwell Payne

Washington always held a special place in the heart of Anne Blackwell Payne, an award-winning poet, because no matter where she went, she always returned home. Daughter of the well-respected Rev. Dr. Charles Payne, she was known to write poetry for her friends and relatives. She was a founding member of the Poetry Society of America, and her only title, *Released*, was the first book of poetry published by the North Carolina Press. (Author's collection.)

Janet Swain Cox

At the age of 12, Janet Swain Cox knew she wanted to be a dance teacher. After years of dancing, she started working with her childhood dance teacher, Marie Wallace, in 1982. Wallace taught dance at the American Legion building in Washington. In 1986, Cox opened her own studio, Le Moulin Rouge de Danse. Over the years, many aspiring dancers studied under Cox. She retired from teaching dance in December 2015, but her legacy lives on, as a new owner has not only continued her studio's well-known classes, she has also expanded to add more options for youth dancers. (Courtesy of Janet Swain Cox.)

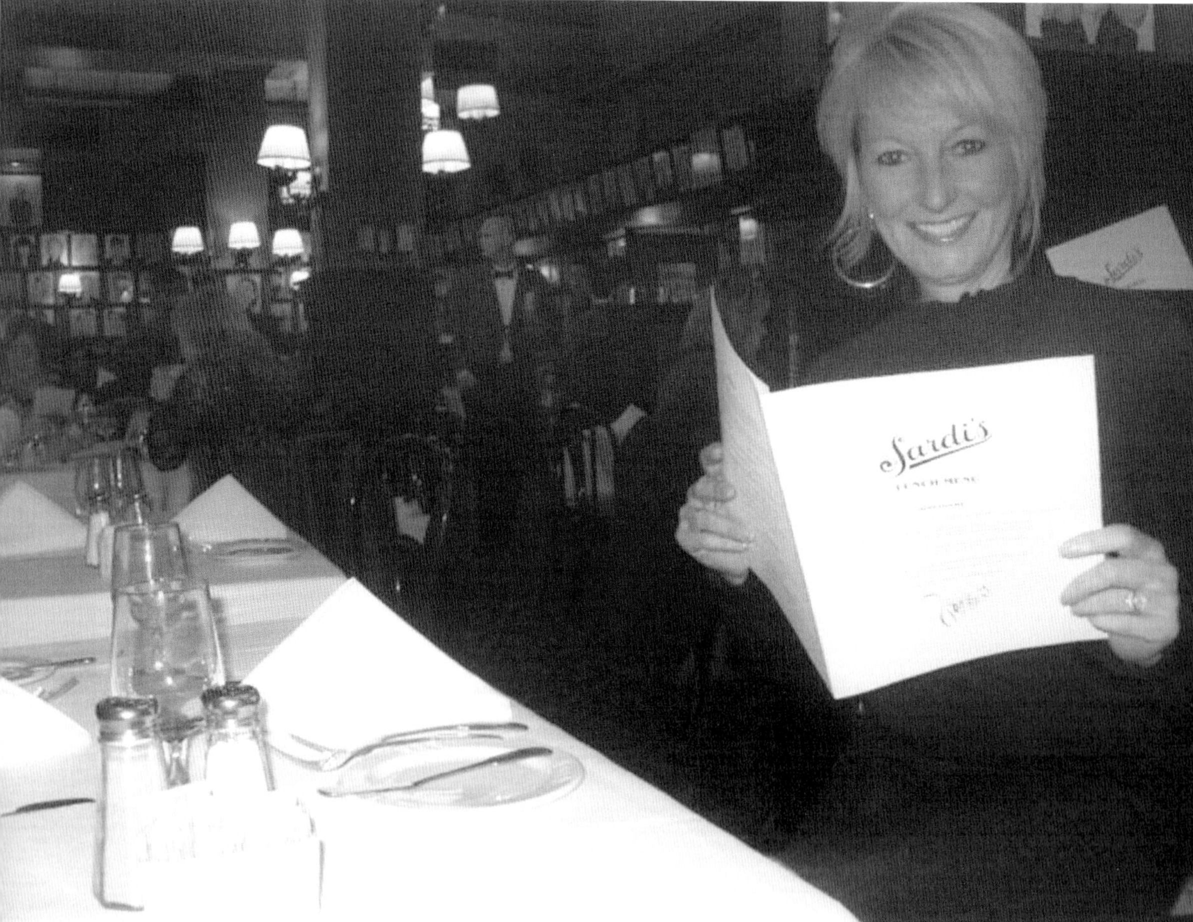

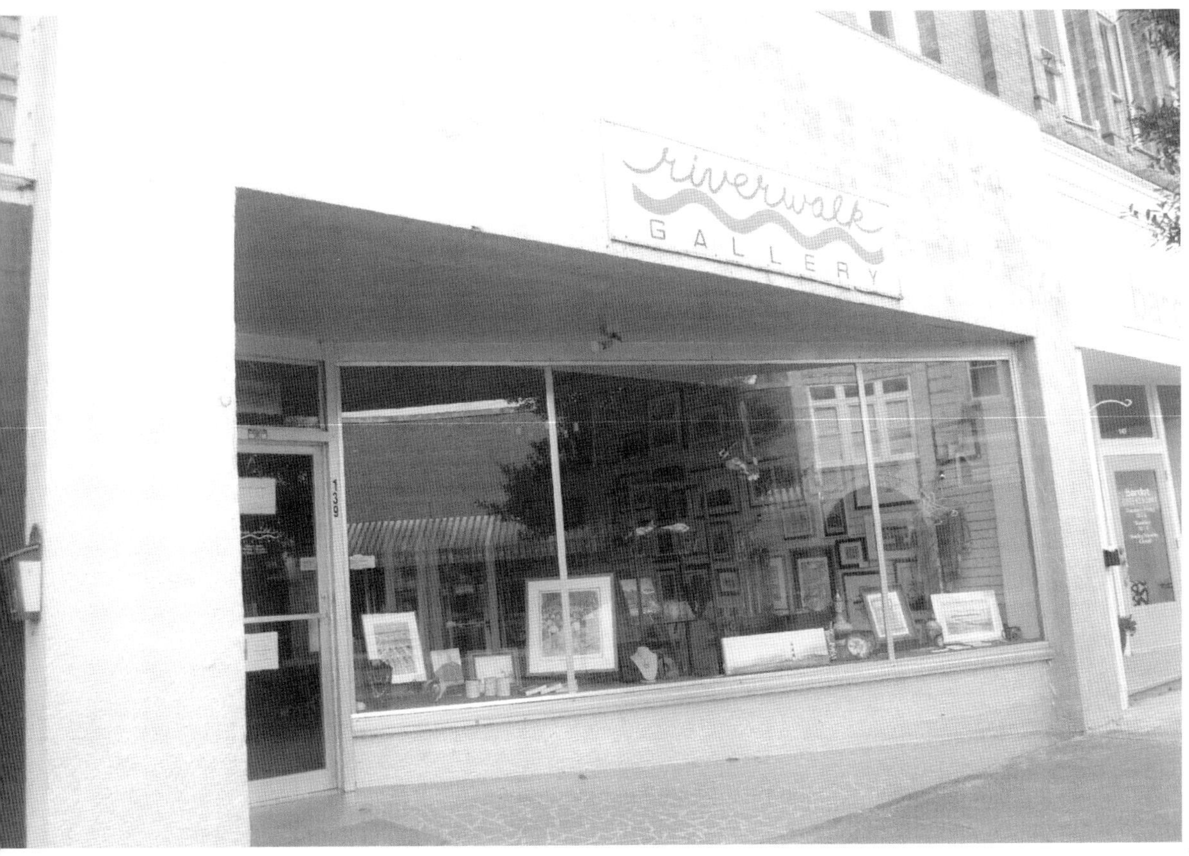

River Walk Gallery

Painter Jane Wall and other local artists found they needed a place to share their art with the community. Thus, they established the River Walk Gallery and Arts Center, an artist co-op on Main Street in Washington, about 18 years ago. The venue gives local artists a place to display their talents and sell their work. (Author's collection.)

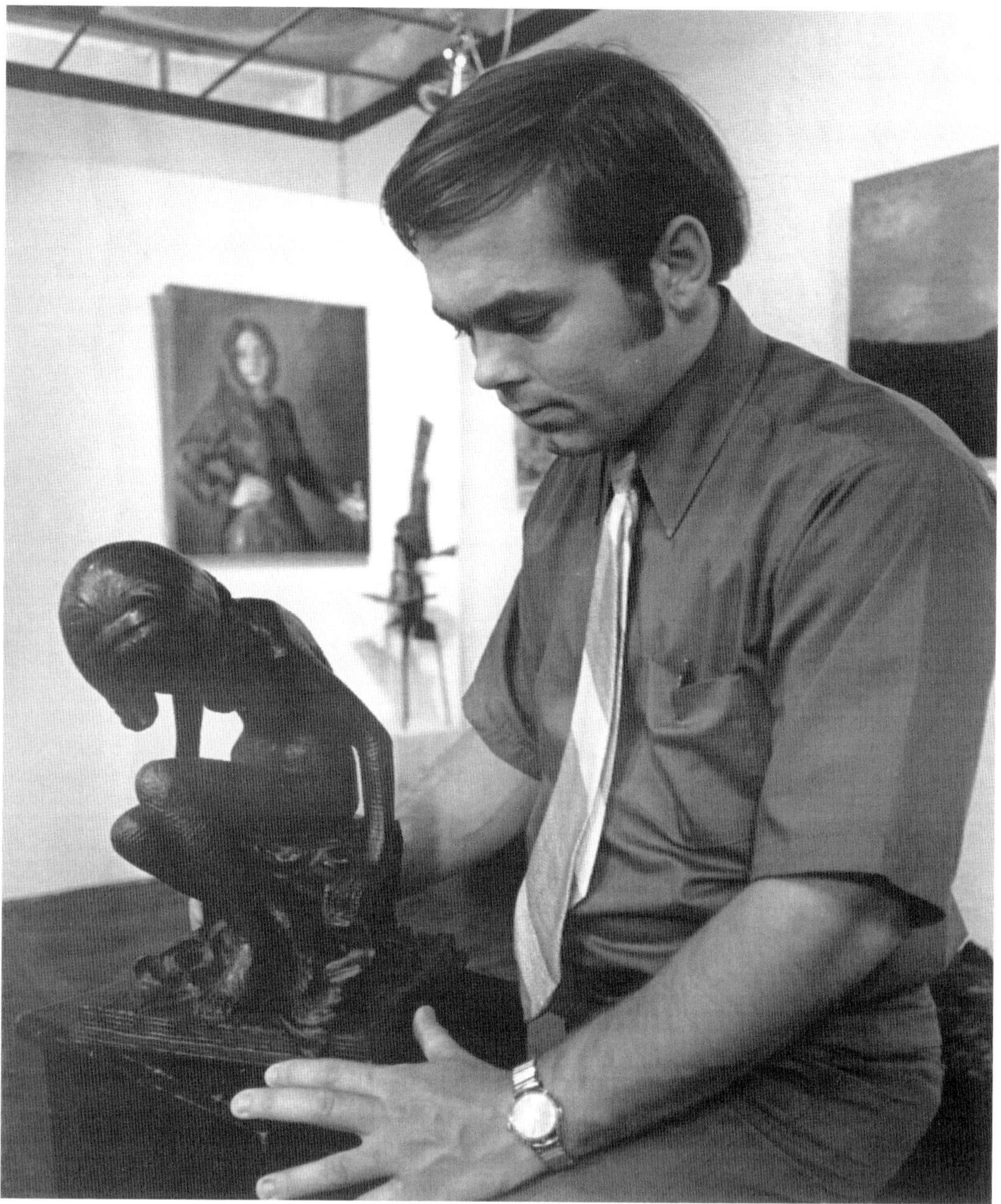

Whiting Toler

Whiting Toler grew up in the heart of downtown Washington, where he found himself an artist without a teacher. His talents grew with practice and encouragement from his mother, who brought home copy paper and editing pencils from her job at the local newspaper for him to use. He is well known for his diverse talents, from designing Fountain powerboats to statues and murals in and around Beaufort County. (Courtesy of Whiting Toler.)

CHAPTER NINE

Throwers and Tossers

The smell of the fresh-cut grass or the sweat of the locker room means that sports are back in season. In Washington, sports seasons continue all throughout the year. Coaches give their time to build sports programs and develop talents among their players. Each season, they train young men and women to be healthy, take direction, and excel at their strengths.

In autumn, the gridiron was where the talent of Choppy Wagner turned into a career of leading Pam Pack champions. Across the field built and dedicated in Wagner's honor, Terrence Copper's career emerged, taking him all the way to the NFL. However, a different talent arises in the early winter months. This is when Coach Dave Smith cultivated his awe-inspiring basketball teams, and it was under Smith's watch that French-born Dominique Wilkins grew to fame.

In the spring, baseball and softball fields are dominated by teams from the Washington area. Many former sports stars have returned to their old stomping grounds to help build programs for the youth in the area, such as Bobby Andrews's 26-year career as the athletic director for the Washington Recreation Department and 48-plus years refereeing. The city's decision to name the local gym after him was well deserved.

"I take pride in my officiating," Andrews said. "We were like family. I loved it."

Like many coaches in the area, he can still recall the names of the children he mentored. Without these coaches, teams, and even those who officiate, many young people in the community would lose their heroes and role models.

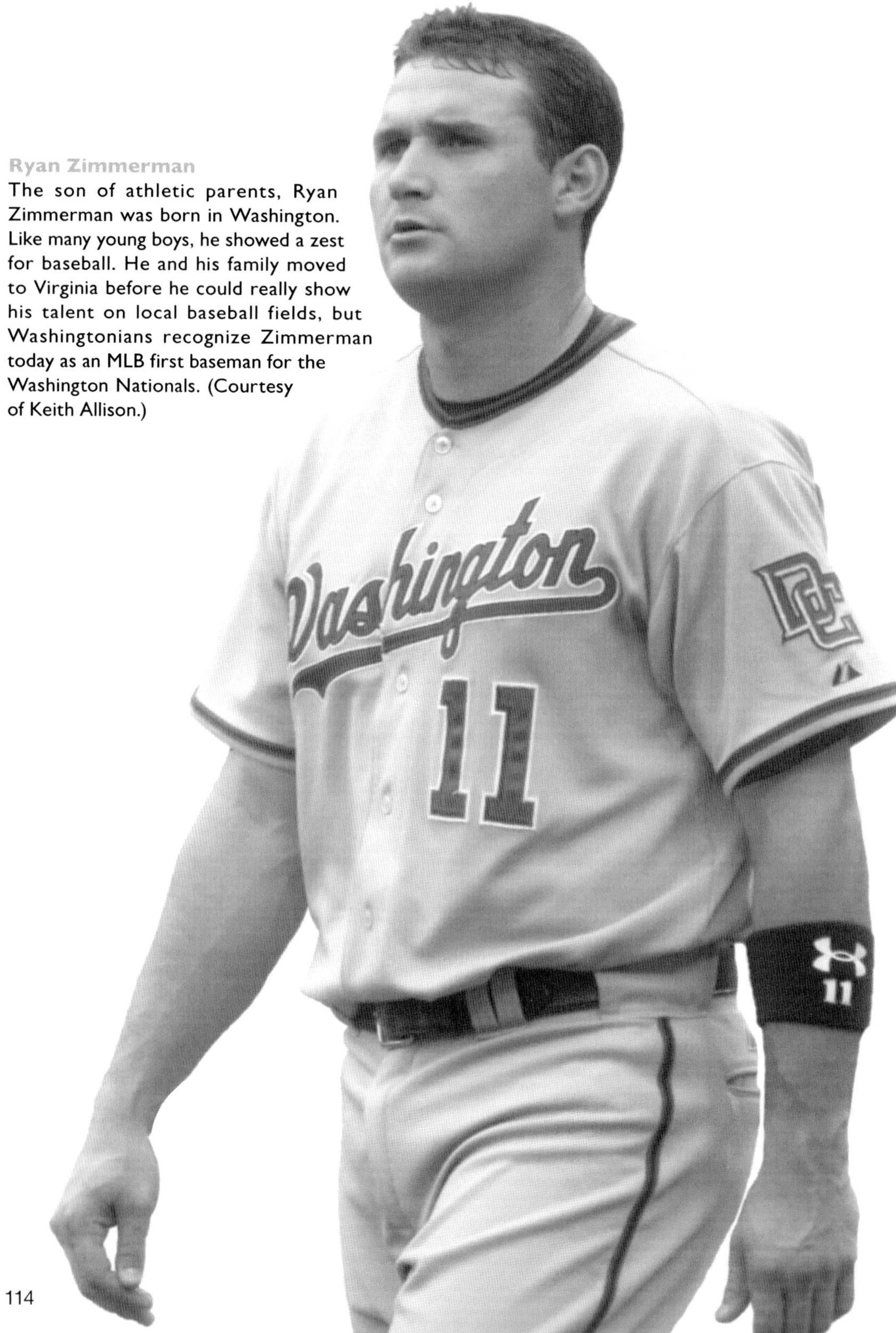

Ryan Zimmerman

The son of athletic parents, Ryan Zimmerman was born in Washington. Like many young boys, he showed a zest for baseball. He and his family moved to Virginia before he could really show his talent on local baseball fields, but Washingtonians recognize Zimmerman today as an MLB first baseman for the Washington Nationals. (Courtesy of Keith Allison.)

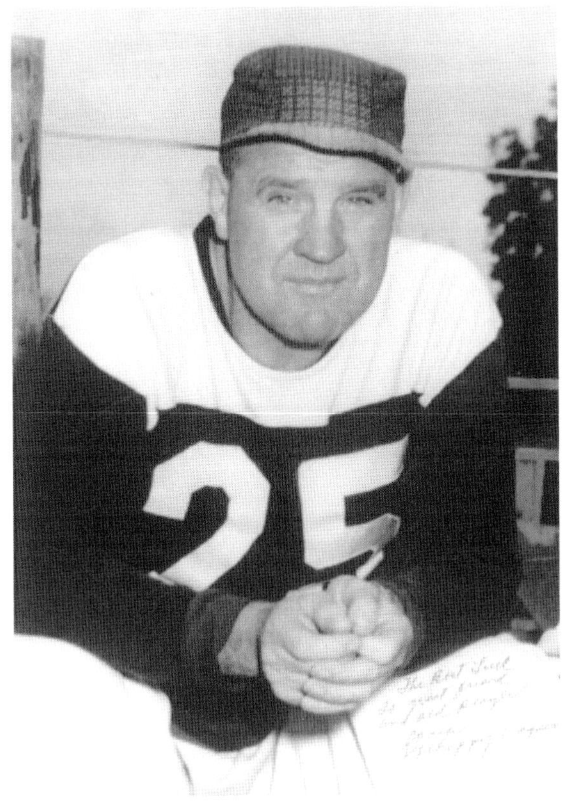

Choppy Wagner

James Glenn Wagner was a pillar of education and sports at Washington High School. Affectionately referred to as "Choppy" by his friends and family, Wagner had a talent for football as a defensive end. When a knee injury ended his own football career, he turned to coaching, creating strong, winning teams. Wagner served the Washington High School for 31 years. He took on many roles, including coach, athletic director, teacher, and assistant principal. In 1990, the stadium at WHS was named in his honor. Numerous former players and students supported the nomination of Wagner to the North Carolina Sports Hall of Fame, where he was posthumously inducted in 1992. (Courtesy of Milton Parker.)

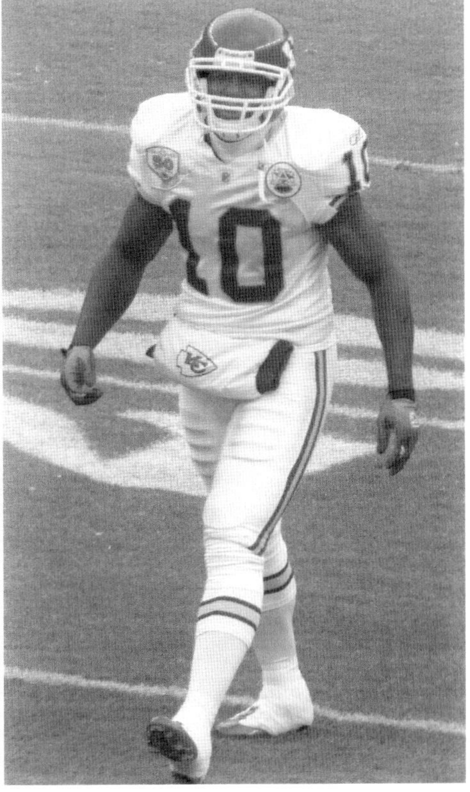

Terrance Copper

On the Washington High School football team, Terrance Terrel Copper was a powerful receiver, breaking school records and scoring 27 touchdowns. He moved on to East Carolina University, where, as a local, he was a fan favorite. Copper has played for several NFL teams, ending his professional career in 2013. (Courtesy of Jeffery Beals.)

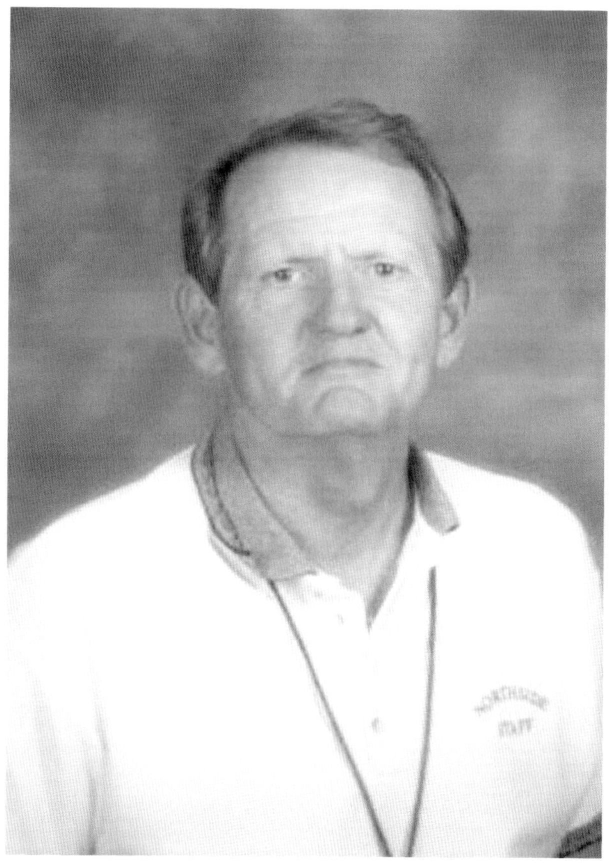

Bing Mitchell
Coach Bingham "Bing" Mitchell worked for many schools in the area, but the majority of his career was spent in Beaufort County at Washington, Bath, and Northside High Schools. A graduate of East Carolina University, he became a well-loved and respected basketball coach and teacher. During his career, he led many winning teams. He also participated in many athletic associations. (Courtesy of Washington High School.)

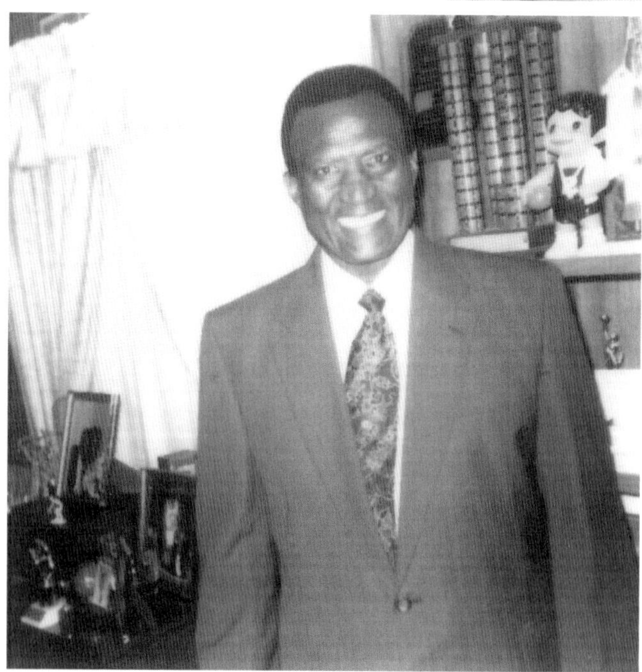

Dave Smith
Coach Dave Smith holds the honor of being the highest-winning basketball coach in the history of Washington High School, with a 520-233 record that included a nearly unbelievable 56-game winning streak. As a teacher and coach, he never missed a day in 34 years of service to his students. (Courtesy of Kenyana Smith.)

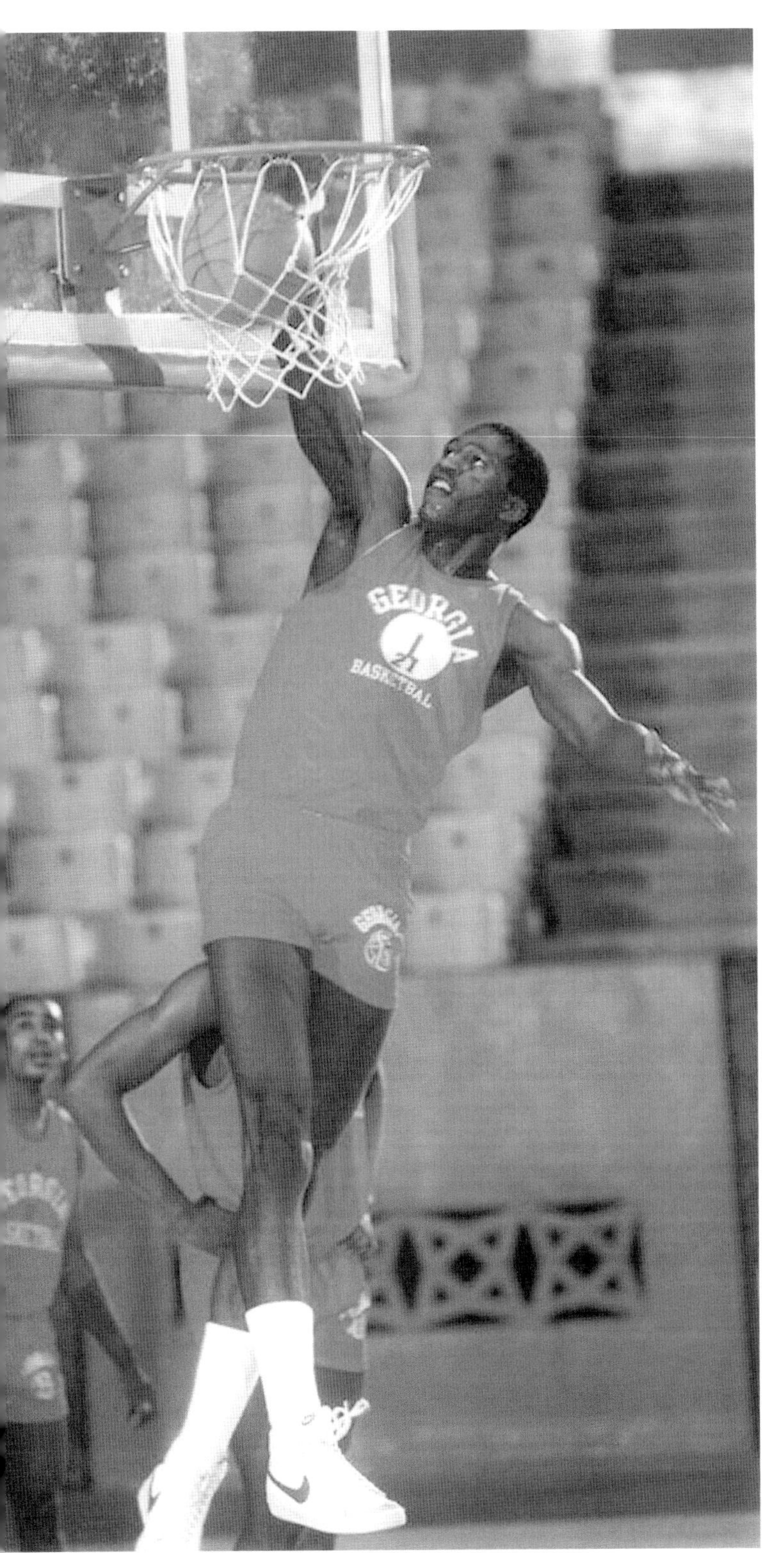

Dominique Wilkins
Dominique Wilkins was a force to be reckoned with on the basketball court. At Washington High School, he led his team to two consecutive state championships. His career continued to the University of Georgia before he was drafted into the NBA, scoring big for several teams. With a total of 26,668 career points, Wilkins currently ranks as the 12th highest-scoring player in NBA history. (Courtesy of Dominique Wilkins.)

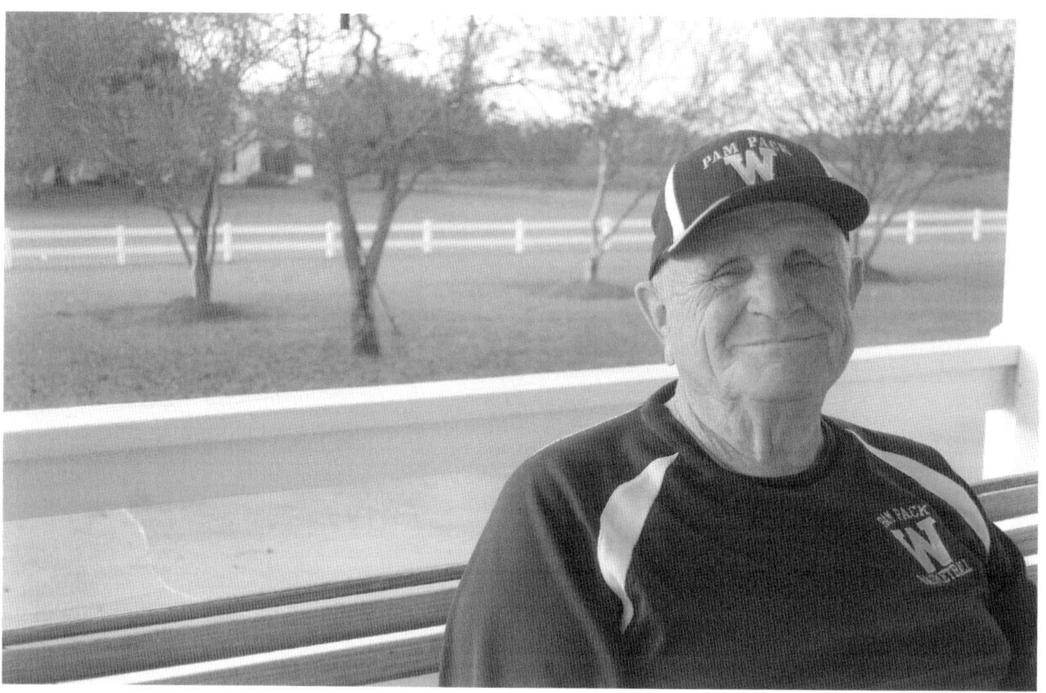

Bobby Andrews

An all-conference ball player at his high school, Bobby Andrews has long shared his love of sports with the young people in and around Beaufort County. "We need something for children to do to keep them from becoming idle," he says. Even after 26 years serving as athletic director for the city of Washington and many more years as an umpire and referee, he remains involved in local youth sports programs. (Both, author's collection.)

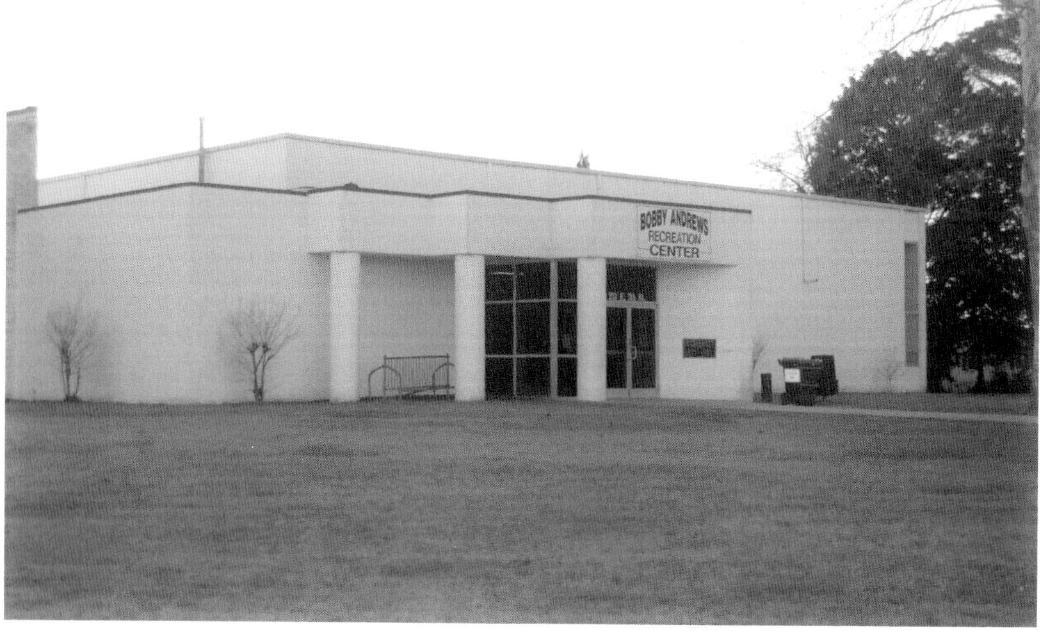

CHAPTER TEN

Educators

It can be said that no one makes more of a difference in a child's life outside of his or her family than educators. In Washington, the spirit of educators has inspired many local citizens to push their boundaries. Whiting Toler, a local artist, noted that if his teachers had not recognized and encouraged his talents as an artist, he might not have been pushed to pursue his passion in a time when there were no dedicated art teachers in the schools. Other artists like Murray Hamilton and William Artis found interest in their crafts when they attended local schools. The same can be said of local sports legends and businesspeople around town. From building educational programs and libraries to facilitating bold and innovative changes in education, these teachers, principals, and librarians have left a significant mark on the growth of the public schools within the town and county.

Similarly, proponents of education have helped build what is now known as Beaufort County Community College. Elliot Graham and others like him worked diligently to establish the former Beaufort County Technical Institute to make sure that public higher education was available to all in the area. Likewise, Katie Paul's dedication to nursing students while teaching at the local hospital led to the development of the college's current nursing program, which has a reputation of being one of the top nursing schools in the area. Due to their efforts, and the efforts of many others, Beaufort County Community College now serves students in Beaufort, Hyde, Tyrrell, and Washington Counties, with additional students traveling to the college from other surrounding counties.

A. Graham Elliot

A. Graham Elliot was the chairman of the advisory committee that helped get the ball rolling on the establishment of a technical institute in Washington. In 1968, he was named the first chairman of the board of trustees for the Beaufort County Technical Institute, now Beaufort County Community College, where a building is named in his honor for his dedication to the education of the people in Beaufort County. (Courtesy of Beaufort County Community College.)

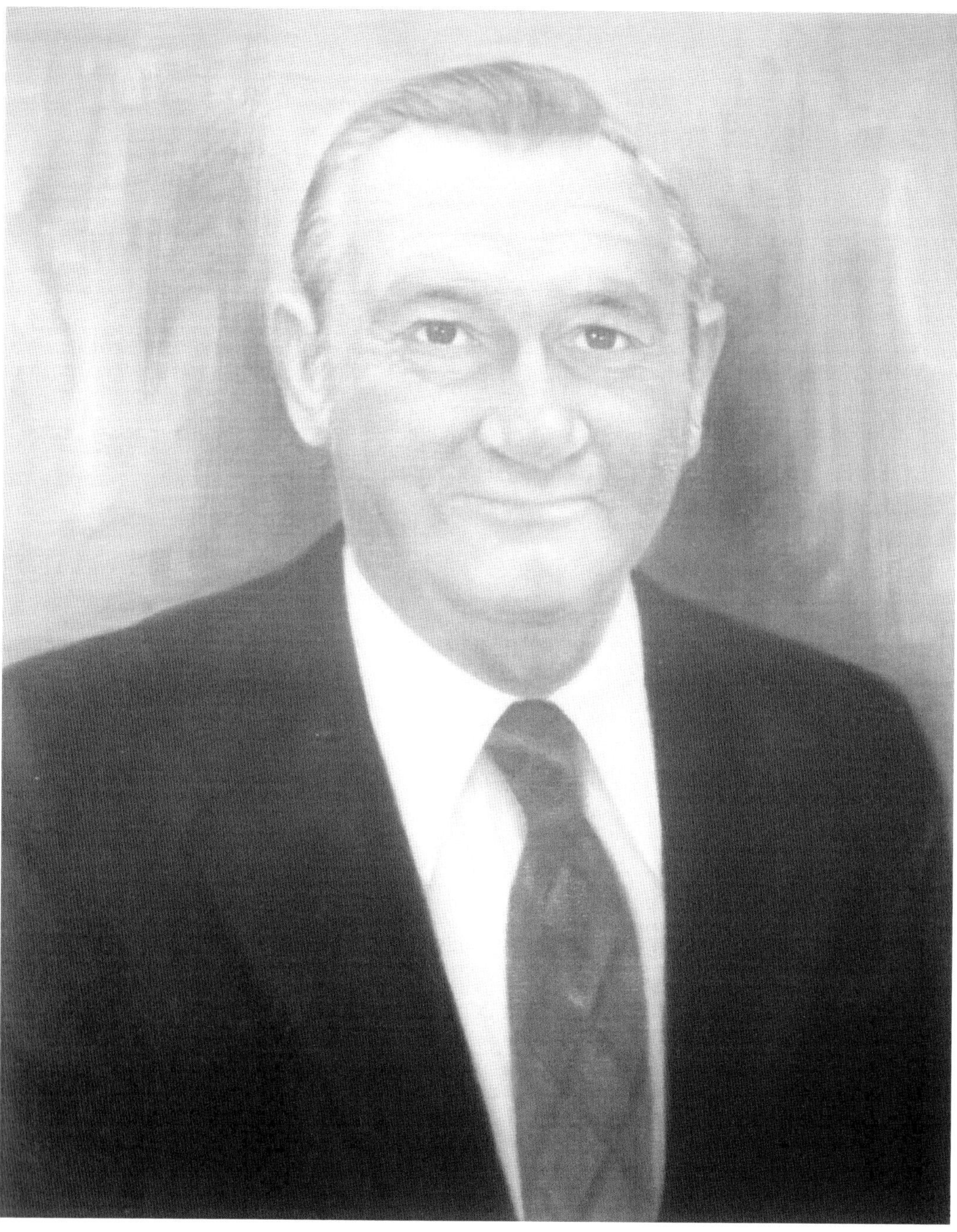

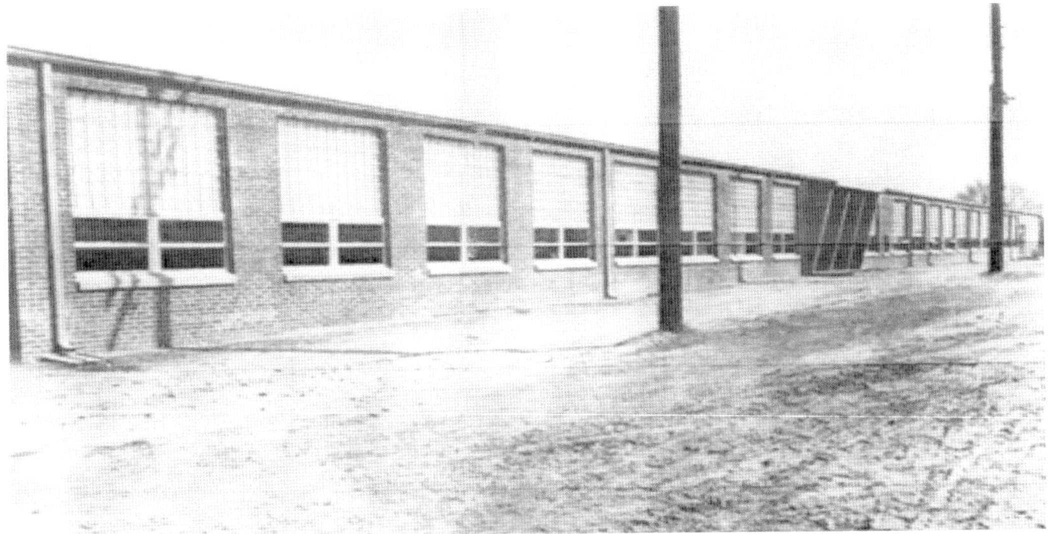

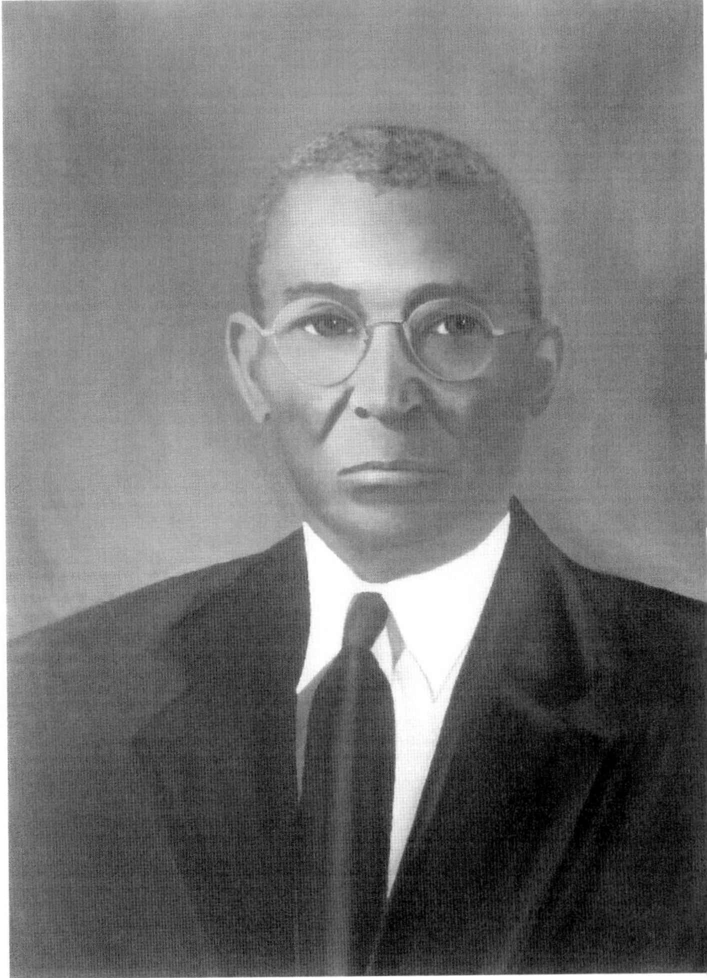

Peter Simon Jones

In 1927, Peter Simon Jones took over principal duties at the local African American school. When he started his tenure, the elementary students were housed on the first floor of the building, with the high school upstairs. For 22 years, Jones was an advocate for his students. He added music and art to the curriculum and started an athletic program, including football, as well as a high school band. Jones expected his students to display courtesy and character. When enrollment increased, another building was added. After Jones's death, a group of students requested that the newer high school be named for him. P.S. Jones High School no longer exists; however, the city has not forgotten his contributions to the community. Today, P.S. Jones Middle School is named in his honor. (Above, courtesy of P.S. Jones Middle School; right, courtesy of Archie Harding.)

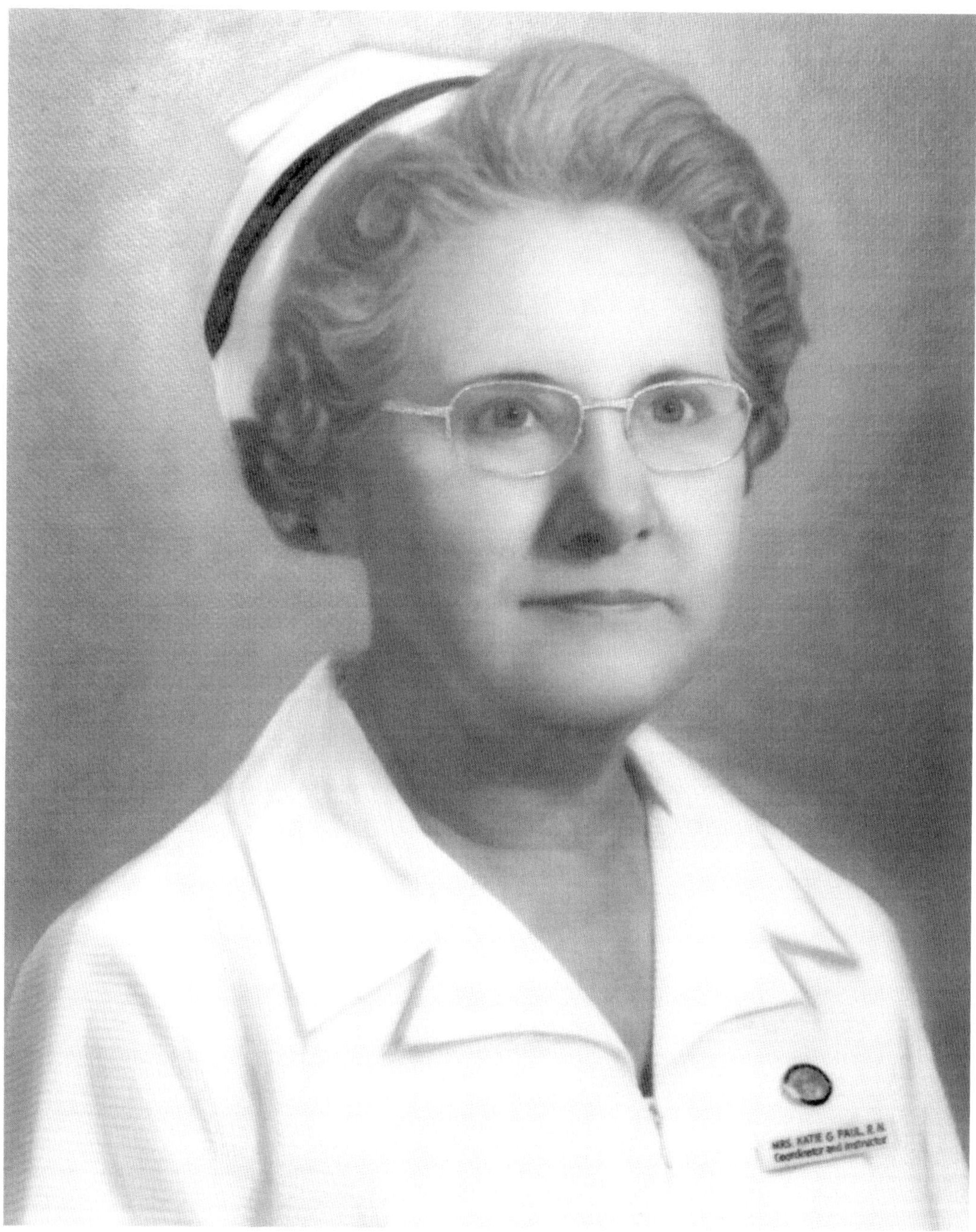

Katie Paul

Katie Paul's name is nearly synonymous with nursing education in Beaufort County. After obtaining an extensive nursing education, Paul became the night supervisor and nursing instructor at Tayloe Hospital. There, she established a practical nursing program. Over the years, her involvement in nursing education programs in the area led to the development of the nursing program at Beaufort County Community College, where the nursing building is named in her honor. (Courtesy of Beaufort County Community College.)

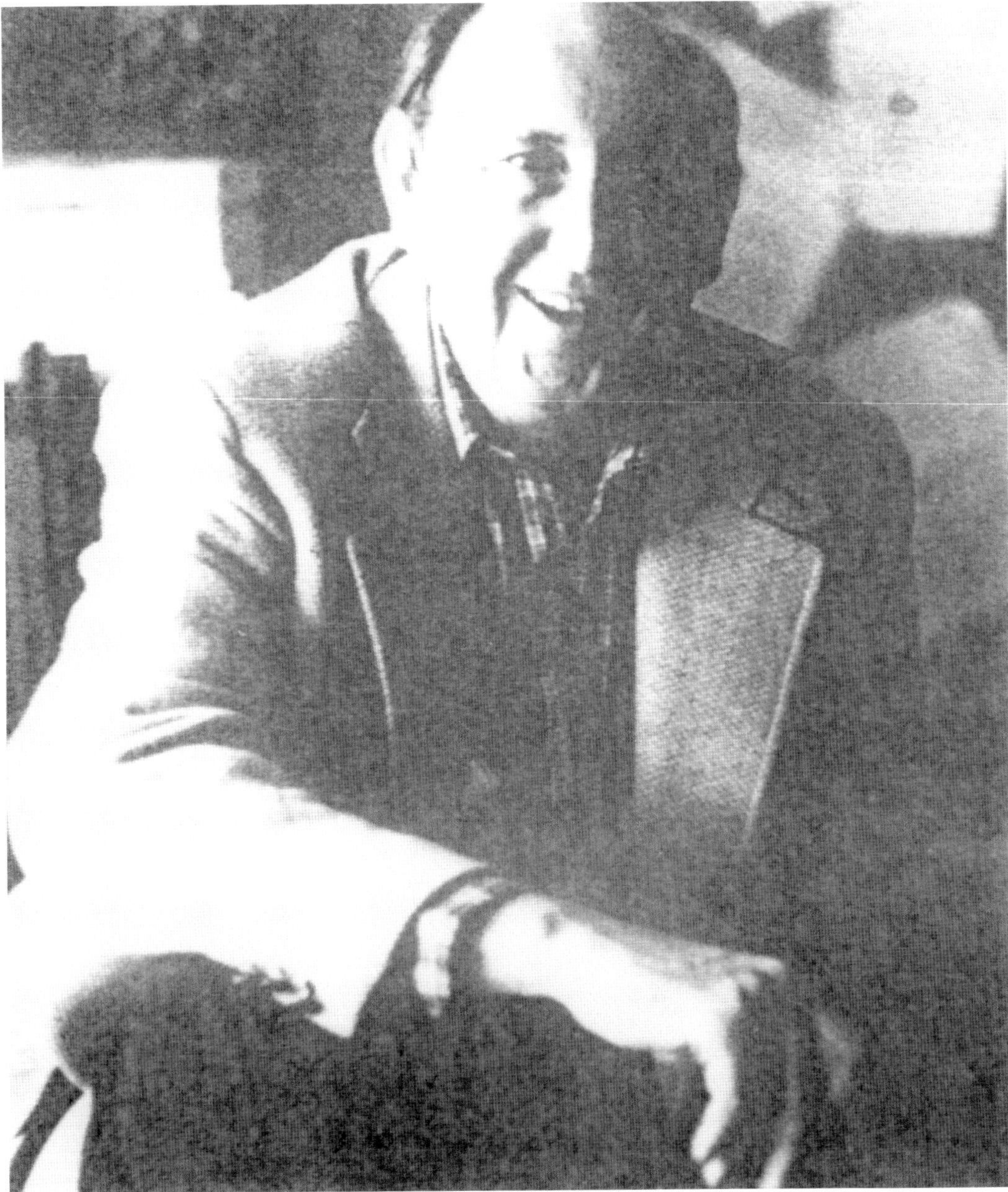

James M. Ferrell

As a teacher, James M. Ferrell is well remembered by the students he taught over his 25-year career teaching English and journalism at Washington High School. He liked getting the students involved with writing. During his tenure, the students created a school newspaper, and his wife, Betty, recalls that his students won many state awards. (Courtesy of Washington High School.)

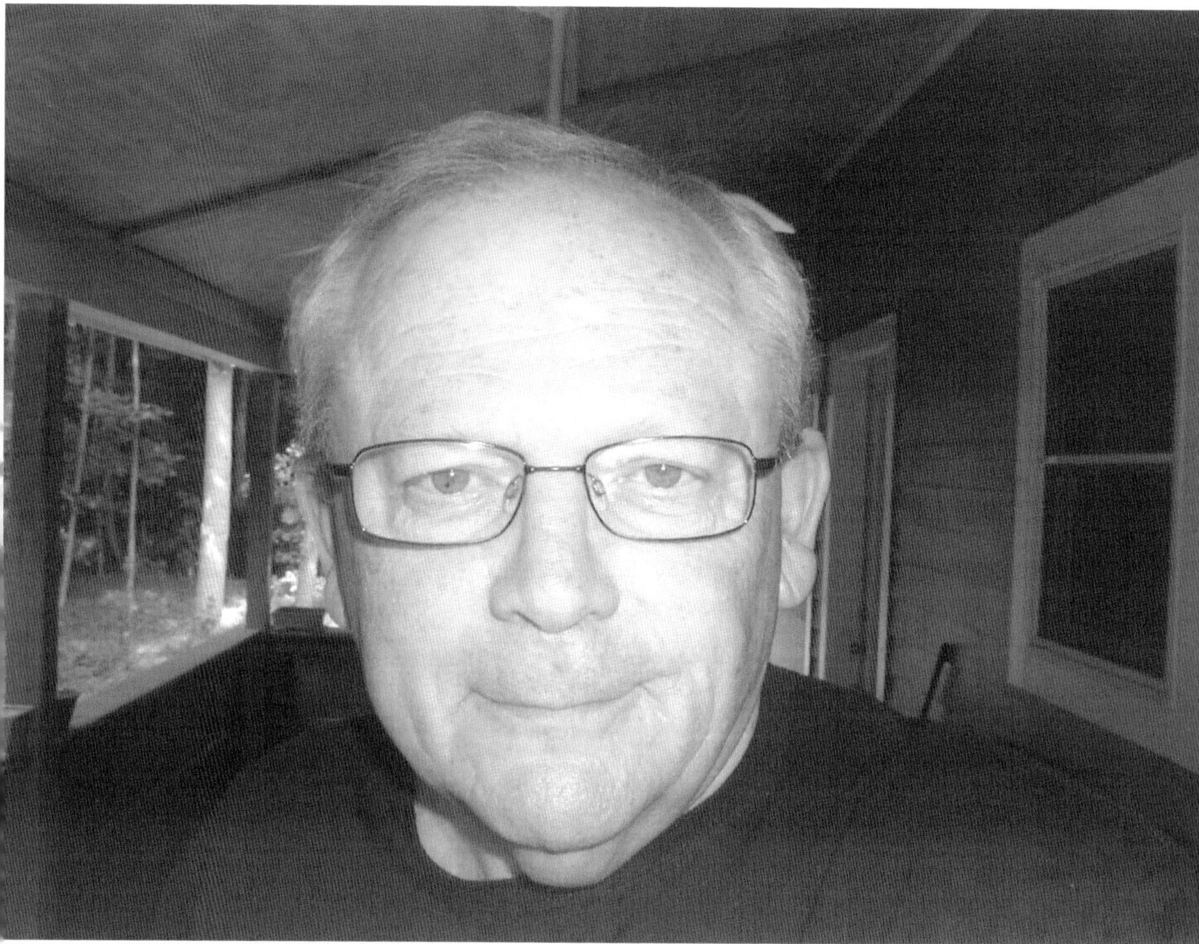

Tim Mattimoe
Mattimoe spent many years teaching at Beaufort County Community College, where his history courses were very popular with students. His students remember his courses as being innovative and exciting, and several students credit him as their inspiration to pursue teaching careers. Now retired, Mattimoe lives in Pittsboro, where he writes and publishes poetry. (Courtesy of Tim Mattimoe.)

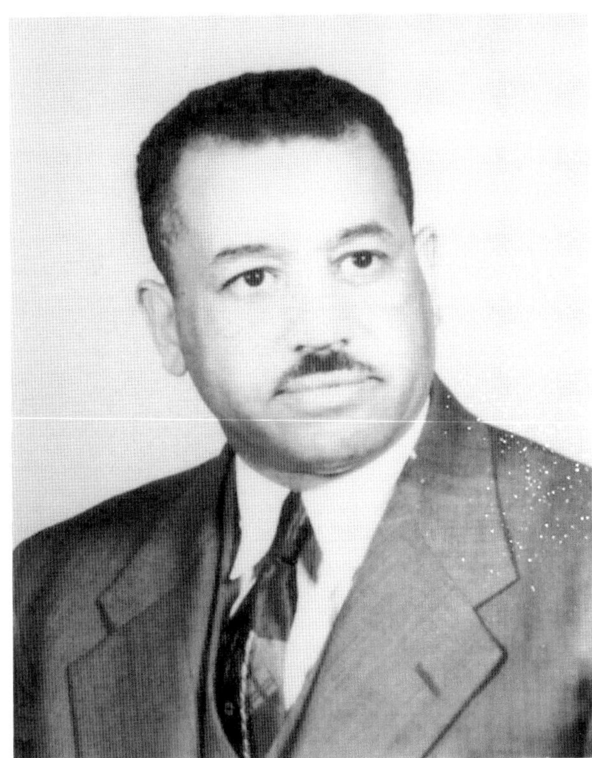

William Mack Daniels

A native Washingtonian, William Mack Daniels devoted 38 years to the improvement of the schools in his hometown. For 22 years, he served as a principal, but his most significant contribution to the schools was assisting in the fluid transition when integration of the schools occurred. Following his retirement, William and his wife, Elwyza, continued to serve their community as active members of the Metropolitan AME Zion Church. (Courtesy of North Carolina Retired School Personnel.)

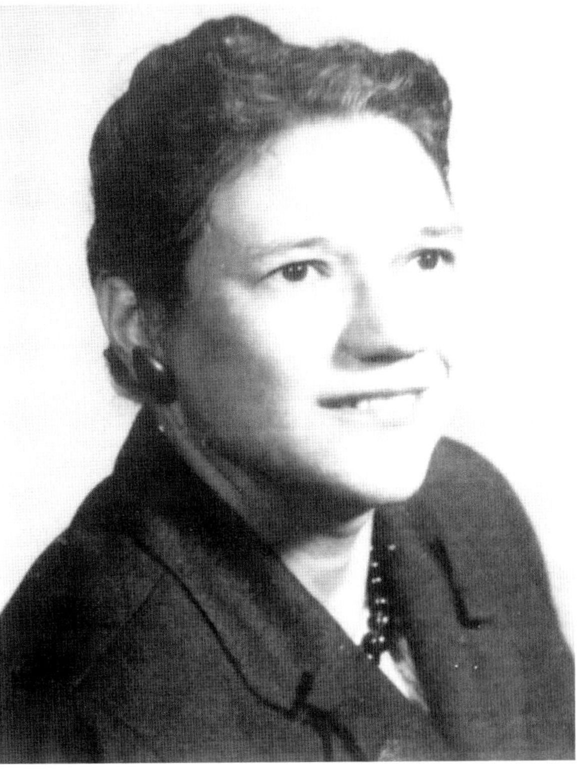

Elwyza Diuguid Daniels

Elwyza Diuguid Daniels relocated to Washington after meeting her husband, William. For 27 years, she made significant contributions to Washington's schools, one of which was to exponentially expand the library selections at the Washington Colored High and Elementary School. She also worked at John Small School's library. Active both in her church and with youth groups, she is well remembered as a thoughtful teacher and librarian. (Courtesy of North Carolina Retired School Personnel.)

BIBLIOGRAPHY

Beaufort County Unit of Retired School Personnel. *North Carolina Retired School Personnel*, 1991.

CIRCA NC East. Beaufort County Community College, 2009.

Loy, Ursula, and Pauline Worthy. *Washington and the Pamlico*. Raleigh, NC: Edwards & Broughton Co., 1976.

Parker, Milton. *The Coach: J.G."Choppy" Wagner . . . a Legend and a Loved Man*. Self-published, 1993.

Powell, William Stevens, ed. *Dictionary of North Carolina Biography*. Vols. 1–6. Chapel Hill, NC: UNC Press, 1979.

State Archives of North Carolina: Natural and Cultural Resources. State of North Carolina, 2015.

Steelman, Joseph F., ed. *Of Tar Heel Towns, Shipbuilders, Reconstructionists and Alliancemen: Papers in North Carolina History*. Greenville, NC: East Carolina University Publications, 1981.

INDEX

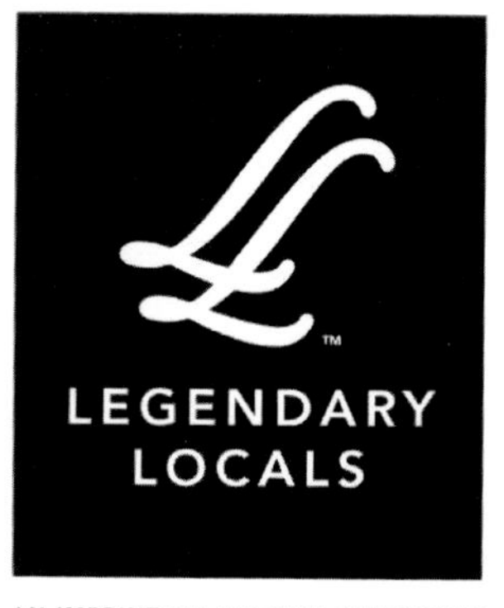

Consistent with our mission to preserve history on a local level, this book was printed in South Carolina on American-made paper and manufactured entirely in the United States. Products carrying the accredited Forest Stewardship Council (FSC) label are printed on 100 percent FSC-certified paper.

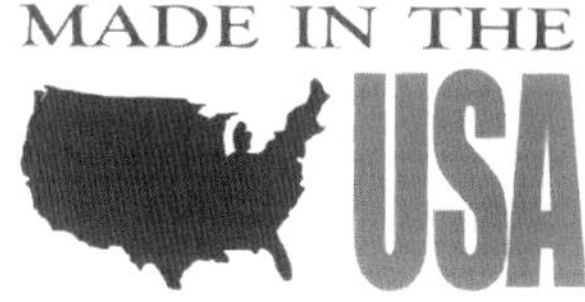